ACPL ITEM
DISCARDED

BEFORE YOU SAY "I DO" IN MARRIAGE, FIRST PROTECT YOURSELF LEGALLY. AND HERE'S HOW.

The National Pre-marital Agreement Kit.

By Benji O. Anosike. B.B.A..M.A..Ph.D.

Copyright © 1999 by Benji O. Anosike

All rights reserved. No part of this manual kit, containing
LEGAL TEXT, FORMS AND PAPERS, plus SAMPLES,
ILLUSTRATIONS and INSTRUCTIONS for their use
thereof, may be reproduced or utilized in any form or by any
means, electronic or mechanical, including photocopying,
recording, or by any information or retrieval system,
without the written permission of the author.

Library of Congress Cataloging-in-Publication Data

Anosike, Benji O.
    Before you say "I do" in marriage, first protect yourself
legally : the national pre-marital settlement agreement kit / by
Benji O. Anosike.
    p. cm.
    Includes bibliographical references and index.
    ISBN 0-93-270434-4 (pbk. : alk. paper)
    1. Antenuptial contracts--United States--Popular works. I. Title.
KF529.Z9 A56 1999
346.7301'6--dc21

                                                                98-56537
                                                                CIP

Allen County Public Library
900 Webster Street
PO Box 2270
Fort Wayne, IN 46801-2270

Printed in the United States of America
ISBN: 0-932704-34-4

Library of Congress Catalog Number:

Published by:

Do-It-Yourself Legal Publishers
60 Park Place
Newark, NJ 07102

The Publisher's Disclaimer

We have, of course, diligently researched, checked and counter-checked every bit of the information contained in the manual to make sure that it is accurate and up-to-date. Nevertheless, we humans have never been known for our infallibility, no matter how hard the effort! Furthermore, details of a law do change from time to time. Nor is this relatively short manual conceivably intended to be an encyclopedia on the subject, containing the answer or solution to every issue on the subject. *THE READER IS THEREFORE WARNED THAT THIS MANUAL IS SOLD AND DISTRIBUTED WITH THIS DISCLAIMER:* The publisher (the same for the author) does NOT make any guarantees of any kind whatsoever, or purport to engage in the practice of law, or to substitute for a lawyer, an accountant, a tax expert, or rendering any professional or legal service; where such professional help is legitimately necessary in your specific case, it should be sought accordingly.

—*Do-It-Yourself Legal Publishers*

Dedication

This Book is Lovingly Dedicated to...

★ ★ Princess Nnenna,
so lovely and loving a wife!

...for making life all too refreshing and re-invigorating all over again for your hubby!

You have, in your own special way , made this undertaking both more purposeful and easier for me.

Table of Contents

Chapter 4
PRE-MARITAL AGREEMENTS: WHAT THEY ARE, WHAT THEY'RE USED FOR, AND THE BASIC LEGAL REQUIREMENTS FOR A VALID ONE

Chapter 5
WHAT YOU MAY PROVIDE FOR IN YOUR MARITAL OR PRE-MARITAL AGREEMENT ...41

Chapter 6
THE BASIC PREREQUISITES FOR A GOOD PRE-MARITAL AGREEMENT 45

APPENDICES

FOREWORD:
THE PUBLISHER'S MESSAGE

To All Our Dear Readers:

This manual is consciously conceived and written with one fundamental objective in mind: for "preventive" law purposes, to spare you the necessity of ever having to go through the all-too-familiar expenses and emotional drains of what could be a lengthy and bitter court battle potentially for a divorce[1], separation, or property settlement, somewhere down the road, if that should ever become necessary!

Using this manual, you can readily draft an appropriate contract with your partner, without a lawyer's involvement, and save yourself the lawyer's hefty legal fees while getting essentially a document of the same legal validity and quality. You can save yourself, quite easily—for the same essential material—upwards of $600 for the simplest type of agreement, and the repeated charges you would have had to pay each time there's a revision or an amendment to be made! BUT THERE'S A MUCH MORE INVALUABLE "SAVINGS" YOU MAKE FROM USING THIS BOOK: the incalculable financial and emotional problems you could later save yourself only because a timely contract with that lady or gentleman of your present momentary romantic fancy later works to keep you out of the courtrooms and the accountants' and lawyers' offices.

Why Seek a Written Couples' Agreement?

As one New York Lawyer and author experienced in matrimonial cases aptly put it, "a contract with your loved ones could [later] keep you out of court and/or the poorhouse!"

And yet another thoughtful lawyer, Toni Kara, a California matrimonial specialist and author on the subject, put it this way, explaining why it's easier but most advisable these days that couples or would-be couples have a written agreement: *"Fortunately, [unlike the situation that obtains with commercial type contracts and lease documents], living-together agreements are different. You are free to design your agreement to say exactly what you want, in words that you can understand... And writing down your expectations is... the best way to stay out of court. Given our adversary domestic relation system, any money or property that exists at the start of a court fight almost always gets consumed by the lawyers. [Hence], in the end, personal disputes [potential or actual], can only be solved well by the people involved."[2]*

The central point, in a word, is that you do yourself a great favor and save yourself (and your spouse or would-be spouse, and especially the children) a world of time, trouble, and your hard-earned money, by simply endeavoring to resolve, in an atmosphere of relative peace and privacy and in advance, any issues or anticipated matters that could conceivably be a source of friction and difficulties between you and your spouse later down the road in your marital relationship—even before it ever gets to be a problem! *And thus, by so doing, by formulating through a pre-marital agreement the proper compromises and rules of conduct and living for your own marriage to accommodate individual sensitivities and areas of potential conflicts, you affirmatively prevent the need for ever having to have the problem in the first place. You, in effect, drastically reduce for yourselves the high risk possibility of ever having to wind up in the lawyer's offices and the court rooms at assured multiples the time, hassles and costs, to you!*

---

[1] The companion volumes by this Publisher, *"How to Do Your Own Divorce Without a Lawyer,"* a multi-volume series, provides interested readers with the same facility with regard to procedures for actually filing for a divorce yourself. The national edition of this manual is packaged for use in almost every state.

[2] Quoted from "The People's Law Review" ed. Ralph Warner (1980) pp. 97-8

This manual tells you, quite simply, that there is one primary legal safeguard and preventive measure available today which you had better seriously considered and used: A GOOD WRITTEN AGREEMENT with your spouse or mate!

With this present manual as a guide, you shall have escaped the fate of millions who are destined to fall into the developing social dragnet of the modern times in America when interpersonal relationship fail or falter. Now, at a time of romance and light spiritedness and good will for the anticipated marriage, you shall have been in a better position to work out an amicable and agreeable settlement of terms with your spouse or mate to make for a lasting, joyful and fruitful married life; and to make for a more civilized and far less acrimonious and expensive divorce or separation, if it were to come to that.

In an age of many varied and often untraditional marital lifestyles, the fundamental if fascinating, point of premarital agreements is positive and constructive, not negative or cynical. Its point is not that, with an agreement a couple will have an easier time or more accommodating tool for disengaging or breaking up in the event of interpersonal difficulties or marital conflicts. Rather, it is that with such an agreement in hand, a couple is better equipped to avoid the areas of potential problems, in the first place, and thus to make the chances of serious disagreements or a break up far less likely, to begin with. The principal advantage of a premarital agreement is that a couple now has an opportunity to set its own guidelines which enable it to structure its marriage to suit its individual needs and personalities.

Gail J. Koff, a New York matrimonial attorney who herself had a prenuptial agreement that worked out very well in her own personal marriage, sums it up quite clearly this way:

> "The notion of a premarital contract is often a threatening one to many people. Some believe that preparing one is too pessimistic, almost bordering on being fatalistic, presupposing the end of the marriage. But in reality [it] is in many cases simply a practical way of dealing with a possible eventuality....A prenuptial agreement can be an effective tool for communication between parties...We drew up our agreement in a light spirit of good will. Nevertheless, it turned out to be a very positive vehicle for communication, and I think it helped set some of the ground rules for our relationship...prenuptial contracts such as ours can be a very useful tool [of marriage]."[3]

Never Mind, You Can and May Draw up the Papers Yourself - Just as Safely, Competently.

At this stage in the nation's legal history, most people probably know this by now: namely, that it is a basic civil and constitutional **right** of every American, who so chooses, to act as his or her own "attorney" in any *civil* matters (which obviously includes the drawing up of matrimonial or living-together papers and agreements). Sure, lawyers have traditionally been looked to to draw up matrimonial agreements, and they can still be useful in a limited way, in some of those undertakings. But in this era of a growing public attitude of let's-cut-down-on-the-rising-costs-by-doing-some-of-it-ourselves, what is more to the point today is this simple fact: *not only is there no law which says that to be legal a marital or cohabitation agreement must be drawn up*

---

[3] Gail J. Koff, *Love and The Law: A Legal Guide To Relationships In The '90s, pp. 84, 89 & 91*. The relevant statistics on the subject also show a dramatic upward trend in the number of cohabitating couples, divorce rates, and rates on non-marriage after divorce. A report in the New York Times (January 1979) reported, for example, that since the nation's premier cohabitation case, California's famous "Marvin case," was decided in 1976, "hundreds of former lovers in New York and 15 other states have filed similar suits alleging that they are entitled to everything from alimony to pension rights."

by a person titled a "lawyer," but there is also no commonsense reason why it could be so. The truth is that any marital or cohabitation agreement (or, for that matter, any agreement of any kind whatsoever) which meets the simple common sense requirements of clarity, fairness, inclusiveness and evenhandedness, is just as legally valid as any other agreement—whether or not it be drawn up by you, the "lay person," or by the best lawyer that Harvard has ever turned out, or even by your house dog!

To sum it all up in one sentence, what it all boils down to, then is this: do you have enough knowledge of the basic law, and of what constitutes the essential elements of a valid agreement, to be able to draw up, by yourself, a document that meets your own basic needs? THIS IS THE BASIC MATTER THAT THIS MANUAL, WHILE DEMYSTIFYING THE LAW, DIRECTLY HELPS YOU WITH—IN PRACTICAL TERMS.

The Changing "New Morality" of These Times Demand Precautionary Legal Measure!

Yet, in this Publisher's humble assessment, never has such an instructional guidebook on a subject such as this been more necessary or timely. With the current trend in America's social and matrimonial scene today, with the escalating trend towards instability and unpredictability in relationships, sooner or later every American involved in a marital or living-together situation of any sort would probably need some form of written agreement with the partner. Time was—indeed, it was a few short decades ago—when it would have been unthinkable, for example, to ever conceive of matters like money, property division, let alone inheritance or divorce, as issues for discussion between lovers engaged to be married. Marriage was, in those "good old days," strictly a social and moral issue, completely divorced from business and monetary considerations.

Not so any more, though! Today, as Max Lichtenberg, a New York matrimonial lawyer, put it, *"Marriage is no longer viewed as something made in heaven by angels. It's (now viewed as) a legal contract with emotions terminating." And since there has been a marked lessening in the emotional contents of marital relationships, the focus of the emphasis, for married parties as well as for cohabiting parties or those contemplating marriage alike, has therefore shifted to exactly those very items which would have been criminal to even think about in years gone by: MONEY, WHO GETS TO KEEP WHAT PROPERTY IF YOU SHOULD EVER BREAK UP OR DIE, AND THINGS OF THIS SORT!* [4]

"Because couples are focusing less on emotional issues today, the accountant and the appraisal of property are much more important than they used to be," said Ruth Miller, Chairman of the California Bar Association, recently.

The Causes of the "New Morality" and What Lessons From it

And what brought about this trend towards unpredictability in relationships? Experts have attempted to explain it in terms of any number of factors: prevalence of liberalized "no-fault" divorce laws and philosophies across the nation, women's liberation, increased mobility of Americans, financial affluence and increased

---

[4] Drs. Phillip Blumstein and Pepper Schwartz, sociologists at the University of Washington who conducted a National Science Foundation-backed research on the secrets of compatibility among couples, found there's a trend toward expressing verbalized arrangements among married couples and unmarried persons just living together alike, involving specifically negotiated allocations of money and more economic independence reserved by the individuals. "There's less of 'what's mine is yours and what's yours is mine,'" they reported.

leisure time, changed social mores[5] concerning loyalty and stability in marital, employment, and social relationships, generally; decrease in the moral influence of the church; the liberal media and advertising promotion of the grass-is-always-greener-elsewhere idea; the coming of age of the post-Vietnam "me generation" of young couples, and so on and so forth. Whatever the real reasons, however, what is far more clear have been the **result and the underlying implication** of the new trend: Those relationships which used to be permanent ties, or at least lasting ties, are now easily severed; people are now more frequently inclined to (and frequently do) engage in informal coupling, casual partnership changing, and an attitude of little concern toward entering and getting out of relationships of all types. And, given these modern realities, you'd be a damned fool not to safeguard and protect yourself !

The Central Message: Safeguard and Protect Yourself

The central message is rather clear, then: The current climate is one that makes it increasingly important, even necessary, to reduce relationships and understandings to writing. And anyone who ignores that reality does so at his or her own risk!![6] (It is no accident, for example, that more and more divorce judgments and terms of court settlements are increasingly being based on written "stipulations" and agreements previously worked out by the parties.) This book gives you all the tools and knowledge you need to be able to do just that, yourself—competently, and without too much expense or redtape. It's "preventive" law at its best!

Nor do you, in fact, necessarily have to actually have a formal agreement in hand, or need to to "do it yourself," for this book to be useful to or necessary for you. Not at all! In the end, even if you were to decide to hire a lawyer to do it for you, or even if you were to choose not to do it at all, yet by doing your homework on the subject matter and doing some of the preliminary work yourself, you would have been able to save yourself substantial amount of money anyway. Even more importantly, you shall have become far better educated and informed about your options, even if you choose never to take advantage of them, and, at the very least, just being educated on the subject matter provides you with the opportunity to make an informed choice.

The Publisher's Continuing Gratitude To You, The Reader

Finally, we urge this of you, our readers: Please send us any comments, opinions or suggestions you might have regarding this manual. Just drop us a few lines at our publishing offices. (We prefer written communication, please.) With us, YOU, our readers, are the KING and QUEEN! We value and welcome your feedback—always!!

Thank You

Newark, N.J.

The Publishers,
—Do-it-Yourself Legal Publishers,

---

[5] The California Supreme Court recognized in its pathbreaking 1976 Marvin decision, that "The mores of society have indeed changed so radically in regard to cohabitation that we cannot (continue to) impose a standard based on (old) moral considerations."

[6] Lillian Kozak, a lawyer who heads New York's Marriage and Divorce Task Force of the National Organization for Women, makes the same point this way: "[Having a good couples' agreement has] the advantage of preserving the parties' hard-earned money, for surely the cost of a marriage contract (even for a high cost one made through a lawyer) . . . will be a pittance compared to the unconscionable lawyers' fees in divorce."

CHAPTER 1

SOME IMPORTANT BACKGROUND CONCEPTS IN LIVING-TOGETHER RELATIONSHIPS AND CONTRACTS

The following terms are defined[1] below, just for the purpose of setting the stage for the materials in the later chapters:

1) Legal Marriage
2) Common-Law Marriage
3) Putative Marriage
4) Legal Separation
5) Settlement Agreement
6. Ante-Nuptial Agreement
7) Cohabitation
8) Homosexual live-Along
9) Palimony

1. Legal Marriage

Every reader of this manual probably has a pretty good idea of what a marriage is all about. But let's just define it here, however, for the purposes of this manual. Briefly, we define marriage here as the status of a man and a woman who have been legally united as a husband and wife for the prime purpose of establishing a family; the union of two persons of opposite sex by civil contract, in which they assume a status granted by the State.

The most important things to bear in mind in a (legal) definition of marriage are basically two-fold: first, that it is a "contract;" and second, that unlike most other contracts, it is one of the few contracts in which parties other than the contracting parties themselves, in this case the State, have a stake. In every legal marriage, the state is said to be a "silent partner" to the marriage contract. It is by the laws of the state (and by that only) that the final results of the rights and obligations of the parties to a marriage contract are fixed, changed or dissolved. Hence, each state has its own requirements for contracting a legal marriage (licenses, medical exams, age of consent, etc.), as well as the requirements by which the relationship may be dissolved or the marital property distributed or inherited.

2. Common-Law Marriage

This is a relationship or arrangement, a much less informal one than a legally contracted marriage, whereby a man and a woman live together and conduct themselves as man and wife *without* formalizing or solemnizing the relationship. Certain states recognize this relationship as a valid marriage while others do not.

States which permit common-law marriages include: Alabama, Colorado, District of Columbia, Georgia, Idaho, Iowa, Kansas, Montana, Ohio, Oklahoma, Pennsylvania, Rhode Island, South Carolina and Texas. The criteria for common-law marriages vary from state to state.

---

[1]For definition of terms, generally see the Glossary of Legal Terms, Appendix C

Generally, it is sufficient if the man and woman live and share their lives together and generally "hold themselves out to the public" as husband and wife. The most common criteria are using the same last name, referring to each other as husband and wife, filing joint income tax returns, opening joint bank accounts, and listing both names on the birth certificate of their children, etc.

3. Putative Marriage

This is a relationship wherein a man and a woman live together, with either one of them or both believing in honest good faith, that they are lawfully married, while, in fact, they really aren't. Example: A woman enters into a marital relationship with a man who claims to have been divorced from his previous wife, while the fact is that he actually wasn't divorced; or, he enters into such a relationship in the honest belief that the man she had previously been married to was dead, when in fact he was not.

4. Legal Separation

The state of living apart by a husband and wife either by a valid written agreement or by a decree (and order) of separation issued by a court. (More on this topic in Chapters 2, 4 & 5)

5. Settlement Agreement

An agreement (same as a "contract"), sometimes by spoken words but usually in writing, between two persons in a married, quasi-married, or cohabitation relationship, by which the parties set out the property rights and entitlements of each other in the event of death or termination of the relationship. (More on this topic in Chapter 4.)

6. Pre-Nuptial Agreement

Conventionally, this is an agreement (same as a "contract") made between a man and a woman at any time <u>before</u> they subsequently married, usually centering around issues of the rights and entitlements each would have with respect to their property. Same thing as "ante-nuptial" or "pre-marriage" agreement or contract. (More on this topic in Appendix C.)

7. Cohabitation

This is the current term generally used to describe the relatively novel but growing phenomenon of two persons of opposite sex living together as partners, roommates, friends, or lovers without being married to each other. (More on this topic in Chapter 10.)

8. Homosexual (Gay and Lesbian) Live-Alongs

This is generally conceived of as the act of living together by two (or more) persons of the SAME sex, not merely as roommates or business partners, but as sexual partners and lovers. When persons involved are female, it's called a "lesbian" relationship, and when they are male it's a "gay" relationship. The relevant rules or living-together agreement which this type of relationships would come under would be the "cohabitation" procedures. (See Chapter 10.)

9. Palimony

This is essentially a term for alimony paid to a live-in lover or "pal" after a relationship had ended. Arising out of the now-famous 1976 Marvin case of California, the logic behind the concept was simple: Since the unmarried partner often fills substantially the same role as a spouse — ranging from taking care of the house, to bearing or raising children and ministering to and providing companionship to a partner— isn't it only fair and logical that he or she should, upon the termination of the relationship, be entitled to a share of the property accumulated during the live-in relationship, just as a married partner would upon a divorce? The Marvin case established, though, that in California (as in most states), there's no such thing as palimony for non-married people in the sense of a statutory duty of support; that, instead, if there is to be any support, it has to arise out of an actual contractual agreement made between two people. Thus, came about the legal significance of entering into a written settlement or cohabitation agreement between partners, whether married or unmarred! (See Chapter 10 for more on this.)

CHAPTER 2

DOING YOUR COHABITATION OR MARITAL AGREEMENT: WHY (AND WHEN) YOU SHOULD DO IT YOURSELF WITHOUT A LAWYER

A. Why You Not Only Can, But Should Write Your Own Agreement, Without A Lawyer

The preliminary question for us here in this chapter is not whether you can, as a non-lawyer, draw up a valid or competent cohabitation or marital agreement. That question has been addressed and adequately laid to rest elsewhere (see page 40). Rather, the question here is even more basic: the practical and strategic reason why it is necessary, indeed advantageous, for you that you negotiate and drawn up the agreement yourselves, rather than involving an attorney.

B. Settlement Agreements are Primarily a Tool for Attaining Less-than-hostile Potential Breakup

As is amply illustrated elsewhere in this guidebook (see pp. 38-40), ultimately the fundamental reason for which cohabitation and marriage-related property or settlement agreements of sorts are drafted or employed in the modern family law practice, is practical — essentially to make an eventual breakup, if and when one were to come, less costly or hurtful, both financially, emotionally and otherwise. Its prime object, in a word, is as a tool for "planning" or "negotiating," albeit on a more peaceful and less costly term, an eventual divorce (or a breakup, in the case of unmarried parties who are planning marriage or merely cohabiting), if that should ever become necessary.

C. Can You Be Your Own "Attorney" Even In Divorce?

The subject of divorce proper is, of course, beyond the scope of the present manual; it is treated elsewhere.* However, in this chapter we shall merely address the general conditions you'd need to have if you are to ensure that you will be in the best possible position to successfully and easily process your own divorce case if you should need to — that is, primarily by making sure to have a good premarital and/or marital settlement agreement.

---

* Readers who are interested in the subject of divorce may consult the nation-wide 10 volume series on the subject, *"How to Do Your Own Divorce Without a Lawyer,"* written by the same author and published by the Selfhelper Law Press of America, a susidiary of Do-It-Yourself Legal Publishers.

With respect to divorce, for one who has to undertake one, there's a simple test to the question: 'Can you do your own divorce?' Let's put it this way: If you can simply read and understand just this manual, and are able generally to make simple practical decisions, follow clear and easy instructions, and fill out simple, standard forms, then you can quite easily do your own divorce (or dissolution of marriage) if you have to. **IT'S THAT SIMPLE!**

On the other hand, as a practical matter, there are just a few situations where it simply may not be advisable for you to do your own divorce or dissolution. These would be in a situation where:

a) your spouse actually goes out and hires an attorney in a divorce case, and then <u>actually</u> files legal papers to oppose you; and/or where

b) your spouse is presently on active military duty **and** will not cooperate with you and sign a WAIVER form granting that he'll not contest the divorce.

In brief, if your case is an "uncontested" one which does NOT come under one of the two exceptions listed above (if there's no lawyer involved in the case and no active military status by the other spouse), and you are honestly certain, after you've read this book, that you have no trouble following simple instructions or making simple practical decisions or compromises, then you can almost certainly do your own divorce — with all ease and facility.

D. What to Look For In Deciding Whether To Be Your Own "Attorney"

First of all, get it perfectly clear: with respect to divorce or other similar "civil" matters (e.g., drawing up a will or writing a premarital or settlement agreements, and the like), the law says that in such matters it is your right to have an attorney represent you, if and when that is what you prefer and want to do, or NOT to have one represent you, if and when that's what you prefer or want. AND NO LAW WHATSOEVER EVER SAYS THAT YOU MUST HAVE A LAWYER REPRESENT YOU. That's the Law! It's pretty simple to decide whether or not you need an attorney. The rule-of-thumb is simple: basically, in a civil matter such as the drafting of an agreement or even a divorce or separation, if your partner or spouse is not putting up a legal "contest" (legal fight or opposition) against the proposed settlement or arrangement or divorce suit, whichever is applicable, you probably don't need an attorney. And, in fact, as you will soon learn below, there are big advantages to not having or involving a lawyer in a case, in any event. In other words, in any situation where the two (or more) principals involved can, on their own, agree on something, or on a proposed settlement or arrangement, no lawyer is necessary!

Thus, in a matter involving a cohabitation or pre-marital agreement or marital property settlement, so long as the matter is an amicable or agreeable one between the parties, then you and your partner can just as easily act as your own attorneys and draw up your own agreements with no lawyer involvement. Now, what if it were a divorce that is involved? In such a situation, in order to be your own attorney in the case, it's most ideal and desirable if and when there is NO opposition (legal opposition) at all from your spouse — that is, if and when the case is "uncontested". Perhaps your spouse is long gone from the house, or for some reason he has no particular interest in what you may do. Or, he or she, too, wants the divorce as badly as you do. In such a case, you will probably have a very easy time doing your own divorce or dissolution. Where, on the other hand, your spouse is in the family picture and cares about what happens, you should make an effort to talk things over with him and try to agree on basic things. This is because there are important advantages for you (the two partners) in working things out. Also, to be suddenly served with legal papers without prior warning or information, might send your spouse the unintended signal and send him nervously running to a lawyer, and thereby get the two of you involved in unnecessary legal tangles and expenditures none of you really wanted but which you'd be unable to stop once it's set in motion!

BUT WHAT IF, ON THE OTHER HAND, IN A MARITAL BREAK-UP SITUATION, YOU HAVE TRIED YOUR HARDEST and you can't work things out, but you are nevertheless not certain whether or not your spouse will actually put up any legal opposition against a divorce action (maybe all that noise is just a bluff)? In such a situation, a wise strategy may be for you to still go ahead and start the divorce case on your own anyway. See what happens. If your spouse does then actually get an attorney who then proceeds to file legal papers in court to oppose your action, then you will have to get an attorney, too — at that point, but only *then.*

As a practical matter, probably the one situation when you definitely ought not to attempt to do your own divorce, is when a spouse is on active military duty but would not cooperate with you by signing the consent or waiver paper for you. In such a situation, either wait for him to get out of the military, or you get an attorney. However, if your military spouse will cooperate with you just to the extent of signing a consent paper (something called a "Waiver") to let the divorce proceed, then it's alright and you can still proceed as your own attorney just as well.

E. There Are Definite Advantages To Being Your Own Attorney

FIRST ADVANTAGE: It's Much Cheaper Doing It Yourself

Perhaps the most obvious advantage of doing you own written agreement or your own dissolution (divorce), is the dramatic SAVINGS IN COST. On the drafting of marital agreements, for example, lawyers will charge you upward of $600 for the simplest type of premarital or settlement agreement, and repeated charges each time there's a revision or an amendment to be made. On divorce, a New York City Department of Consumer Affairs survey in 1992 reported, for example, that the lawyers' fees for doing just a simple uncontested dissolution ranged from $600 to $1500, with most falling between $400 and $700, not including the out-of pocket costs and charges, such as the filing fee, cost of serving the papers, and the like, which separately averaged over $300 additional. Many attorney argue that they have to charge that much because, they claim, few cases stay uncontested! In deed, they have a point; in almost every case where one spouse gets an attorney involved, the other spouse will almost surely run out and get one too, and the legal cost will then be at least DOUBLE!

Here's how Nancy E. Albert[1], herself a practicing Chicago divorce lawyer and author, summed up the prevailing fee practice and habit of her fellow lawyers:

"Lawyer's fees vary dramatically.   Few of the "downtown" lawyers will touch your case before you put $1,000 on the table. Many insist on a $2,000 "retainer" (advance fee). One Chicago firm advertises that they will do divorces for $50 plus costs, but when asked in person will respond that they charge $350 for their high volume, simple, uncontested divorces. A few lawyers advertise divorces for anywhere from $30 to $250, but may tell you that, while the advertised fee is for a simple divorce, your divorce is much more complicated, and will cost more. A standard fee for a simple, uncontested divorce charged by many lawyers if $750, plus court costs."

Yet, even at their often prohibitive prices, lawyers would generally not give you much time, attention or information, and this is especially true in the supposedly cut-rate offices. You may find it very difficult to get

---

[1] As quoted in "Insider's Guide To Divorce In Illinois: The Practical Consumer Divorce Manual," by Nancy E. Albert (Nancy E. Albert, Publisher, Evansville, ILL. 1984) at p.33.

personal advice and attention.   You almost always end up wondering what's going on in a situation, but there's no one to talk to about it.

      The point here, is simply this: that as a general proposition, you can save at least $400, more like $600, and as much as $1200 or more, by doing it yourself!

SECOND ADVANTAGE: Without A Lawyer's Involvement You Can Better Keep It Simple

On a matter like the drafting of pre-marital or property settlement agreement, for example, try involving a lawyer in the negotiations just when the parties are full of all the goodwill and compromising spirit and are slowly but surely working their way through their differences on many tough, sensitive issues. And you'll soon discover that with the lawyers in the picture, one on <u>each</u> side but none for "both" sides, they will only make it more dfficult, not less to reach an agreement. Perhaps even impossible to do so, in the end! And the same is even more true in a divorcing situation. Most separating or divorcing couples, for examples, start off with a simple case alright. But then, all of a sudden the case doesn't end up that way. Lawyers, many experts agree, have a way of making almost anything more complicated. This is primarily because of the way they are trained, the way they think, and the way the legal system works. A lawyer is, in a word, a combatant. Our system of justice is known as "the adversary system". The principles and attitude we see in the courtrooms of today are said to have begun on the medieval field of honor where trial by combat meant that whoever survived in the end was "right."

Law schools generally have no course requirement in counseling or communication skills, and generally offer none. Instead, the training strongly emphasizes aggressive and defensive strategy and how to squeeze out the most financial advantage in every case. Is this the attitude you want in your marital agreement? Or a divorce?

A New Mexico publication on the subject summed it up this way: [2]

    "Most dissolutions are fairly sensitive and it doesn't take much to stir things up. Your average attorney is just too likely to make things worse, instead of better. Here's a typical example. Let's say a couple is separated and they have things more or less stabilized, in a situation where lots of sleeping dogs are being left to lie. Then one spouse goes to an attorney to start the dissolution . Often the attorney encourages the client to ask for more property and support than is actually expected. Lawyers think it pays to ask for extra so they can bargain their way back down. When the other spouse hears of this, it's a big shock, and that person will feel deceived. There's tension and trouble, not to mention mistrust and hurt. In most cases, just receiving formal legal documents from an attorney will motivate the other spouse to go see their own attorney for an independent opinion. Then the fun really starts.

      The two attorneys start off costing just double, ***but pretty soon they start writing letters and filing motion and doing standard attorney-type things, just like they were taught. Now we have a contested case,*** more fees and charges, and a couple of very upset spouses. Sure hope they don't have kids. The fees in contested cases run from a lot all the way up to everything." (Emphasis added by the writer)

---

[2] "Uncontested Divorce Kit, New Mexico," p.3.

One veteran divorce lawyer, Gail J. Koff [3], a partner in the New York branch office of Jacoby & Meyers Law Firm, while extolling the essentiality of the lawyer's involvement in marital settlement affairs, concedes that such kinds of trouble-creating lawyers are prevalent whose main role in marital disputes is to build confrontation and exacerbate tensions between spouses in order to build up legal fees. Attorney Koff, obviously an avid advocate of attorney involvement in the handling of all marital agreements and divorce, contends, however, that that breed of lawyers was a major factor only in the past when fault based divorce was the law. But not any more, she says. True, says Attorney Koff, in that "past" era, the kind of lawyers who controlled the system were the ones whose "specialty was getting in there and then 'sticking it' to the opponent, often using intimidation as a potent weapon. More often than not these attorneys simply exacerbated the problems, sometimes forcing a formidable wedge between the spouses. But just as often, they were enormously effective and got the job done for their clients."

But, says Koff', the rules have since changed: "once fault was no longer an issue and the emphasis shifted from sin to economics, this brand of attorney went the way of the dinosaurs."

Koff's perspective is certainly not lacking in imagination and inventiveness! In substance, though, her account is grounded more in fiction or hope than in reality. For, even at the same time, even as she claims that the old rules have "changed", she's enthusiastic about the use by attorneys in her own firm of tactics that were purely a throwback to the same old adversarial order lawyers are noted for. For one thing, she endorses the tactics of a lawyer in her firm who pressed on for shared custody, anyway, as a "negotiating tool" even though the client had perfectly been willing to settle for less, and another lawyer's tactics of calling in the police and accusing a parent of sexually molesting his own daughter in order to use the law as a "sword or as a shield" in a custody fight! [4]

So, again, the point here remains simple: ***If you do your settlement agreement or divorce yourself, you (and your spouse or partner) are much more likely to keep a case that started out simple that way—SIMPLE!***

THIRD ADVANTAGE: You'd Get A Unique Sense Of Personal Satisfaction Doing It Yourself

Admittedly it's a bit more work for you if you do it yourself. But this way, though, you stand to understand every step. You are completely in charge of your own case, your own decisions, and your own life.

The beneficial fallouts of this aspect of doing your own marital agreement or dissolution is subtle and is, hence, often under-estimated. But for you, it can become the most important advantage of them all. Doing it yourself helps to overcome the helpless feeling that often comes at this time. It will focus your mind on the

---

[3] Koff, *Love and The Law: A Legal Guide To Relationships in the '90's*, pp. 165-166. Another report, a more recent one to add its voice to the perennial debate, makes much the same point almost in identical words: "The simple addition of two lawyers to the problems encountered by a couple considering divorce will merely intensify any conflict.

    The reason for this is rooted in the way that most lawyers approach divorce. They want to "win" a divorce... (and in this), they set up an enormously costly game of legal chess with the spouses and any children of a marriage as pawns in the game.

    The legal maneuvering generally begins with the lawyer preparing a list of demands... The client is urged to ask for everything: the house, the car, custody of the children, huge amount of alimony and child support, the household possessions... Of course, the other spouse will be outraged when confronted with such a list of demands and will immediately seek out a mercenary lawyer to draw up a list of equally outrageous counter-demands. Thus, the battle lines will have been drawn. The attempt to amicably dissolve a marriage and get on with one's life will have escalated into an economic and psychological war which will cause enormous suffering and long-term misery for the participants." The report added: "(But) there is an alternative to turning a divorce into a war waged by competing lawyers... The alternative is a no-fault divorce by agreement." (Daniel Sitarz, a Florida attorney, in *"Divorce Yourself"* (Nova Publishing Co: 1991) pp. 11-12)

[4] Ibid. pp. 55-71. It should only be added that Koff concedes that individuals "may feel capable of writing their own separation agreement," but maintains that "it is not advisable when children are involved... (and) are best left to an attorney who is fully familiar with such cases." (p.175)

practical things, get you moving in a positive and constructive way, and give you a sense of movement out of the past and into the future. It feels good to stand on your own two feet, without being dependent, for a change, on a third party, whether it be in the form of a spouse or one who goes by the name "lawyer"!

FOURTH ADVANTAGE: *You Get To Make The Major Decisions On Your Own Life Yourself*
In theory, if you hired a lawyer, part of the service you are supposed to get from him or her is help with making decisions about your affairs. They are practically all-knowing, the theory goes, and they know which things have to be decided and the general standards and rules by which things are done in the courts. Or, at least, they are supposed to know!

However, by doing it yourself (and learning the court or legal procedures and using the help provided you by this manual), you shall have **YOURSELF** known a lot about what needs doing and the way things are generally done in cases such as you may have. You will understand the vital issues involved in a matter since you will yourself be the one that makes your own decision or settlement on your marital matters — the so-called "collateral" and "ancillary" issues — based on YOUR OWN knowledge and on YOUR OWN best self-interest! You won't now have to depend on someone else, some "expert", to do that for you!!

F. The Major Collateral Or Marital Issues That Must Be Decided:
- That the parties have to separate, and/or that the marriage should be ended, or not ended;
- Who is to be entitled to what property or asset of the parties?
- How to divide any property and outstanding bills that you may have accumulated before the marriage, or during the marriage; and
- Whether there is to be spousal financial support, and if so for whom and how much.
 Where there are no minor children, that's just about all there is to it.

If you have children, you must also decide:
- Who is to have custody of the children;
- How visitation is to be arranged; and
- How much is to be paid by whom for child support.
 (See Chapter 3, (pp. 15-30) for detailed discussion of collateral and ancillary issues in a divorce situation)

As a practical matter, this is what the overwhelming majority of premarital, as well as marital, settlement agreements and divorce (dissolution of marriage) cases is basically all about — settling the practical affairs of the couple and watching out for the well-being of the minor children, if applicable. If the parties were to be seeking a divorce, for example, these are the things you must decide about in order to get a separation or divorce. And if your spouse is in the picture and actively cares about what happens in the divorce, then you must be able either to talk over the issues with your spouse and come to some agreements, or you must be sure that your spouse is not likely to get a lawyer and actively oppose the divorce action.

G. You Should Try To Have Either An "Agreed" Or A "Default" Divorce or Settlement
When a separation arises, or a divorce or dissolution lawsuit is filed, it raises the issues outlined above. These issues can be resolved in one of only three ways:
 1) by *"agreement"* of the parties; or
 2) by *"default"* of the other spouse; or
 3) by *"contest,"* one spouse against the other.

In the **"AGREED"** case, the parties get together and settle the issues themselves and then, in effect, submit their agreement (written agreement) to court for its approval. In the **"DEFAULT"** situation, the respondent (the defendant-spouse) is properly notified of the fact that a lawsuit for divorce has been filed, but he does nothing about it, hence, as far as the court is concerned, no response or opposition is deemed to have been filed by the defendant in that case, and hence, the Petitioner-spouse (the plaintiff) is awarded the divorce **"BY DEFAULT"** — that is, by the failure of the other spouse to show up to object to or contest the divorce case. In the third situation, the **"CONTESTED"** case, the respondent-spouse, usually through a lawyer, files a Response to the divorce action and comes to oppose and do battle with you in court. (It will usually be a more difficult task, though by no means an impossible one, for you to do your own divorce under this last (the **"CONTESTED"**) category.

1. The "Default" Situation

In this kind of situation, the divorce is easy to do, providing you can only get the divorce papers "served" on (i.e., properly delivered to) your spouse. After a short wait following the service of the divorce papers on your spouse, you just go ahead and file the rest of the divorce papers with the court and get your judgment. Even if your spouse is angry and unsupportive of the divorce action, it's considered that so long as no actual, formal "Answer" or Response is filed by him, there is no legal apposition, and hence in official terms what he may otherwise be feeling means nothing — with respect to the divorce action.

2. The "Agreed" Divorce Situation

If your spouse is in the picture and actively cares about what happens, then it would be extremely advisable that you should make efforts to reach an agreement with him (her) on the "collateral" or "ancillary" issues that are involved in your marriage (property division, child or spousal support, child visitation or custody, and the like).

Here are some of the many things you stand to gain by having an agreement or understanding with your spouse, whether in an oral, or, preferably, in a written form, in **advance** of your going through with the divorce:

I) It is much easier getting the divorce, especially since you won't have to chase your spouse around to have the papers served on him. This makes it faster, and a lot cheaper, too.

II) It is more certain as to how the Court will likely decide matters in the end. The judge will very likely follow or adopt the terms of any agreement you and your spouse shall have had, providing such terms are not obviously unfair.

III) It will help the "defendant" or "respondent" spouse feel better about letting the divorce go through without contesting or having to hire a lawyer to "represent" him, since the terms of the Divorce Judgment (the final order) from the court would have been pretty much settled between you and him ahead of time.

IV) It invariably leads to better relations with your ex-spouse. Where there are children, this is extremely important.

In a word, the "agreed" type of divorce simply has so many big advantages and that's why it's generally agreed that if at all there is any chance of settling and working things out with your spouse — or, even better still, with your would-be spouse through premarital agreement even before marriage — you should struggle for it long and hard! It's absolutely worth the try and effort you can muster for one!!

H. Avoiding A "Contested" Divorce, Separation, Or Settlement Situation

When you really get down to it, when it comes to a divorce or separation, to fight, or not to fight, say the experts, is the point that divides the "easy" cases from the "hard" ones. The main reason, experts say, for a difficult time with a divorce situation, for example, is that such couples want to fight, or that they just can't keep from it! Such people are angry or hurt and want to hurt back. They want to use the law as a weapon, to revenge or force their spouse into some sort of response. The law, however, rarely has this result. *Instead, what usually happens is that "the law" and the legal system almost always turn a **contested** divorce into a very unpleasant and very expensive failure. The divorce will still always go through in the end, but no one will be happy about it. What a cruel hoax! NO ONE EVER REALLY "WINS" IN A DIVORCE COURT BATTLE!!*

Hence, if your case may turn into a fight, remember this: **It is one thing to get a court order against someone, but it is very much another thing to be able to enforce that order.** Especially in cases where there are children, a divorce is not a final solution since you have to deal with each other in the future because of the kids. In more ways than one, it really pays to work things out.

Whatever You Do, Please Avoid Ever Involving An Attorney!

Can you get a non-selfish, "friendly" pre-marital agreement negotiation, or separation or divorce (not to talk of a simple or affordable one!), once you and/or your partner hire a lawyer and involve him in the process? **NO! YOU JUST DON'T STAND MUCH OF A CHANCE!!** It's too late already by then. Here's how a Chicago practicing divorce attorney and author summed up the reality:

> "Perhaps you have been making a valiant attempt to avoid hostility and deal fairly with each other in resolving property and parenting issues. Enter the lawyers. All that is over now. After all, this is an adversary proceeding; each side must be represented by different lawyers…Step back three paces — Draw!
>
> *Now the contest has only begun. But there will be no winner among the parties…Except for the lawyers…The longer the contest, the greater their share of the spoils.*
>
> Are there alternatives to that scenario? Yes! One is to sit down together [with your spouse] and hash out your differences so that you can come up with an agreement. Then you can either handle your own divorce or present the substance to your respective lawyer…
>
> The second alternative is to go to a divorce mediation service…that helps the two parties come to their own voluntary agreement about disputed issues…"[5]

Try Working Things Out With Your Spouse

To negotiate a mutually acceptable agreement or arrangement, if you can't agree about basic things peacefully, maybe you should let some time pass. This is one strategy suggested by many experts. Wait to see if things settle down. It may probably help if you order another copy of this marital agreement manual and send it to your spouse, and then try to discuss various sections of it with him or her directly — i.e., with no lawyer being involved on either side.

---

[5] Nancy E. Albert, writing in *"Insider's Guide To Divorce In Illinois: The Practical Divorce Manual"*, at p.11. Another experienced divorce lawyer, Burton L. Monasch, past President of the New York Chapter of the American Academy of Matrimonial Lawyers, has this to say: "…the courts are the last place a person resolving a matrimonial dispute should be… Because of the adversary nature of the law, an atmosphere of heat and ill-will is immediately created… I believe that the day a matrimonial problem gets in the hands of lawyers the individuals are in deep trouble." Monasch in <u>Marriage and Divorce Today</u>, a New York City bi-weekly newsletter, December 19, 1977.

This is a good idea because your spouse or partner may misunderstand what a property settlement or a divorce (dissolution of marriage) is all about, or what exactly you are seeking by the divorce or settlement action, and informed people are usually less emotional and irrational. It can get the two of you talking about practical, constructive things.

Also, this manual, especially the informational material contained in this chapter, can help to drive the following points across to your mate or spouse:

- Fighting will not automatically prevent the divorce if at all you're at that point, it will only make it more unpleasant and much more time consuming and expensive — to BOTH parties (not to mention the children, if you have any in the marriage).

- Even dissolutions that are "contested" by the parties are decided according to the standards discussed in this manual. Any monetary advantage gained by a court fight is usually wiped out by the legal fees and other costs of the battle, such as the emotional and psychological costs. How much price tag do you place on the emotional strain and future relations with your spouse and children, for example?

If the reason you can't agree is emotional, or a basic inability to communicate, you can still be very successful if you can both agree to involve a third person. A trusted friend, a priest, a rabbi, a member of the clergy, or a professional mediator or counselor (but, please no lawyers!) can often be very helpful at getting things worked out.

Listen to the wise words of **Gail J. Koff,** a seasoned veteran New York matrimonial attorney with long, first hand court-room experience in the practical aspects of matrimonial court fights, about the detrimental, almost-always-negative effects of child custody court battles, for example, to everyone involved:[6]

> "All too frequently child custody battles [between parents]become a matter of pride [for them]. Parents sometimes believe that a custody battle is necessary to prove how much they "love" their child. Or perhaps they do it because they feel it is expected of them. Other times it's a way of demonstrating the bitterness one spouse harbors for the other. *What parents blinded by emotions, sometimes fail to understand is that those truly hurt are the children. For this reason, before undertaking any custody battle, it's a good idea to ask yourself: Am I doing this for myself or for the child?"* (Emphasis added by the present writer)

> Koff adds this piece of advise: "Even under the best of circumstances a court battle can be devastating and may result in irreparable harm to the children. For this reason it's almost always in the best interests of the child to avoid these confrontations. Divorce is difficult enough on children without a vicious custody battle between their parents. *Parents should make a serious attempt to work out a reasonable agreement before it reaches the point where the matter must be resolved by the court... this can be accomplished either in a separation [or other type of settlement] agreement or be negotiated at the time of divorce."* [Emphasis added by the present writer]

And finally, listen to another wise words, this time of ***Sandra Kalenik***, an experienced, long-term Washington D.C. area author and expert on divorce matters:

> "Over the years I have talked with many divorce lawyers, mediators, and people involved in the divorce process. If there is one common problem divorcing people have, it is that they are

---

[6] Koff, *Love and the Law*, op.cit., 214, 212-3.

emotional and often do not think clearly about what they are doing. Many are extremely angry, and revenge against their spouse pops up as the only answer to their problems. They allow revenge to replace cogent thinking. When this happens, bad decisions often result to the detriment of both parties...

If I were to offer advice, it would be this: stay as calm and unemotional as you possibly can. Learn what your rights are, decide what you need and want, and keep as cool as possible. When you are feeling depressed, overwhelmed, spiteful, or furious, talk it over with a respected friend, therapist, or member of the clergy...***Whatever you do, try not to act out your emotions by making them a legal battlefield among you, your spouse, and any children you might have. Unless you are very wealthy and wish to transfer a good chunk of that wealth to your attorney's coffers, don't argue over everything.*** Be selective with your fights. This detachment can save you more later than you might be able to realize now." [7] (Emphasis added by present writer)

I. If Direct Negotiations Don't Work, Use Mediation

But, even if all efforts at direct-negotiations between you and your spouse (or cohabiting partner) have been exhausted and they are unsuccessful, or such negotiations are not feasible, all is still not lost yet. Far from it! In fact, quite to the contrary, fortunately there is a new potent devise that has increasingly gained approval with the courts and popularity among divorcing and separating couples across the country. Such device can come to your rescue. It's called: **MEDIATION.**

Mediation basically involves using the assistance and services of a professional negotiator, called a "mediator", to help couples negotiate their agreement or settlement. Often, the mediator is a social worker, or even a lawyer, but well trained specifically in the art of family conflict negotiations and resolution. In recent times private mediation services and centers have sprung up across the country, their specialty being mediating divorce and separation cases — including property settlement, and child custody and support arrangements, alimony, etc.

Perhaps not surprising, at the beginning divorce lawyers had been among the major detractors of mediation. The lawyers claimed that, because mediators are often not lawyers, their services often fail (they claimed) to protect the right of either party in that mediators, the lawyers contend, are sometimes unaware of the legal ramifications of their decisions. Nevertheless, mediation has gained increasing popularity with that segment of the public who are aware of and educated about it.

The chief attraction of mediation which has accounted for its growing popularity especially among upper middle-class and wealthier persons (but not necessarily among divorce lawyers!), are two-fold: first, unlike "arbitration" (negotiation arrangement in which the parties must abide by the decision of the arbitrator), mediators are involved in the process only to facilitate agreement by offering objective, professional, third-party alternatives acceptable to both sides; and secondly, use of mediation have been noted to save the parties both substantial time and money relative to the traditional method of using the lawyer-dominated settlement arrangements, and often includes in one flat fee package the cost of preparing and filing the necessary written agreements and court papers to finalize the separation or divorce judicially.

For a national mediation organization which provides referrals to mediators meeting its strict standards, contact: The Academy of Family Mediators
     5 Militia Dr. MA 02173 0
     Phone: (781) 674-2663

---

[7] Sandra Kalenik, in *How To Get A Divorce* (Washington Book Trading Company, 1991) pp. X-xi

Use County Counseling Services, If Possible

In addition to privately-run mediation, many counties in certain states across the county (e.g., Arizona, Washington, Oregon, Wisconsin, New Hampshire, New Mexico, etc., to name just a few) now have a Conciliation Court or unit thereof, which provides marriage counseling for troubled marriages, either before or during a divorce action. They would help you save your marriage if and when there's still any hope, but when it's too late and hopeless they can also help you dissolve it on a more peaceful and civilized basis. Conferences with the counselors are often free or at a nominal fee, and their confidentiality is usually protected by the law, so all you can lose is time. You can first try it. And if, in the end, you don't like their services, you can always go back to your legal proceeding and pursue your divorce or separation accordingly.

J. Putting It All In A Written Agreement

THE BOTTOM LINE QUESTION: So you'd want to have an "agreed" or agreeable divorce (or separation) with your partner or future spouse — if a break-up were ever to become an issue for you at some point? Then it's simple. You simply must put it all down IN WRITING NOW, any and all agreements and understandings the both of you shall have had about your lives together and your future relationship. And that's where the drawing up of an appropriate pre-marital or property settlement or separation agreement (or such other agreement of other types), the primary subject matter of this guidebook, comes into play — and handily. (See Chapter 6 for the actual drafting procedures for such agreements).

As is more elaborately covered elsewhere in the manual (See Section F of Chapter 4 at pp.38-40), in these contemporary times written settlement agreements between couples who are either married or about to marry, or those merely cohabiting, have become the basic instrument of effectuating peaceful, compatible divorce or breakups, accepted and encouraged by the courts. In a word, once a good written settlement agreement is drawn up, if an action for a divorce or settlement were later to be filed by either party (or by both), the divorce action will almost automatically be resolved in accordance with the provisions of the written agreement, thereby leading to a far more amicable "uncontested" case in which at the final hearing only one spouse need attend. The court, in effect, will basically review and approve the agreement you and your spouse had reached; and, providing the terms are half way fair, it will incorporate it into the final divorce **DECREE** to grant you your divorce and/or agreement. (Or, in very rare occasions, it may require changes in the agreement before approving it and granting the divorce in a situation where, for example, it finds the agreement to be too one-sided or grossly unfair).

How To Do It

Hence, the message? It's simple: that you had better tried and at least exerted every effort, and if at all it's all possible, by all means work out and sign a written agreement with your partner spouse, whether before or after marriage or cohabitation. If you try your darnest but in the end you and your partner still cannot agree on signing one, well that's too bad; you can still proceed without one then. (The procedures for the actual drafting of agreements are in Chapter 7)

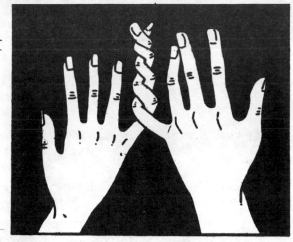

CHAPTER 3

THE TYPICAL PROPERTY AND OTHER "COLLATERAL" ISSUES THAT ARISE BETWEEN MARITAL (OR COHABITING) PARTIES: YOUR BASIC LEGAL RIGHTS & ENTITLEMENTS

1. The Most Important Thing: Try Reaching A Fair, Reasonable Understanding & Agreement With Your Partner On The Issues.

In chapter 5 (pp.41-44), we fully set forth the kinds of issues and subject matters which couples are permitted to address in a pre-marital agreement under the Uniform Pre-marital Agreement Act guidelines — a guideline used in almost every state. An interesting observation is that, upon a closer look, one quickly finds that those provisions of the Uniform Pre-marital Agreement Act (UPAA) are essentially identical to those pertaining to couples already married, and to marital situations and divorce. In fact, the provisions of the UPAA seem to closely mirror the Uniform Marital Act of 1983 which preceded it, particularly on matters of property disposition rights, spousal support, and other issues of relevance in marital relations other than child custody and support. Indeed, except for one major issue, namely child support issues where the UPAA prohibits couples from making binding provisions on such matter in a prospective divorce, both Acts are virtually indistinguishable on the major issues.

Consequently, what we shall address in this chapter, are seemingly the same basic issues as are generally applicable in marital situations involving married partners in a divorce situation or a separation or settlement agreement situation. And, given below in the rest of the chapter for your education and general information, are the basic legal rights of the parties with respect to the various typical issues in a relationship (property division, income, child custody or support, etc.) for different states, and the legal principles by which such matters are generally resolved by the courts in the event of a divorce or a separation or other settlement.

A Word Of Caution: As a couple contemplating to be soon married, if any of the issues addressed herein are applicable to you — or realistically likely to be applicable to you in the future — the point is to be sure to reach an understanding that is fair and reasonable with your partner about the issues, using the principles outlined in this chapter as your general guide. As a general rule, the court will all too likely uphold whatever terms an adult man and woman couple freely agree upon, providing they are lawful, pretty fair and reasonable, and not unconscionable or harmful to one party, especially to the welfare of the minor children, if applicable.

Hence, as a general principle, if you wish to formulate a good pre-marital agreement that will stand the test of the law or challenge, then or any time in the future, the key is really for the both of you to work earnestly with each other on the "collateral" issues of your marriage and learn to practice the art of human compromising and reasonableness, even generosity, with each other in working out the terms of your agreement. It's that simple!

2. The Settling Of Different Issues Between Marital (Or Cohabiting) Partners, The Legal Rights & Principles Involved

Let's go in some detail into the collateral (they're also called "ancillary" or "incidental") questions that typically arise in divorce. The following issues will be discussed:

A. Property Division

B. Settlement of Insurance Pension & Retirement Funds, Stock-Option/Profit Sharing Plans, Social Security Benefits, Etc.

C. Division of Marital Debts & Bills

D. Alimony (Maintenance)

E. Custody of Children, if Applicable

F. Visitation Rights With Children

G. Child Support (if Applicable)

H. Other Issues

A. PROPERTY DIVISION

In a nutshell, the legal principles by which marital property is divided or allocated upon divorce, fall under three basic categories under various states' rules:

i) **The "Community Property" States.** Here, in such states, the spouses split **equally** on a 50-50 basis all property acquired by either or both parties DURING marriage, generally excluding as each spouse's "separate property," those acquired by them either before the marriage or by gift or inheritance. There are nine community property states in the nation; they are: Arizona, California, Idaho, Louisiana, Nevada, New Mexico, Texas, Washington, and Wisconsin.

ii) **"Equitable Distribution" Property States.** Here, in such states, marital property acquired or owned by the spouses DURING the marriage is distributable to them "equitably" — that is, on the basis of what is just and fair, with each couple's circumstances determined on a case-by-case manner.[1] In other words, aquitable distribution does not necessarily mean equal distribution.

---

[1] New York's Equitable Distribution Bill of 1980 is typical of provisions made by equitable property division states. It treats marriage as an "economic partnership" for which the property accumulated by it at the time of it's dissolution is to be distributed to the partners (the spouses) on an "equitable" basis — i.e., on a fair basis, although not necessarily 50-50. The law states that, except for couples who settle peacefully without contest, or have privately entered into a written "opting-out agreement" setting out how marital property is to be divided up in the event of a divorce, marital property (defined as "all property acquired by either or both spouses during the marriage") is to be distributed upon divorce by the court "equitably between the parties, considering the circumstances of the case and of the respective parties."

Rather, what it means is that the courts, when allocation the marital property, are required to make a fair and just allocation taking into account such factors as the length of the marriage, ages of the participants, earning capacities, the respective economic and non-economic contributions of the spouses, the relative financial circumstances of the parties during the marriage, etc. *The basic idea, in a word, is to ensure that each spouse receives a fair share of the financial fruits of the marriage, the assets and property.*

In general, under the rules of most equitable distribution states, the separate property which a spouse owned **PRIOR** to marriage and any property which a spouse receives by gift or inherits (either before or during the marriage), is usually treated as his/her own "separate property" not subject to division, and only any other property accumulated by the parties (including any income from such separate property that was earned during the marriage), is distributable. However, in a few states (Alaska, Connecticut, Georgia, Hawaii, Indiana, Kansas Massachusetts, Michigan, Montana, New Hampshire, North Dakota, Oregon, South Dakota, Utah, Vermont, and Wyoming), ALL of the spouses' property is possibly subject to being divided on an equitable basis, regardless of when or how it was acquired or held even including any gifts and inheritances — providing the court sees good reason to feel it's just and proper to do so.[2]

iii) **"Common Law" or "Title" Property States.** Here, the ownership of individual property is allocated to the respective spouses according to who purchased it, or who has legal title to it or who had his/her name on it at the time of the divorce. As of this writing, only Mississippi appears to be the one state in this category. Under the common-law, basically an individual owns any property purchased with his or her own assets or out of his or her own income, as well as any assets in which sole ownership is shown on a title, deed, or other legal instruments of ownership.

Almost all the states, in deed except for Mississippi which is a "title" state, are today either community property or equitable distribution-based. In brief, except for the nine "community property" based states listed above (and Mississippi), the other 40 states plus the District of Columbia are equitable distribution-based in terms of their marital property allocation principle.

NOTE: Rather fortunately for us, though, as a practical matter it turns out that in marital situations most couples involved in divorcing situations don't really have to worry about the problem of "property division" in the first place, since in the first place, they either have no major property to fuss over, or they shall have already given up whatever property there is to one or the other spouse even long before they decide it's time to file for divorce! Hence, for most couples seeking divorce, this issue will probably be an irrelevant one, anyway! Furthermore, bear in mind that, again, as a practical matter, the issue of what state law or what method of property division to apply, will only arise where the judge has to come into the picture to rule on it because the spouses themselves are not able (or not willing) to come to agreement on their own regarding the way to divide up their property.

The point to remember is that these rules are, in the final analysis, only guidelines and 'talking points' for negotiating and discussion; if you and your spouse can mutually agree on dividing up your property in any manner or proportion, that division, even if only half way fair and reasonable, will be just as valid and sufficient for all intents and purposes!

---

[2] Included among the group which divide marital property "equitably," are also the following territories: the District of Columbia, Puerto Rico and The Virgin Islands.

Who Should Have The Family House?

For most couples, a home is often the most important and most expensive acquisition they ever made, and "partitioning" (dividing up) of a house is not easily acceptable to either spouse. Fortunately, as a practical matter, in the majority of cases the spouse who does not have custody of the children (usually the husband) will usually agree to an arrangement whereby the other spouse may have the use of the house in the interest of the proper rearing of the children or, he will frequently agree to deed his interest in the property over to the spouse when the equity in the house (the current market value of the house, minus the outstanding mortgage debt on it) isn't large.

But what if you and your spouse can't agree on anything, by what principles do you (or, does the court) decide who is to have the house? There are a few options, the more common solutions, you can consider:

- Put the house (or apartment) up for sale and divide its "net" proceeds, if any (the balance from the sales proceeds, if any, after subtracting the mortgage debt on it, and the estate taxes, commission, etc). This method, by the way, is the simplest way. Or,

- One spouse, especially the one who does not have custody of the children in a marriage involving minor children, may grant the other spouse the right to "exclusive use and possession" of the marital house for a specified number of years, say, until she remarries or the youngest child attains the age of 18 or 21, without actually giving her the ownership, at which time the house would be sold and the net profits shared equally. Or,

- One spouse may simply agree to buy out the other's share in the house — i.e., he or she is allowed to retain possession of the home, with the title to the house transferred to her at divorce, while she either takes out a second mortgage to pay off the house to the other spouse, or gives the other spouse a note to pay him off either installmentally or upon the sale of the house or the attainment of a designated age by the last child. Or,

- One spouse, the one not having the pension plan (say the wife), may balance the house against the other spouse's (the husband's) pension; the wife simply receives full title to the house in return for waiving all rights and claims to her husband's pension.

NOTE: One "sticky" issue that often arises in relation to how to apportion a house, has to do with the down payment on the house when it was bought. One spouse, for example, might have made the down payment out of his or her own separate resources — that is, money which was neither part of the community property (if they lived in a community property state) nor part of the marital property. Subsequently, however, all mortgage payments were paid out of marital funds. Thereupon, at the time of separation or divorce it is legitimate to have the down payment written into the settlement agreement or divorce judgment stipulating that he or she will receive that amount up front, before the final split is made (assuming it's a community property state), and any appreciation divided up.

B. SETTLEMENT OF INSURANCE, PENSION & RETIREMENT FUNDS.[3] STOCK-OPTION/PROFIT-SHARING PLANS, SOCIAL SECURITY BENEFITS, ETC.

a) Insurance Funds: In a marital dissolution situation where either or both spouses maintain some retirement or insurance policies (e.g., life insurance, health insurance, pension right, etc.), it is not unusual to find that one spouse may have named the other as the beneficiary of the proceeds. One thing the spouses should remember to discuss — and arrive at an agreement on — in such situations, is who should retain or give up which beneficiary rights in which policy or funds? Couples may also agree on maintaining a medical or life insurance policy for the benefit of the children, where applicable, and how it should be paid for and by whom.

b) Pension & Retirement Plans: In the last several decades, pensions have become one of a couples' largest marital assets, and almost every state now considers the value of benefits from retirement and pension plans, and from stock options and profit-sharing plans during the course of a marriage, as part of a spouse's assets or marital property subject to sharing upon divorce. Consequently, figuring out how to value such plans and to divide them equally is important in divorce or separation settlements. The issue can be a thorny one.

Assuming that your spouse has an employment which has a pension plan (only 76.1 million Americans or just 46% of all American workers, for example, were covered by a pension plan in 1990), an important question is: how do you evaluate the pension and divide it in a divorce settlement? *Here are a few options that can be considered:*

Option #1: Other assets could be given to the non-pensioned spouse in lieu of a 100% right to the pension. The way this works is this: you let the pensioned spouse (the covered employee) keep the pension benefits and give the other spouse cash or other assets worth half the <u>current</u> value of that part of the benefits accrued during the marriage. (But this, however, requires that you be able to figure out what the current value of the benefits are, meaning basically that you'd need the services of an insurance actuary). In other words, let's say the parties jointly own a house, the employee spouse (the one with the pension) keeps his or her full pension but waives his rights to the house, and in return, the non-pensioned spouse receives full title to the house but also waives all her rights to the pension.

Or, as another example, one spouse, say the husband, may retain his entire interest in his retirement fund by giving up to his wife his one-half interest in a jointly held bank account with his wife, or by giving his car he wholly owns, to his wife in return. Trade off arrangements are generally preferred among couples because retirement plans are often very difficult to divide up without terminating it and cashing it in. Hence, often it is customary to give other assets to the non-pensioned spouse in lieu of a right in the pension as it usually saves everyone a whole lot of headaches.

Basically, you'll have to hire an actuary (a pension or insurance evaluation specialist), since the calculations involved are usually very complicated even for lawyers and other experts, who'll employ the proper methods to substitute the present value of the unemployed spouse's share of the pension with other marital property, and thereby place a present value on the pension. And, with that figure, the pension can then be divided equitably, as agreed to between the spouses. [To get an actuary to appraise the value for you, just look under "actuaries" and "insurance consultants" in your local Yellow Pages].

---

[3] Common among retirement plans, are the following: Individual Retirement Accounts (IRA's); IRS 401 (k) Retirement Plans; HR-10 Retirement Plans (KEOGH'S); Self-employment Person's Individual Retirement Accounts (SEP-IRA's); Tax Sheltered Annuities (TSA's); and Employee Stock Options (ESOP's).

If the parties are living, for example, in a "community property" state, the pension rights will be treated as an asset to be split 50-50 at its calculated, present value; and if living in an "equitable distribution" state, the pension rights will be treated as an asset to be split in other "equitable" proportions as agreed to by the spouses.

Option #2: The pension may be allocated to the non-employee spouse based upon the ratio of years the employee-spouse worked during the marriage and his/her total years of employment. (Example: husband worked five years prior to marrying wife, and fifteen years during the marriage, during which time they lived in a community property state before they divorce. This means that the wife will be entitled to share in only three-quarters (i.e., 15 years of marriage out of 20 years of work) of the pension, and she should look to split that three-quarters share 50-50 being that they live in a community property state. [With this method, though, the non-employee spouse may not collect until the employee spouse actually retires, and who knows, he may die or lose the job in the meantime before retirement, or the pension fund may go bankrupt, in each case the non-pension spouse would be left without any recovery.]

Option #3: The value of the employee spouse's anticipated pension could be treated as a future asset in which the other spouse (the non-employee spouse) could have some share. You'll give, in other words, the non-employee spouse the right to receive part of the retirement benefits when those benefits are eventually paid out.

Qualified Domestic Relations Order (QDRO)

Under the above third option, it is not necessary to figure out the current value of the benefits; both spouses will simply have to wait to receive any payments until the employee-spouse is eligible to receive the benefits. **HOWEVER, HERE'S AN IMPORTANT POINT:** if you choose this option, your settlement agreement with your spouse must generally contain a provision for what is known as a "Qualified Domestic Relations Order" (QDRO) as applicable under the retirement plan rules. Furthermore, your settlement agreement, along with the final decree of dissolution of marriage, must be filed with, and be accepted by, the administrator of the retirement plan involved before it will be effective.

A Qualified Domestic Relations Order, or simply QDRO, is a court-signed Order which, if and when it gets signed at the time of a divorce, authorizes the administrator of the pension plan to "qualify" (comply with) the stipulations of the order — that is, for it to make certain that the plan meets certain requirements which principally ensures that the pension assets are split according to the couple's agreement.

Note, though, that QDRO orders apply ONLY to pension plans of two types — the "defined benefits" and "defined contributions" types, such as 401(K) and profit-sharing plans. They do not apply to Individual Retirement Accounts (IRA) or to special arrangements that companies set up for high-paid executives.

But You May Not Be Entitled To Share In Your Spouse's Pension, In The First Place!

Whatever the method of sharing the pension that applies, it should be emphasized, however, that unless you have been married for a fairly long time, the value of the retirement plan (and of your share of it) may be insignificant and not worth the trouble. Furthermore, as stated above, surely it's true that nowadays there's generally no disputing the fact that benefits from pension or retirement plans, or from stock option or profit sharing plans which are earned during the marriage, are legitimately classifiable as assets which could be subject to sharing by the other spouse upon a divorce. *But where the problem arises on this issue, however, is with respect to determining what the actual* **PRESENT VALUE** *of these items is — in particular, the current value of the benefits that accrued (the amount of money that was contributed) during the marriage. On your* part, here's the simple advice to follow: simply ask the employer or administrator of the plan (or an insurance actuary, or accountant or CPA) for help with working out this information.

What about social security benefits, or military and federal pensions and benefits? With respect to social security, under the law any benefits received by a spouse are not classifiable as marital property or subject to division upon divorce, the rule being that these are federal benefits and are not subject to state laws. Paradoxically, though, on the other hand military retirement pensions and federal civil annuity benefits, though federally administered, are in most states subject to division upon divorce, especially for marriages of long duration (generally over 10 years).

C. Division Of Marital Debts And Bills

How do you settle the marital debts and bills incurred by divorcing parties? Who is to pay or be responsible for what? Whichever ways the parties voluntarily agree to divide up the debts they jointly signed or co-signed for between them, will ordinarily be acceptable to the court. Generally, only debts and obligations incurred by the parties DURING their marriage are applicable, and any such obligations that are incurred prior to the marriage are deemed a "separate" obligation for which the spouse who incurred them is solely liable. Just to make sure, however, include in your negotiations and agreement **ALL** of the debts that are outstanding for each and both parties and that legitimately apply, and stipulate clearly and in detail who should be responsible and liable for what debts or bills and why. More importantly, make sure that you promptly take away those charge cards or joint check books from each other and physically destroy them. That way, you prevent the possibility of finding that there are more debts for you later!

In those states which fall under the equitable property principle of property ownership (see p.16), the marital debts are to be divided "equitably," as reasonably seen fit by the couple; and for those who fall under the community property states (p.16), the community debts are split 50-50, unless a different arrangement is otherwise agreed to by mutual consent of the parties.

i) An Important General Rule To Follow In Apportionment Of Property Or Debts

In respect to partners involved in a cohabitation situation or engaged in entering into a premarital agreement (or even any other types of property settlement agreement), perhaps the single most important piece of advice about going about the appropriate property arrangement or appointment of their personal debts, is simply this: BY ALL MEANS, TRY TO AVOID MIXING THEM UP; KEEP THOSE OF EACH PARTNER SEPARATE!

As a general rule, the net assets of the vast majority of divorcing families are relatively small, in the first place, and not worth litigating for by parties. However, even regarding those limited special cases where there are substantial assets in the relationship, experts have noted, for example, that in almost every state where there are strict laws that clearly delineate what share of the marital property each spouse would be entitled to in a division of the marital estate, and which leave no apparent legal "loophole" for landing a different result, there has been a remarkable lessening in the amount of litigation over property issues following the enactment of such laws. In the state of Wisconsin, for example, a 1989 study of its strict Marital Property Act (1985) which made all marital property at divorce subject to a 50-50 division between the spouses, found that only about 5 out of 2,000 cases went to trial specifically over property division. The major reason accounting for such sharp decrease in litigation over property division, the experts say, is the strict and unambiguous property distribution law. For, as one observer of the Wisconsin experience notes, divorcing parties rapidly got wise to the reality that, "If property is going to be divided 50-50, lengthy litigation means that both parties will substantially lower any proceeds they might receive from the divorce."[4]

But what is even more interesting, even of greater relevance, here, for the purposes of those primarily concerned with writing up a good premarital agreement before getting into a marriage, or with merely avoiding making an unwise property arrangement with a cohabiting partner or would-be spouse, is another reality. That is, the discovery that even in such strict "community property" law states, such as Wisconsin where property is clearly required to be divided 50-50, the primary reason that equal property division is challenged by spouses, is that assets in one partner's name has been **CO-MMINGLED** with assets of the other.[5] This sometimes happens, it is found, when one person owns a house and then remarries. During the marriage, both parties pay the mortgage and house repairs. But then come divorce; and at this point, the other partner, the non-owner of the house, now claims that house to be "marital property" for the reason that he has paid for some of the house mortgage and its upkeep, and litigation ensues!

In sum, the lesson is clear. *The central point is that one major way to avoid potential future litigation over property division, is to strenuously avoid the co-mmingling of assets between marital parties, and further to be also sure that in writing your premarital (or other) agreement between you and your partner, you do so in strict adherence to that basic principle.* In fact, it is advised that you avoid doing any commingling in any kind of assets — whether in real property, or by having joint bank account or jointly owning a vehicle, or whatsoever. Don't agree to pool and share earnings and accumulations, either. In deed, this rule is more especially applicable when your partner has debt troubles, actual or potential. This way, by keeping all property and financial arrangements <u>separate</u>, there'll be no elements of confusion or mistaking by anyone, you'll never have to take legal responsibility for your partner's debts, and your separate property cannot be taken to pay for your partner's overdue bills. In short, both in actual living as well as in the drafting of your cohabitation or pre-marital agreement with your partner, a wise general principle would be to strictly avoid the co-mmingling of gifts, inheritances and individual assets owned solely by you with assets jointly owned by you and your spouse or partner!

ii) Consideration Of "Fault" In Award Of Property

As could be seen from a review of Appendix B (pp. 108-120), virtually every state now has some type of 'no-fault' ground for divorce or separation, and a judge can simply decide on a divorce case without consideration of any allegation or testimony about a spouse's marital conduct in bringing about the break up of the marriage. The important thing to realize, however, is that even in those same states where divorce can be obtained without regard to marital fault, the same marital fault (a spouse's conduct) can still be considered with respect to the division of their marital property. Thus, in such states a judge may still award more property or less to one party based on the evidence of marital fault or conduct presented before him — adultery, mental cruelty, desertion, sodomy, non-support or neglect, and the like.

The following 20 states are those which, under a provision of the state law, a spouse proven guilty of marital 'fault' (adultery, mental cruelty, desertion, sodomy, non-support, neglect, etc.) may be made to receive <u>less</u> than the share of property to which he/she might otherwise be entitled: Alabama, Massachusetts, Michigan, Mississippi, Missouri, New Hampshire, N. Dakota, Rhoda Island, S. Carolina, Texas, Utah, Vermont, Virginia, and Wyoming.

D. ALIMONY (MAINTENANCE)

Alimony (it's now more commonly referred to also as "maintenance" or "spousal support" in some states) is, of course, the term given to court-ordered allowance a husband (or wife) pays to his wife (or husband)

---

[4] *Wisconsin Fathers Guide*, p.92

[5] l bid

for her separate maintenance after divorce. Nowadays, in the wake of the women's liberation movement, the trend among most divorcing women is not to demand alimony payments from their husbands, and even when they ask for it, the judges are no longer quite as willing to grant it, any way. Furthermore, in the present era, alimony is no longer the sole or exclusive right of the wife, as it once was in the past. Today, the husband is just as eligible to apply for — and to be awarded — alimony by the courts under the laws of most states, as the basis for spousal support has dramatically shifted from the sex of the spouse to the need of the spouse. If, however, a separation or settlement agreement between the spouses had called for the payment of alimony, the judge, viewing the agreement essentially as a separate contract, would generally enforce the provision.[6]

Also, you should note that generally award of alimony is not commonly made nowadays, either. According to one estimate, only in approximately 15 percent of all divorces are alimony or spousal support of any kind made or even considered necessary or applicable. And the length of time during which alimony payments are paid after divorce has also been decreasing in recent time; it now runs an average of 2 to 5 years. And such payments, for the specific duration they are fixed to be made, is specifically for one purpose, namely, for "rehabilitation" — that is, to allow the recipient (dependent) spouse just that limited time he/she needs to get himself/herself self-supporting.[7]

The Important question that often arises when alimony is paid at all, is: what amount of alimony should be asked or paid? There is no set amount that is applicable for all cases. As one informed analyst, a lawyer, put it, "The dominant rule in the United States is that such an award rests in the discretion of the court. Basically, alimony depends on the spouse's needs and conduct, and the other spouse's ability to pay."[8]

All that is safe to say is that any amount the husband can afford, and to which his spouse can readily agree, would probably receive the signature of approval by the judge. And, indeed, even in situations where the states have established, by law, guidelines for awarding alimony, the decision by the court as to when to approve or order an award, or the length of time or amount of the award, or as to the spouse who should make the alimony payment, will still have to be determined by consideration of certain criteria, such as these: the standard of living of the parties, their relative income, their assets and obligations, the earning ability and prospects of each spouse, the length of the marriage, the needs of each of the parties and of their children, the occupation and vocational skills of each spouse, the employability of each, the age and health of the parties and of their children, and what other responsibility each party may have for the support of other persons, such as the couple's minor children from a previous marriage, etc.

The two most important considerations among judges seem to be the length of the marriage and the earning abilities of the spouses. In general, alimony award has the best chance of being favorably ruled on and approved where there has been a long marriage, particularly if one spouse earns considerably more than the other, or one spouse earns all the income and the other earns practically no income while, say, having to raise the couple's children. Alimony is not favored much, on the other hand, where the marriage is relatively short or

---

[6] Note: Note that alimony payments (providing it is based either on a written agreement or a court order) is tax-deductible to the payer, while the recipient, on t he other hand, is required to report it as taxable to herself. Child support payments, on the other hand, is not taxable to the recipient.

[7] Here's how one recent report summed up the prevailing state of affairs: "With the exception of marriages that have lasted 20 years or more, in which one spouse has no employment skills or is physically or mentally unable to enter the work force, the concept of long-term alimony has generally become a thing of the past. Instead, the courts now more frequently provide dependent spouse with short-term payments that, at most last for five to seven years and never longer than the duration of the marriage. (From our experience, the average is somewhere between three and five years)... During this period, the dependent spouse, who in almost every case is the woman, is expected to acquire skills so that she may enter the work force and eventually earn her own living. In other words, the law is now written to avoid placing a permanent responsibility [of support on] a divorced spouse indefinitely." (Koff, *Love and the Law*, Simon & Schuster, N.Y., 1989, p. 192)

[8] Edward Siegel, How to Avoid Lawyers. Ballantine Books, new York 1989 p. 125

very short, or where there are no minor children and both spouses are healthy and relatively young and can presumably take care of themselves.

You should note, though, that as a practical reality, compared to child support, spousal support (alimony) has a lower priority to child support in divorce proceedings. The reason this is so is related to several practical reasons. For one thing, in many families, once adequate child support payment is made, there often isn't much left over for more than a token spousal support to be attempted; secondly, alimony is deemed to concern grown adults who, presumably, can cater for themselves far better than the minor children of a marriage.

Consideration of 'Fault' In Award Of Alimony

As has been previously emphasized in this Chapter, in virtually every state today, some type of "no fault" ground for divorce is available. [See Appendix B for detailed coverage of the grounds for divorce on a state-by-state basis]. To put it briefly, in a no-fault divorce case, basically the judge would not entertain any testimony or evidence about which spouse or the other committed marital offenses that brought about the breaking up of the marriage. Rather, he'll simply consider whether or not there's evidence showing that the marriage has hopelessly broken down and cannot reasonably be mended, irrespective of which of the parties might have been at fault for it.

The no-fault ground is not exclusive, however, in most states; rather, most states (some 35 of them) still retain the fault-based grounds in addition to the no-fault one as a basis for the settling of marital affairs. And furthermore, even in many of those no-fault states where marital fault or conduct cannot be used against a spouse on matters concerning his or her divorce, it can still be used, nevertheless, in regard to assessing the division of the parties' marital property (or the award of alimony or spousal support). Additionally, in other states, a spouse's alimony could be reduced or terminated if the recipient ex-spouse cohabits with another person, especially if it appears that this reduces the ex-spouse's need for support.

But if a spouse is the 'guilty' party or the party who's 'at fault' in a divorce, does that automatically affect his/her alimony award? It depends. It depends on what state and the nature of the fault or misconduct. Not every misbehavior will disqualify a spouse, but serious offenses, such as adultery, or an attempt on the spouse's life, might still bar a spouse from receiving alimony or at least affect the amount or duration of the award. A growing number of states, however, (29 of them) now award alimony without regard to marital misconduct.

States in which marital misconduct is either considered or is a bar to alimony (21 states plus District of Columbia and Puerto Rico):

Alabama, Connecticut, District of Columbia, Florida, Georgia, Idaho, Kentucky, Louisiana, Massachusetts, Michigan, Missouri, New Hampshire, North Carolina, North Dakota, Pennsylvania, Rhode Island, South Carolina, South Dakota, Tennessee, Virginia, West Virginia and Puerto Rico.

States in which marital misconduct is not considered (29 states and the Virgin Islands):

Alaska, Arizona, Arkansas, California, Colorado, Delaware, Hawaii, Illinois, Indiana, Iowa, Kansas, Maine, Maryland, Massachusetts, Minnesota, Mississippi, Montana, Nebraska, Nevada, New Jersey, New Mexico, New York, Ohio, Oklahoma, Oregon, Vermont, Washington, Wisconsin, Wyoming and the Virgin Islands.

One way of gauging how much alimony a given spouse should pay in a given situation is by gauging what proportion of his income should reasonably be granted to the receiving spouse as alimony. Determination of that figure will be based on a number of factors: how much the paying spouse makes, what assets he has, the social status of the parties, the standard of living the parties have been accustomed to, and, not the least of all, the amount of child support he also has to pay. One analyst ventures a 'rule of thumb' of combined alimony and child support of between 15% and 50% of the man's pay, but adds that "more commonly, the average would probably be from 20% to 40%, although there necessarily is a wide variation, based on the individual case."[7]
Furthermore, many states now make use of a chart that offers a standard spousal (alimony) as well as child support figure, which sets forth the minimum, average and maximum amounts per week or month. Upon working out the figures on such a chart, the judge merely decides on the amount to be awarded based on the individual case. [Ask your court clerk for a copy of your state's alimony/child support chart.]

When alimony is applicable, however, parties had better make sure of the following: 1) that the **exact** amount of alimony to be paid is specified in the documents in **periodic** terms (weekly, bi-weekly, semi-monthly or monthly);[8] 2) that alimony payments are not lumped together with, but are stated separately from, child support payments, if applicable; and 3) that the time at which the alimony payments are to terminate is expressly specified (e.g., whether it should be at the death of the husband, remarriage by the wife, graduation from a trade or profession, etc.)

E. CUSTODY OF THE CHILDREN, IF APPLICABLE

Ordinarily, by and large, the courts tend to award the "sole" custody of the children to the mother almost automatically, unless it can be adequately shown that she is an "unfit" mother (usually meaning there's and immoral or criminal habit in her past or lifestyle which she is likely to transmit to the child.) This policy is based on the so-called "tender years doctrine" traditional thinking (which is probably valid in most instances) that holds that mothers are generally better at caring for babies than are the average fathers. *As a general rule, however, any child custody arrangements the plaintiff is able to present to the court which is mutually agreed to by the spouses, if half-way reasonable, would usually be respected and approved by the judge.*

The overwhelming majority of states now permit a form of custody arrangement that is known as *"joint custody"* allowing the both parents together to have a shared legal custody of the child and equal voice in the major decisions involved in the raising of the child. In deed, as of this writing only 6 states, and the District of Columbia — Georgia, North Dakota, Rhode Island, South Carolina, Virginia, and Wyoming — do not specifically authorize or provide for a joint custody form of custody under their state law.

If your state's laws permit a joint custody system, and you and your spouse want this to apply in your written agreement or divorce, then you must so stipulate in your pre-marital agreement (or other agreement that applies), as well as in your divorce petition or complaint, and more importantly, you must be prepared at the time of divorce to provide the court with some information and explanation (it's called a

---

[7] Siegel, Ibid. p.126

[8] The need for this is essentially to avoid being trapped in all of the "tax consequence" complications that might arise. For a fuller treatment of the tax ramifications of property division in marital situations, See Chapter 11.

"parenting plan") as to why the judge can expect that you and your spouse will now exhibit, *as parents*, the kind of maturity and mutual cooperation that you never showed *as spouses*, so as to be able to convince the judge that you can BOTH make such a joint custody arrangement workable and practicable. Joint custody permits both parents to take turns keeping the children, if the parents so decide, and then to have the usual right and responsibility to jointly make major decisions concerning the child(ren). *Currently, however, the trend regarding the matter seems to be strongly in favor of joint custody arrangements, as it is increasingly viewed by many in and out of the judicial system as a desirable way of encouraging greater contact of the child with BOTH parents, which is generally believed to be in the child's best interest.*

Other states, very few in number, also permit a third form of custody called **"divided"** or **"alternating"** custody, whereby each parent will exercise custody of the child for alternating periods of time, say six months out of a year, or for every other month or week.

And, on the vital question of who between the spouses should have custody, how do you make that determination? By what criteria? One recent analyst gives this informative but enthusiastic summary of the "commonsense" standard now being generally employed by the courts in making such a decision:

> "The most recent trend in custody legislation and court decisions provides one of the most common-sense approaches to the problem. Increasingly, courts are looking at a child's day-to-day circumstances in an effort to determine which parent has been the primary caregiver of the child. The parent who has provided most of the day-to-day care for the child during the marriage is then considered to be the most likely candidate to continue on as the primary custodian of the child after the divorce. The preference is given to the parent which has actively participated in caring for the child and performed the majority of the parenting activities: preparing meals, readying the child for sleep, sharing in their playtime, dealing with medical problems, participating in their education, etc. This method does not presuppose that either parent has an entitlement to being awarded custody, but rather is based on an examination of the reality of the burdens of parenthood. The decision is based on the practical considerations of which parent has provided the most time, care, and guidance to the child prior to the actual divorce. It allows each parent an equal right to *earn* the custody of a child by providing care for the child before the divorce proceeding begins. This method of selection of the parent to have physical custody places the greatest emphasis on which [one of them] has been providing the most parental care for the child prior to the divorce. Selection of the primary care-giver as continuing custodian generally fosters a home life of stability and continuity for the child. In the family upheaval caused by divorce, this factor deserves considerable attention."[9]

F. A PARENT'S VISITATION RIGHTS WITH THE CHILDREN

Under most states' laws, one parent, usually the mother, gets custody of the children, while the other parent makes up for it by having the rights to visit with (or take out) the children on given days of the week or month. In general, it is not difficult to work out a reasonable visitation arrangement with the other spouse, once you let one overriding consideration be your guide: consideration of what is in the **child's** own best interest, and **NOT** of what is in the special interest of this or that parent. The facts about this are not in dispute: most child psychologists and experts are in complete agreement that the interest of the child is best served and maximized whenever he can get a "balanced piece" of **both** parents as much as practicable, whether in marriage or after divorce.

---

[9] Daniel Sitarz, *Divorce Yourself: The National No-Fault Divorce Kit*, Nova Publishing Company, 1991, p.102

SAMPLE VISITATION GUIDELINES

The following is a sample of the type of Visitation Guidelines that some courts and counties are adopting. This sample is from Hamilton County of Ohio. Be sure to check with your local county Clerk of Court's office to determine if your county has adopted visitation guidelines for the non-custodial parent. In any event, you can always adapt some (or all) of these provisions for use in your own case, if agreeable, to draft your own visitation terms.

Note that you need not (no one couple needs to) pick any or all the terms specified here. You can pick and choose, and modify or expand on any terms as better preferred.

■ The non-custodial parent shall have visitation on *alternate* weekends from Friday at 6:00 p.m. to Sunday evening at 6:00 p.m.

■ The non-custodial parent shall have visitation from 5:30 p.m. to 8:30 p.m. on a weeknight *preceding* the weekends during which there is visitation.

■ During *even*-numbered years, the non-custodial parent shall have visitation on New Year's Day, President's Day, Memorial Day, Veteran's Day, and Thanksgiving. Each of these visitations shall begin at 10:00 a.m. and continue until 8:30 p.m.

■ The non-custodial parent shall be entitled to four weeks of additional visitation each year, this visitation may be exercised during the child's school break, at Christmas time, the child's break from school and summer visitation, or at any other appropriate time during the year.

■ During *odd* numbered years, the non-custodial parent shall have visitation on Martin Luther King Day, Easter, Fourth of July, and Labor Day. Each of these visitations shall begin at 10:00 a.m. and continue until 8:30 p.m.

■ On Mother's Day, the children shall be with the mother, and on Father's Day the children shall be with the father, no matter whose turn for visitation it is. Visitation shall begin at 10:00 a.m. and continue until 8:30 p.m.

■ During even numbered years, the non-custodial parent shall have visitation on the child's birthday. If the child's birthday falls on a non-school day, the visitation shall take place from 10:00 a.m. and continue until 8:30 p.m. If the child's birthday falls on a school day, visitation shall take place from 5:30 p.m. to 8:30 p.m.

■ The non-custodial parent shall not exercise visitation on holidays other than those which the non-custodial parent is entitled as described in the above paragraphs, except as otherwise agreed by the parties.

Note: The holiday schedule may be modified to accommodate the parties' religious preference

■ Make-up days shall be given if due to an emergency, the child or non-custodial parent cannot visit at the scheduled time or if the custodial parent denies visitation without just cause. All make-up days shall be rescheduled and exercised within thirty days.

■ Extended visitations are to be arranged within seven days from the time the parent's vacation schedules are posted by their employers. The non-custodial parent shall notify the custodial parent in writing of the time desired for extended visitation no later than 30 days prior to the requested extended visitation.

■ The children and/or custodial parent do not have to wait for the non-custodial parent to arrive for visitation more than 30 minutes. The non-custodial parent who is more than 30 minutes late for a particular visitation, shall forfeit that visitation.

■ The non-custodial parent who is more than 30 minutes late in returning the children without calling to make arrangements, shall, for just cause, be subject to contempt.

■ The custodial parent may not remove the children from the State of _____ and establish residence for them in another state without a Court order or an agreement signed by the parties.

■ In the event that the parties are unable to reach an agreement regarding transportation for visitation, (_Plaintiff/defendant)_ shall provide transportation at commencement of the visitation period and _____ shall provide transportation at termination of the visitation period.

■ The custodial parent shall arrange for the appropriate school officials to release to the non-custodial parent any and all information concerning the children.

■ The custodial parent shall authorize the release of any and all medical information and records concerning the child to the non-custodial parent. In the event the child's illness requires medical attention by a physician, the custodial parent shall promptly notify the non-custodial parent. Elective surgery shall only be performed after consultation with the non-custodial parent.

■ Any child who is twelve years of age or older may set and determine visitation with the non-custodial parent.

NOTE: Willful non-compliance with the visitation order of the Court may result in a Finding of Contempt.

G. CHILD SUPPORT OBLIGATIONS (IF APPLICABLE)

Closely interrelated with the issue of child custody is the issue of child support. It is the legal obligation of parents, both the mother and father, but more so for the father, to provide adequate and continuous financial support for THEIR minor or infant children — that is, generally children under 18 years of age. Under most states' laws, though, it may extend to 21 years of age, where the child is provably in actual, _active_ attendance at a school or college for that duration.

What is "adequate" support for a non-custodial parent to pay in a divorce situation? The rule is to determine what is adequate by the circumstances of the parents, as well as of the children, on a case-by-case basis. The factors considered are pretty much the same as those in an alimony case: The need of the children, the ability of the non-custodial parent (usually the father) to pay, etc. And even if the custodial parent has substantial capacity, the other parent is not relieved of his own obligation.

Some of the questions that would determine this, include: How much money does the father (or the mother, if there's no father) earn? Is the father a man of independent wealth, or not? Does he have other children he's supporting from a previous marriage? Is the child a normal child requiring no extraordinary expenditures, or is he, say, a diabetic who would require special care and extra expenditures, etc.?

One eminent analyst gives an estimate of the "fair" amount that the paying parent should pay for child support and alimony, combined, as some 20% to 40% of the paying parent's income "in the average case," depending on the section of the country, and the income and the living standards of the couple.[10] *In any event, it should always be remembered that, in general, when the husband and wife can, on their own, agree on the amount of child support to be paid, there's not much of a problem and the court will usually go along. But it's only when they can't work out this matter (or agree on a figure) by themselves that there's a problem.*

In recent times, however, largely because of a provision of the 1984 Federal Child Support Enforcement Amendments, and of the Family Support Act of 1988 passed by Congress, by which all states were required to provide some type of formula or child-support guidelines by October 1989 on how much a parent should pay for child support, virtually every state in the nation now has a child support guideline schedule on the books which provides a set of numerical formulas for setting child-support awards. Under the circumstances, to set a child support amount, all that you would practically need to do is simply to follow the percentage guidelines or formula set forth in your given state's rules (unless, however, you can prove that the percentage amount would be unfair in your particular situation.)

In general, each state's guidelines require that the non-custodial parent (unless he lacks sufficient income to do so) must provide a specific level of monthly support to the parent having custody of the child. Furthermore, a common feature of today's child support arrangements is to provide for other non-monetary needs of the children that go beyond simply the monthly payment. For example, in addition to his paying support of a set amount of money, the supporting parent may also be required to carry health insurance on the children, or pay for their medical bills, or to provide life insurance for the custodial parent as the sole beneficiary.

As stated above, generally provided for under each state's divorcing procedures are specific statutory child support guidelines for meeting the state's child support obligation. *The good news for a do-it-yourselfer who is doing his or her own settlement agreement or divorce, is that in the present times virtually every state has a package of forms giving the approved guidelines and percentage standards for child support which are often readily available from the state's Family and Divorce Courts, as well as from the state's Department of Social Services.* Specific worksheets for use in working out the exact amounts of support to be paid are generally a part of the state's official guideline package of forms. If you are unable to find these forms otherwise, always ask the divorce clerk of your court for where you can obtain them or for copies of the local child support guidelines or rules that might be in effect.

To conclude this topic, perhaps a word of advice may be appropriate and useful as the ultimate 'guideline' to aid you in the making of your final determination as to what is the 'fair' amount of child support to ask from your spouse. One knowledgeable analyst probably says it as well as anyone, as follows:[11]

> "The [child support] guidelines provided [by the state laws] are just that: guidelines. They are not intended to be an ultimate method for determining support payments in all cases. They should be reviewed and used while considering all of the other relevant factors in your particular situation. The determination of the proper amount of child support in each case will always be difficult. *A careful balance must be obtained between providing an adequate level of support and overburdening the parent who must pay the support. If the support payments are set at a level which becomes a tremendous financial burden to the paying parent, there will be a tendency and temptation to default on the payments. On the other hand, if the payments are too low, the child will suffer the consequences.*
>
> Both parents must work together carefully to actually determine a fair and reasonable amount of support. Care must be taken to keep the negotiations on a mature and rational basis. Discussions involving child support have the very real potential of deteriorating into hostile arguments. Of all of the aspects of divorce, child support obligations have spawned more post-divorce lawsuits than any other." [Emphasis added by the present writer]

---

[10] Siegel, op. cit. p. 126

[11] Starz, *Divorcing Yourself: The National No-Fault Divorce Kit* p. 122

H. OTHER ISSUES

Other issues that may arise in a settlement agreement or divorce situation, though not frequently with most couples in uncontested situations, may concern agreement on who should have the right to claim the children (or some particular ones) as his/her dependents when filing the annual income tax return; whether or not the children should be educated in a private school or a particular religious denomination, or up to a certain level of education at the expense of the supporting parent; whether one or the other parent should be responsible for the future medical bills and expenditures of the children (or spouse); and whether a parent is forbidden to take the child(ren) outside certain boundaries of the city or state without the written consent of the other parent, etc.

These matters do not occur as issues often. They rarely become problems with the overwhelming majority of divorcing couples. However, if you happen to think any of them might become a problem in your situation, there is a Simple practice solution: just include a provision in your written agreement, and in your divorce papers (essentially in your "Petition" or "Complaint" and the "Final Judgement" papers, or even in your settlement agreement, if applicable) spelling out exactly such terms and conditions as you would want, or as have been agreed upon by the parties.

CHAPTER 4

PRE-MARITAL AGREEMENTS: WHAT THEY ARE, WHAT THEY'RE USED FOR, AND THE BASIC LEGAL REQUIREMENTS FOR A VALID ONE.

A. The Nature of Living-Together Agreements in General

Under the laws of just about every state in the nation, parties who are about to be married may enter into an appropriate Premarital (also called Prenuptial) Agreement. Likewise, parties who are unmarried, whether heterosexual or homosexual, may enter into an appropriate Cohabitation or Living-Together agreement. And parties, whether married or unmarried, may also enter into a valid Property Settlement Agreement before, during, or after marriage; and following the separation of the (married) parties, they may enter into a Separation Agreement. If a couple is married, at the moment the relationship comes into being, certain legal rights and duties spring into being. And, on the other side of the spectrum, if a couple is unmarried but living together, certain legal rights and duties they may otherwise think they have do not actually spring up. These rights and duties may, however, be varied and regulated by the act of signing a valid Premarital Agreement for a couple that later went on to be married, or by the signing of a valid Cohabitation or Living-together agreement, for a couple that never got married. In the absence of a Premarital Agreement (or a Cohabitation Agreement for the never-married couple), these rights and duties (or lack thereof, for the never married) continue, nevertheless, even when the parties separate, and will remain so until such time as the parties enter into a valid separation or property agreement, or until their rights and duties are decided upon by a court of law in a divorce or otherwise.

In a word, the central point of importance here, is that a written property or other types of settlement agreements could legitimately be entered into between married persons, as well as between non-married persons who plan to be married, or between persons who are just cohabiting with each other, whether in a heterosexual or homosexual relationship.

A. Pre-Marital Agreement Defined

A premarital agreement (also called prenuptial agreement) is a formal agreement or contract made between a man and woman in clear <u>contemplation</u> of marriage, but which is made <u>BEFORE</u> they subsequently marry, primarily centering around issues of the rights and entitlements which each would have with respect to their property, among other things, after their marriage. A premarital agreement does not take effect until AFTER the contemplated marriage takes place, if it does. And if the marriage never materializes, the agreement is of no force or effect, either.

*A central point to remember, is that to be legally valid, a pre-marital agreement must meet one fundamental requirement: it must be signed and entered into **in** deliberate, explicit **contemplation** of marriage by the parties, and must be made <u>before</u> their marriage, say within two or three months or so thereof.* Thus, for example, a mere living-together or property settlement agreement between two parties does not necessarily or automatically qualify as a valid prenuptial agreement. Nor can such contract, even though valid otherwise, be automatically carried into your marriage and be enforceable. *In short, unless the contract you make with your partner is made within a reasonable time before your marriage, and in explicit contemplation of marriage by both parties, it will not be a valid premarital agreement or enforceable as one under the law.*

A premarital agreement between prospective spouses could provide for just about every applicable thing that a regular separation or settlement agreement between married persons could provide for, ranging from the ownership, control and management of the parties' property, to their distribution at separation, death or divorce, custody and upbringing of children, alimony and spousal support, life insurance beneficiaries, and so on, except that there may be certain limitations on making provision for the support and the raising of minor children of the marriage. [See Chapter 5 for more on this]. And, so long as the same rules of fairness, evenhandedness, and full disclosure, are adhered to, such an agreement will be recognized and upheld by the courts just as well. These agreements are now universally legal and popular with the courts because having a good pre-marital agreement would be in keeping with the courts' basic preference, nowadays, for settlements that are voluntarily pre-arranged between couples and which employ devices that facilitate smoother disengagement in troubled marital or quasi-marital relationships.

One major strength and advantage of a pre-marital agreement, is that since premarital agreements are not, like separation or settlement agreements, a product of disputes born in times if troubles, they do not have to be a public record. Hence, the fact of the existence of a prenuptial agreement, let alone its specific contents, could be kept as secret and discreet as the parties themselves want to make it, thus increasing its potential for constructiveness.

As could be seen from at least one of the three sample prenuptial agreements provided in this manual (see the versions on pp.65-75 and pp.76-8), an agreement of this sort need not necessarily be constructed in the traditional impersonal or threatening legal language of contract law that would give the impression that the parties are somehow suspicious or untrusting of each other. Rather, it could just as well be written in a mild, personal, accommodating language. *A good pre-nuptial agreement (as well as a good pre-cohabitation agreement) is one which honestly sums up the financial and other facts and conditions of the respective parties, and sets forth the reasonable aims, objectives and expectations of each from the prospective relationship.* **And for the agreement to be most effective, the man and the woman must reasonably presume they are dealing with each other in "good faith" – that is, in an atmosphere of mutual trust, honesty, and full disclosure, on important facts about themselves** (the extent of property owned, if any; any prior marriages or commitments to family and children, prior debts owed, physical infirmities, sexual impotency, what each expects of the other or out of the relationship, their respective likes and dislikes, etc.).

C. Circumstances Which Prompt Persons to Enter into Pre-Marital Agreements in These Times

1. The circumstances vary from couple to couple, of course. But generally, pre-nuptial agreements (also called "ante-nuptial" or "pre-marital" agreements) begin to become important when the financial status of the parties who are contemplating marriage are radically different -- when, for example, the man (or woman, as the case may be) has got considerable wealth (and, probably greater age differential too) relative to the woman. In such situations some questions may be entertained about the real motives and intentions of one party or the other, particularly the one with less or without much money. The man, in this case, may therefore wish to use a pre-marital agreement to protect himself, and to allay any suspicion and concern that it may not be him that the spouse-to-be really wants, but his wealth.

    It is the classic case of the wealthy older gentleman marrying or proposing to marry a younger woman without a lot of cash! And, as one woman, an experienced family lawyer, put it, "in such a case the guy would have to be a two-headed idiot not to protect himself."

2. Or, as is usually the case, one of the spouses-to-be, or both, may have had some earlier marriages, and may have earned or inherited substantial property from a deceased spouse or relative, or been awarded considerable sums as a settlement from an earlier divorce. In such circumstances, often involving children, debt allocations and other commitments arising from the earlier marital relationships, a pre-nuptial agreement could properly be drawn up to keep the separate commitments of each party separate in the interest of peace and harmony of the new union.

3. Another situation would be where one of the spouses-to-be, or both, have prior or anticipated commitment to parents, brothers, sisters, a business or profession and what have you, which will soak up a part of the estate in the event of death. The party involved may, therefore, want to limit or modify the property which the prospective spouse shall be entitled to inherit from the estate. There are also instances where a spouse-to-be may just prefer to give a specified amount of property or asset to the other as a pre-marital settlement so that if it should ever become necessary for the parties to divorce themselves, the done spouse (the one to whom the partial assignment has been made) shall have foreclosed his or her right to make claims on the remainder of the estate.

4. *But it is no longer just the previously married, or just those with property, who are undertaking premarital agreement in these times. Rather, recent evidence shows that there has been a dramatic rise in popularity for premarital agreement among middle-class couples – professional couples, those with thriving businesses, and even those getting married for the first time, who are starkly aware that nearly one out of every two marriages today are said to end in divorce.* These days pre-marital agreements appeal to men and women who are getting married later. (Men over 30 account for 41 percent of all new marriages, with 32 percent involving women over 30). They are popular with the 45 percent of newlyweds who have been married before, who know first-hand how nasty break-ups can get or who don't want a new relationship to prevent them from leaving money to heirs by a previous marriage, or who simply are gun shy from their previous experience with divorce and merely want to protect themselves before going into another marriage one more time.

As James Novak, co-founder of the Wisconsin Fathers For Equal Justice and a frequent speaker at seminars and workshops for divorcing fathers, summed it up, noting that 80 percent of divorced people remarry within 5 years after their divorce, "Lest a man repeat the same mistake, he should have a premarital agreement in his next marriage....[As without it] it would be easy to fall into the same traps as in past marriage."

Thus, in the 1990's (and the 21st Century), pre-marital agreements once used almost exclusively by the very rich and mainly to protect substantial wealth differential held by one partner, have become accepted practice among middle-income couples as well, who have little or no wealth at the moment. Mostly, such agreements are concerned with the so-called *"soft" issues of marriage*, issues that the courts will not and cannot enforce – matters ranging anywhere from who does the dishes in a marriage, to guidelines on how the parties will spend their vacation, how many children they'll have and at which intervals, their religious affiliations and how to bring up the children, to economic issues such as who will be responsible for what household bills and expenses, or the terms of support or property division to be used in the event of divorce, and so on.

5. Furthermore, there is yet another factor that has contributed to the increasing popularity of pre-marital agreements in recent times: the social trend towards marrying later in life which has made it more likely that substantial assets shall have been accumulated by one or both of the parties by the time of a contemplated marriage. Women are now more often employed outside the home, hence there is an increased probability that the wife as well as the husband will have substantial personal assets, or at least have the capacity to be self-supporting, by the time the marriage takes place.

Noting that in recent times "prenuptial agreements have become more prevalent and popular" among Americans, Gail J. Koff, a New York matrimonial lawyer who herself had at her husband's prodding reluctantly entered into a premarital agreement that she was later to applaud as a "very positive vehicle" some 10 years later, sums up her assessment of the principal reasons for the growing popularity and use of pre-marital agreement in recent times, as follows:

> This is probably the result of two major changes that have occurred over the past twenty-five years: There are now more second marriages, and prenuptial contracts have become the accepted tool in terms of inheritance issues involving children from those first marriages. Along the same lines there has been a rise in two-income families, thus there is an interest for some to protect each spouse's individual property. These economic reasons for having a prenuptial contract reflect the growing trend of looking upon marriage not only as an emotional partnership but also as a business partnership.

> The other reason for the growth of prenuptial contracts is the many changes in the divorce law. Prior to no-fault divorce, community property, and equitable distribution, the rules of divorce were far clearer. Alimony was almost always granted, for instance. But the new divorce laws are far more flexible, and it's uncertain in many instances how the courts will rule. As a result, in creating prenuptial agreements, people are attempting to formulate the rules of their own marriages and, if it comes to it, their own divorces, at least to a point. [The new equitable and community property laws, for example, because it no longer guarantees a spouse sole ownership of property simply because his or her name is on it, has caused some spouses, fearful of losing property they consider theirs alone, to go for prenuptial agreement in order to hold on to such property]. *Thus, even though it may not be romantic, it is often practical to be clear*

up front, especially in the case of second marriages or when there is a good deal of property involved.

In general there are two [basic] motives for making a prenuptial agreement. The first is purely financial and made in order to protect property that is brought into the marriage. It can also be used to ease relationships with each spouse's family, protecting heirs, for instance [as when used in]….second marriage where children are involved or for couples who marry somewhat later in life and each wishes to protect some assets. The second kind of agreement is primarily issue-oriented [involving emotional and personal aspects — matters that range anywhere from whether or not the parties will keep their surnames socially and/or professionally, to where they will live, whether they will have children and how many, agreement to discuss any major purchases over a certain amount, how to bring up the children and in what religion, whether or not to get counseling if any serious problems arise in the marriage, and the like]. Sometimes prenuptial contracts are a combination of the two. [Emphasis added by the present writer]

6. Finally, there is one other reason, a somewhat salient one, why pre-marital agreements are commonplace among American couples nowadays: the changed nature of marriage in America and lack of structure to marriage today. Only a few short decades ago, the rules and the roles of the man and woman in marriage were well defined and quite clear. The man, to be sure, was the family breadwinner and worked, while the woman was the family homemaker and stayed home to look after the home and children, and didn't work. Furthermore, the lifestyles for a married couple was unmistakable: both lived together strictly under one roof, and saw each other and stayed with each other virtually every single day.

Not so any more, though! Today, both spouses invariably work outside the marital home, and in deed in many a home the man now stays home to take care of the home while the woman works outside the home; "commuter marriages" are common today where couples live in separate places and try to see each other at arranged times, and so on.

Because there is no more formal structure to marriage, premarital agreement becomes essential as it provides couples with legally and socially acceptable means by which to set their own guidelines to enable them structure their marriage to suit their individual needs and personalities.

D. Doesn't Pre-Nuptial Agreement Detract from Love?

But isn't a pre-marital agreement, in effect like mapping out a future break-up just when a relationship is gushing with romance and passion? Isn't drafting such an agreement tantamount, in a way, to anticipating the breakdown of the marriage and thus tends to destabilize marriage and encourage divorce?

Absolutely not, say the experts and, lately, increasingly the courts. Indeed, it is said, quite the contrary is the case. For a long time, that argument, that agreements of the kind primarily promote divorce, was one of the most compelling arguments used with the courts against upholding pre-nuptial (and post-nuptial) agreements, as the courts had felt that such agreements anticipated the breakdown of marriage and thus tended to encourage divorce. In recent times, however, the courts have taken an apposite view; the courts, under the new, liberal, social environment of 'no-fault' divorce laws that now holds that the state no longer has an interest in preserving a marriage that is irretrievably broken, now takes the position that rather than destabilizing marriage, such agreements actually promote marital stability by defining the expectations and responsibilities of each partner.

A good pre-marital agreement, it is now generally held among matrimonial lawyers, family counselors, mediators and the courts, could actually be a constructive force for developing relationships, not, as many lay people often think, a destructive or divisive force. It can help the two partners learn more about their mates, clarify what they want and expect from the marriage, and avoid unpleasant misunderstandings or disagreements down the road. By confronting such sensitive issues as finances and property rights beforehand, experts say, couples may even be able to determine earlier on whether they are sincerely meant for each other before getting in deeper. As Bernard Clair, a Manhattan divorce lawyer , aptly put it, "A written (pre-marital) agreement need not detract from love. In fact, in the 1980's [and beyond] it may be one of the most sincere ways to prove it."

What is to be admitted, however, is that there is a definite psychological "downside" involved in making a pre-marital agreement, though one of a special kind: the undertaking is an unpleasant affair with most people, and many are naturally uncomfortable with the prospect of drafting one! At the very least, writing an agreement as a prelude to marriage simply strikes many soon-to-be-wed couples as distasteful, as they don't want to talk about divorce at such a time of romance, hope and optimism, let alone construct what smacks like a detailed map for it! Making a pre-marital agreement may not quite be exactly the planning and writing of a divorce. But the reality is that it sure "feels" like being one! To be sure, negotiating and writing a pre-marital agreement does bring up precisely many of the same issues parties feel when they divorce, and certainly this feeling seems awkward as it directly contrasts with the hope and aspirations for an upcoming marriage and optimistic relationship.

Negotiators report that the process of hammering out the terms and details of a pre-marital agreement is often a very touchy affair, and that there are many instances when arguments and disagreements on the terms are just so bitter and emotional that the parties are just not able to see eye-to-eye, causing the proposed marriage to fall through altogether.

The "distaste" factor in the making of pre-marital agreement are, however, simply the psychological downside inevitably involved in having to confront the sensitive issues addressed by a pre-nuptial agreement. In the view of the vast majority of the experts in the field today the advantages of having an actual agreement in hand, they contend, far out-weigh the disadvantages, nevertheless. *Here are statements from across the entire spectrum of the professionals engaged in matrimonial law practice, all of whom display almost rock-solid position in support of having a couple's agreement:*

- "I've had a few of those [relationships in my practice that fell through over inability to agree on terms of the contract]. But let's face it. If it's that iffy that the relationship goes down the sewer over financial arguments, what do you think are the odds that the marriage would have succeeded?"
  —*Shelley Ann Dickson, matrimonial attorney, Hartfield, MA.*

- "I think making an agreement conscious, deliberate and concrete, makes you put your money where your mouth is. Otherwise, what happens is that couples slide back into traditional roles."
  — *Kate Woolner, Mediator and Director of the Franklin Mediation Center in Greenfield, MA, who herself had such an agreement with her husband.*

- "The notion of a pre-nuptial contract is often a threatening one to many people. Some believe that preparing one is too pessimistic, almost bordering on being the fatalistic, presupposing the end of the marriage. But in reality it is in many cases simply a practical way of dealing with a possible eventuality, in much the same way that writing a will simplifies what happens to your estate after your death. An agreement can be an effective tool for communication between parties."

> — *Gail J. Koff, a New York City matrimonial attorney and author of Love and the Law: A Legal Guide to Relationships in the 90's, who herself had pre-nuptial agreement with her husband.*

- "(You) should take heed... to make a valid and enforceable agreement before or during marriage... for surely the cost of a marriage contract will be a pittance compared to unconscionable (lawyers) fees in divorce." — *Lillian Kozak, New York attorney and head of New York State's Marriage & Divorce Task Force of National Organization for Women.*

- "A written agreement need not detract from love. In fact, in the 1980's [and beyond], it may be one of the most sincere ways to prove it."
  — *Bernard Clair, a New York divorce lawyer.*

- "Lest a man repeat the same mistake, he should have a pre-marital agreement in his next marriage....[without one] it would be easy to fall into the same traps as in a past marriage... One has a choice in marital agreements...the [better] option is for the two parties to write their own marital agreement." — *James Novak, Co-founder, Wisconsin Fathers for Equal Justice and author of Wisconsin Father's Guide to Divorce & Custody.*

- " I always have the feeling that people who have them are literally less likely to divorce. I've found that people who take care of the financial side of the relationship before they get married, have that aspect done with and have eliminated a huge subject for argument. It's a big relief."
  — *Shelley Ann Dickson, the matrimonial attorney.*

D. Is Pre-Nuptial Agreement for Everyone?

True, over the past several years the courts across the country have been taking these agreements far more seriously than before, and there has been a noticeable growing demand for them among Americans. Still, it should be recognized that pre-marital agreements are not for everyone. Most "clean couples" (young first-timers without significant assets or dependent children) probably shouldn't bother with one, according to experts.

In fact, with the advent of equitable distribution rule for property division in about 44 states in the country, certain key assumptions of pre-nuptial agreements have already been incorporated into law. For instance, the equitable distribution principle primarily allows married couples to keep finances separate during marriage if they wish, or to make a "gift" of pre-owned assets to their spouse. Equitable distribution laws admit that marriage is an economic partnership and that if the partnership ends, each partner should get a "fair" share of the assets acquired during the marriage — based on a dozen or so state-defined criteria: age, employability, conduct during the marriage, financial security of minor children, to name a few. ("Community property" laws, on the other hand, which are still operative in 9 states, allow that a spouse gets only support no matter what she might have done to further the other spouse's career or to help him acquire property.)

Secondly, there will be a category of people whose relationship and commitment to one another simply cannot bear the weight of a pre-marital agreement. As a practical matter, those are going to be couples for which, as in any contract, negotiation of the terms will become so bitter and irreconcilable that the deal will just fall apart – the proposed wedding will have to be called off on account of the impasse on the agreement. And for this class of couples, many lawyers and marital negotiators and counselors have often taken the position that it is far better that such a marriage be called off this sooner, in that such marriage is obviously doomed to failure!

E. The Main Practical Legal Purposes For Which Pre-Marital or Marital Agreements Are Used

To put it simply and briefly, in the final analysis, as a practical matter it may not matter which specific type of agreement you are talking about, or whether you are talking about a marital, quasi-marital or nonmarital situation between partners; *the prime object and use for which a couples' agreement of any sort is made, is essentially the same: namely, they are made in preparation for an actual or potential breakup or divorce action to dissolve a marriage or relationship*. Such an agreement (which, in the context of a divorce action is often called a "stipulation" or a "petition" in most jurisdictions) become, then, the document by which couples (whether married or otherwise) set forth how they want to allocate their property and income while they live together in marriage, or in cohabitation, as in the case of a pre-marital or cohabitation agreement, or upon divorce or a breakup, as in the case of a separation or property settlement agreement. *In either case, by defining privately and BEFOREHAND the rights, obligations and entitlements of each party in the event of serious personal difficulties in the relationship, or by doing so right after it has become clear to the parties that the relationship is headed for an eventual break-up, you minimize having to unnecessarily enrich the lawyers in what could otherwise be a bitter, protracted, costly battle in court proceedings.*

Thus, as a matter of practical reality, among most legal practitioners in the field of matrimonial law, whether the specific document is a pre-marital agreement, or a separation or property settlement agreement, they are generally viewed today in the same light as, above everything else, a wise and least painful tool for "planning" or "negotiating" an eventual divorce, if that were ever to become a reality. In the words of one Washington D.C. divorce lawyer, it is now "the practical device used by a husband and wife about to embark on the road to divorce; the basic instrument to effectuate a compatible divorce."

As elaborated in Section D Above, in years gone by, under the old system in operation during the pre-no fault days, the governing philosophy then operating was that any agreement or arrangement which appeared to have made it easier to dissolve a marriage or for couples to separate, was "against public policy." Such agreements or arrangements were therefore discouraged and frowned upon by the courts. Not so any more, though! *Today, under the "new morality" of no-fault philosophy in settling marital affairs, the courts are more interested in one thing and one thing only: speeding up and smoothly resolving the process of dissolving the marriage and dividing up the common property among couples who wish to split.*

One principal and generally acceptable tool by which this is frequently accomplished, is through the use of Written Agreements (or "stipulations") by couples. Today, most states now have laws or legal interpretations on the books by which the provisions of a pre-marital agreement, or a separation agreement or other "stipulation" or written agreement worked out by couples on just about anything (the state of their marriage, child custody or visitation rights or support, division or property, etc.), are accepted by the courts as the "*grounds*" or the primary basis for eventual settlement. [1]

---

[1] The Uniform Marriage and Divorce Act of 1970, from which the laws of most no-fault divorce states borrowed their moral impetus, provides as follows: "To promote amicable settlement of disputes between parties to a marriage... (they) may enter into a written separation agreement... (and) in a proceeding for dissolution of marriage or for legal separation, the terms of the separation agreement... are binding upon the court unless it finds... the agreement unconscionable." The drafters of this act then acknowledged, in a special "Note", that "this section, entirely reverses the older view that property settlement agreements are against public policy because they tend to promote divorce." (See also Appendix B for the "grounds" for securing a divorce in all 50 states.)

In most states, the way it generally works out these days, is this: when a couple has a valid pre-marital or separation or other written settlement agreement, one or both of the spouses would be allowed to use that document either as a sufficient "ground" or basis for divorce at a later date, or as the basis upon which the terms of a later court settlement is based. Thus, rather than leave the matters completely to chance or to uncertainty, or to an unpredictable judge at the very time of final settlement or divorce, the provisions of a couples' settlement agreement previously drawn up and signed by the parties are, in effect, simply incorporated into the divorce decree, with little or no modifications. Because of this reality, *many divorce lawyers now view a written couples' agreement as a "real passport" to a divorce, a "negotiated" and "compatible" method of achieving a divorce*; and state legislators and judges who preside over divorce and matrimonial issues now favor, even love,[2] situations where the partners themselves have already worked out and signed a settlement agreement before coming to trial.

There is a second practical purpose, just as major and important if not more so, for which such couples' agreements are used, particularly the pre-nuptial type agreements. *That purpose is of a more positive and constructive nature: namely, for use for stirring up and promoting greater communication between marital partners.* Thus, by identifying vital issues and areas of potential conflicts for the would-be spouse, and compelling the parties to confront them much earlier on, parties are not only in a much better position to make an objective evaluation of the workability of a marital union in a climate of realism that is devoid of sentimentalism, but are also better able to formulate, through their pre-nuptial agreement, the proper compromises and rules of conduct and living which harmonize individual sensitivities and areas of potential conflicts between the parties. And, hopefully, the end result of this will be to make for a more harmonized, stronger, and more lasting marriage and marital relationship between couples through their pre-nuptial agreement experience.

Gail J. Koff's personal experience with her own pre-nuptial agreement is somewhat instructive in this regard. Koff, a matrimonial attorney who had at first reluctantly entered into a pre-nuptial agreement in her own marriage that she was later to applaud a decade later as a brilliant act, notes, for example, that her own pre-nuptial agreement primarily dealt, not with the "hard" issue of marriage (economics), but with the "soft" issues of marital life – issues that, by their very nature, the court will not and cannot rule upon or enforce, such as a provision on who does the dishes, or on the parties spending a set amount of time with each other, or on observing a period of mourning for a deceased spouse in the event of death by one party, and the like. Yet, Koff states, although such are not the kinds of provisions a court may ever have to enforce, such provisions do serve a special, useful purpose nevertheless: The fostering of communication between the parties. As she put it, they serve the vital function of being "thought-provoking and might even work to avoid future acrimony in a marriage…[and demonstrate how a pre-nuptial agreement can be] used on a personal level to promote better communication in marriage."

---

[2] One Illinois judge expressed the courts' preference this way: "Parties to divorce suits are to be commended for their attempt to settle their property differences amicably. This not only saves the courts from being fraught with details and the necessity of repeated, recurrent hearings, but leads to better feelings and peace of mind…" Quoted from *"Everything You've Always Wanted to Know About the Law"* by Edward E. Colby, p. 255.

Koff sums up, this way, through her own personal experience with it, how a good pre-nuptial agreement experience of today could potentially make a constructive, positive contribution to the health, life and vitality of a future marriage:

> "[Our agreement] turned out to be a very positive vehicle for communication, and I think it helped set some of the ground rules for our relationship. Issues we hadn't really articulated or even thought of before were spread out on the table, issues that were best discussed before we got married. I think pre-nuptial contracts such as ours can be a very useful tool [particularly] in the first couple of years of marriage…[Until] after a certain number of years of marriage [when you shall have known your spouse better and are in a position to] begin to accept your spouse for who he or she is, and you find other ways of working out your problems."[3]

F. Can You Properly Draw Up Your Own Couples' Agreement Without A Lawyer?

The answer is YES, YES, YES! You not only can, you indeed should!! First of all, one fundamental point needs to be gotten perfectly into the minds and heads of everyone right away. That point is that: *the correctness or the legal validity of a settlement or couples' agreement, or , for that matter, any legal contract or agreement of whatever kind, does not, in any way, depend on what the professional calling or title of its preparer is. Not at all!* Generally speaking, any agreement voluntarily drawn up, signed and agreed to by any two (or more) adults themselves, may be just as legally valid as the one drawn up by the world's best lawyer, and the courts will normally give full recognition to such an agreement — as long as that document meets certain basic tests of reasonableness, mutual fairness, clarity and public policy propriety. IT IS COMPLETELY IRRELEVANT WHETHER SUCH AN AGREEMENT WAS DRAWN UP BY A LAWYER, A DOCTOR, A MAILMAN, OR EVEN YOUR HOUSE DOG!

The second point is: It's the commonly acknowledged legal and civil right of every American, who so prefers, to draw up his or her own legal papers, and even to represent himself, in any legal proceedings involving civil matters. That's what the courts have consistently ruled —whether it be in a divorce, bankruptcy, probate, tenant-landlord disputes case, will-drafting, incorporating your business, or what have you. That's the law! The only relevant question you really ought to concern yourself with is this: DO YOU KNOW HOW TO PROPERLY DRAW UP AN AGREEMENT THAT MEETS THE MINIMUM LEGAL STANDARDS? Well, if you can say "yes" to this basic question (and what else is this manual meant for!), then you really don't have to hire a lawyer to do the agreement for you — unless, of course, you're rich, or enjoy throwing moneys away, or just plain lazy!

The third point: Finally, there's an even more important issue here for you from your standpoint as a consumer. *And that is that, you not only can do it yourself, you should*. With regard especially to the making of matrimonial agreements, there are just so many advantages and *benefits for you in doing it yourself that it will be highly perplexing if you were to do otherwise:* it's much cheaper doing it yourself; you can better keep matters simple and agreeable without a lawyer's involvement; you improve, by far, your chances of cooperating with each other and making delicate but needed compromises for your future life together when there's no lawyer on each side to "fight" for each party's "interests" and to constantly remind you of your separate "rights"; you get to make the major decisions on your own life doing it yourself, and, most importantly, if you draw up your agreement based on the same standard that are outlined in this manual, you'll have exactly the same quality agreement that's just as legally solid as any that can be written by the best lawyer around, but at a fraction of the cost and hassles; and so on and on, as fully elaborated in Chapter 2 (see, esp. pp. 6-11). So, why wouldn't you rather just do the agreement yourselves (you and your spouse), and leave the lawyer out of it!

---

[3] Koff, Love And The Law In The 1990's, p. 89

CHAPTER 5
WHAT YOU MAY PROVIDE FOR IN YOUR PRE-MARITAL AGREEMENT

A pre-marital agreement between prospective spouses could provide for just about every applicable thing that a regular separation or settlement agreement between legally married persons could provide for, but with just a few exceptions.

And, as long as the same rules of fairness, evenhandedness, and full disclosure, are adhered to, the agreement will be recognized and upheld by the courts just as well. The same rule against including in the agreement the terms or conditions considered contrary to the society's public policy, also applies in pre-marital agreements.

Prenuptial Checklist

What to Include:

- All property and assets owned separately or jointly.
- Checking and savings accounts, credit cards, loans, cars, real estate and other property.
- How assets and liabilities will be dealt with in a divorce.
- How new assets will be divided.
- Who keeps the house or apartment.
- Allowances (such as percentage of assessed value) for the party who agrees to leave home.
- How future income will be shared. (A woman who puts her spouse through med school may want a share of his medical practice, even after divorce.)

Can Also Include:

- Number of children you'd like to have.
- What religion will be practiced.
- How household duties will be divided during the marriage.
- How childcare responsibility will be divided during the marriage.
- How household expenses will be covered.
- The option of renegotiating in a certain number of years.

Should Not Include:

- How children of the marriage will be supported or raised should the couple divorce. (State child custody and support laws supersede the agreement.)
- Statements allowing infidelity or encouraging divorce.

The laws and legal rules governing pre-nuptial contracts are relatively new in the nation's legal history, and are still evolving. However, there is now in place the Uniform Pre-Marital Agreement Act, already adopted by at least 20 major states [1], which give the essential principles broadly followed in most states and the appropriate subject matters to address in the making of written contracts prior to marriage. Indeed, even for those states that haven't specifically adopted the Uniform Pre-Marital Agreement Act, the precise state laws that govern the writing of pre-marital agreement in such states often generally differ in only minor ways from the Act, nevertheless.

Thus, for all practical intents and purposes, the following guidelines, extracted from the Uniform Pre-Marital Agreement Act, represent the dominant legal principles that govern pre-marital agreements in most states:

1. Property acquired <u>during</u> marriage is MARITAL PROPERTY; and after they're married, both the husband and wife have an undivided one-half interest in their "marital property".

2. Property owned <u>before</u> marriage, or acquired before or after marriage <u>by gift</u>, or by inheritance, as well as appreciations in value of individual property not resulting from substantial personal effort of the other spouse, are considered "SEPARATE PROPERTY" individually and separately owned by each spouse.

3. On the other hand, however, any substantial <u>appreciation</u> of separate property (or of marital property) which is a result of, or is demonstably attributable to the <u>marital</u> effort of the parties, is a marital property to which BOTH parties are entitled to share. To put it another way, even if an initial money or property (say real estate) was originally spouse A's property separately owned by him, and was obtained by him prior to the marriage or as a personal gift or inheritance, if it can be clearly shown that its value *appreciated* during the course of the marriage and that the other spouse, spouse B, had a hand in bringing that appreciation about, then spouse B, as spouse A's husband or wife, would be entitled to share in that property—to the extent of the value of the appreciation, only. The share determined to have been the appreciated value during the marriage, will simply be prorated to each spouse fairly and equitably according to each spouse's believed "contribution" to that share—depending on whether the state involved follows the "equitable distribution" or "community property" principal of property distribution (See Chapter 3).

4. In cases involving "marital" and "separate" property components of such items as life insurance, pensions, and other deferred employee benefits that seem to spread through and across the date of marriage (i.e., items that seem to favor both sides of the issue), the court will follow simply the rule of presuming that certain property used by both parties are owned by both parties.

5. Husbands and wives have broad scope to enter into marital property agreements that may vary the effect of the Uniform Property Act.

6. Parties may contract with respect to:
   a) The rights and obligations of each of the parties in any of the property of either or both of them, whenever and wherever acquired or located;

---

[1] As of 1996, the following 20 states had specifically adopted the Uniform Pre-Marital Agreement Act: Arizona, Arkansas, California, Hawaii, Illinois, Iowa, Kansas, Maine, Montana, Nebraska, Nevada, New Jersey, North Dakota, Oregon, Rhode Island, South Dakota, Texas, Utah, Virginia.

b)   what to do with property upon separation, divorce, death or the occurrence or unoccurrence of any other event;

c)   the modification or elimination of spousal support;

d)   the making of a will, trust or other arrangement to carry out the provision of the agreement;

e)   the ownership rights in and the disposition of the death benefits from a life insurance policy;

f)   any other matters, including the personal rights and obligations of the parties, that are not in violation of public policy or a statute imposing a criminal penalty;

g)   the right of a child to (financial) support, except that the agreement may not adversely affect the said right;

h)   amendment or revocation of the agreement, providing it is provided that such an amendment or revocation may be done only by a written agreement signed by the parties;

Here Are Some Of The Kinds Of Provisions That Have Been Known To Be Included In Pre-Nuptial Agreements*:

- Wife shall keep her surname (or shall change it to the husband's), but couples' children would have the husbands' surname.

- Wife would use her maiden name professionally only; alternatively, professionally as well as in social situations.

- Upon marriage, parties would maintain their present separate residence in different locations, but shall live together after a specified period of time, or only on weekends.

- During the period when the parties live in separate residences, they would spend a certain number of weekends (specified) per month together each winter and summer in each party's residence every other year.

- Each party would be responsible for his or her expenses, such as for clothing, entertainment and transportation. A joint checking account would be established for common expenses such as rent or mortgage, utilities, food and the like. Bookkeeping would be rotated on a yearly basis.

- Any major purchases over a specified amount would be discussed and agreed upon before it may be implemented.

- Each party would be responsible for developing and maintaining his/her own credit history as well as his/her own medical plan.

- Each party would be responsible for maintaining an IRA account with yearly contribution goals of $1000.00

- In the event of a divorce, if there were any disputed property the matter would be submitted to arbitration to settle, and the parties would accept whatever decisions it renders as final.

---

* Much of this exposition is summarized from *"Love and the Law: A Legal Guide to Relationships in the 90's"*, by Gail J. Koff (pp.86-90, 95-96), to whom the present author is highly indebted.

- The parties are to have children, starting by a set time (e.g. when the wife reaches a given age); there would be an agreed number of children.

- Parties would make it a priority to be sure to have a vacation (or a set amount of time) together each year for nurturing the marital relationship, but on occasion may also have separate vacations, if desired and if possible.

- Parties are to start a retirement fund of a specified amount per month or quarter by a given time.

- Provision concerning religion; how to raise the children; and in the case of death of either parties, there is to be a period and act of mourning by the rest of the household (one couple, for example, stipulated that a photo of the deceased parent is to be always prominently displayed around the house as a way of assuring that the children would never forget the deceased parent); clauses about sex in the marriage and about other kinds of relationships outside the marriage.

- Parties would readily seek and submit to counseling in the event that any serious personal problems or disagreements arise between them in the marriage

- The parties shall set aside one weekend day and one week night, when possible, for nurturing the marital relationship, no matter how career-orientated or busy. In addition, a full weekend once every two months, shall be set aside for recreation or non-office related work on projects.

- The husband shall have the option of spending the night of December 24 each year with his family; the wife has the option of spending one holiday a year with her family.

- Each party does not necessarily have to accept without discussion the inevitable personality peculiarity or behavior that the other party has or may exhibit, but each retains the right to express his/her disapproval when warranted. Once such disapproval is expressed, the other would make good faith effort to look into the complaint and to take steps to change such behavior.

- Fidelity is expected, and a lapse by either party is grounds for divorce.

- Each party has the right, reasonably, to refuse specific sexual requests, and the parties shall make special effort not to make unreasonable, unfair, or insensitive demands of the other.

- Each party is expected to have friendships of both sexes and is expected to exercise appropriate sexual behavior.

NOTE: Note that, as can be seen from a review of the above listed provisions includable in a prenuptial agreement, one distinct advantage of a prenuptial agreement is that these kinds of contracts are highly flexible, and are capable of being tailored to cover not simply the "hard" issues of marriage (economics), but also the "soft" issues of marital life—the issues that by their very nature the courts will not and cannot rule upon or enforce, such as a provision as to who does the dishes, or on spending time with each other, or the vacation arrangement of the parties, or their sexual privileges, and the like. The "soft " issues in the agreement, though not ordinarily enforceable by a court, are however of immense usefulness, nevertheless, as they serve to provoke thoughts between the parties, and to promote better communication in the marriage.

Not everything whatsoever that you can think of, however, ought to be put into an agreement. In the final analysis, the parties must still be flexible and trusting of each other, as there will always be a difference between what is put in the agreement and the reality of what actually happens in the marriage in real life.

CHAPTER 6
THE BASIC PREREQUISITES FOR A GOOD
PRE-MARITAL AGREEMENT

If you and your would-be marital partner can meet the following conditions in the making of your premarital agreement, and produce a final document that contains these basic elements, you can be almost certain that your agreement would be just as good as any that is drawn up by the best lawyer around anywhere in the business. *In any event, these are the key elements that a good, legally valid pre-marital agreement (or other types of agreements) should strive to have.*

They are:

1. Specify the beginning of the term of the relationship. (To avoid the tendency to exaggerate the length of a relationship).

2. Clearly identify in the agreement the two principal parties to the agreement by their real names and in full, including the respective ages[1] and addresses of each at the time.

3. Make mention of the specific kind of relationship you are involved in at the moment (is it a legal marriage, a common-law marriage, a putative marriage, a non-marital cohabitation or a pre-nuptial relationship?); as well as the kind anticipated in the future, if any; and give the date and place where the marriage was performed, if applicable, or the non-marital relationship commenced. **IMPORTANT:** *Never make reference to sexuality or explicitly refer to rendering services as lovers in exchange for property or support. For example, never identify yourselves as "lovers"; rather use the term "partners."*

4. The effective date of the agreement should be specified, and the parties should define when the proposed future relationship should take hold and what specific event should occur to trigger it (e.g. occurrence of legal marriage). The manner by which the termination of the agreement may occur, or what should trigger it, should also be spelled out.

5. ***This is extremely important***: *Each party must provide the other a full, complete, reasonable and fair disclosure of all relevant information on the value and extent of his or her property and financial and other obligations, prior commitments to family and others, and the like.* This way, you're able to guard against the possible claims of fraud, conflict of interest, misrepresentation or overreaching, later, any one of which could void the agreement. In a word, the financial position and status of both parties should be honestly and fully stated. Each person should have a complete, clear and understandable explanation of what he or she is giving up, and what he or she is receiving in return, in their relationship and agreement, if anything. REPEAT, TO AVOID ANY POSSIBILITY OF A LATER CHARGE OF FRAUD, THE FINANCIAL

---

[1] You may just say something like: "We are each over the majority age of 18 (or 21) at this time."

POSITION OF EACH PARTY SHOULD BE DISCLOSED FULLY TO THE OTHER. (To be enforceable, it is necessary that a contract be negotiated "at arms length"—i.e., that one party give something of value to the other in return for something, and that events shall have been transacted in an environment free of any fraud, with neither taking advantage of the other.)

6. The assets and liabilities of each party should (ought to, ideally) remain separate. This is best accomplished by setting forth who owns what particular property at the time of entering the relationship. The parties may also agree on what funds are to be commingled, if any at all. (**Note**: As much as possible, avoid altogether any commingling of property whatsoever!).

7. A paragraph should be included in the agreement to assure each party exclusive title to any gifts or inheritances that might have been (or will in the future be) received by each.

8. The parties' earnings should be considered as <u>separate</u> to each individual.

9. A paragraph should be included that concerns how earnings should be applied to cover joint living expenses and purchases.

10. The agreement should make clear, in explicit terms and language, that its principal purpose is marriage in the immediate future (should be no more than 3 months) and the <u>mutual</u> promise of each non-marital cohabitant to provide care, companionship and home-making services to or for the other, *and should affirmatively foster the idea and impression that the agreement was not made primarily for sexual services.*

11. A major test is, does there exist between you and your partner, a demonstrable, mutual intent on and understanding of the pre-marital agreement, and concerning the marital relationship you later got into? **This is an absolute Number One requirement for a good couples' agreement**, because if you do have this, if both parties do really have a good and reasonable understanding of the agreements you eventually signed and it's basic implications, then everything else frequently would logically follow from that as you both at least presumably knew what you were getting into.

12. Each party shall have fully read the contents of the agreement (or had them read to him or her) several times over, and shall have had a fairly good understanding of the terms and provisions of the agreement to which he or she puts his or her signature at the time of signing. (One way of showing this is to be sure to give in the agreement a general idea of (emphasize!) the extent of each party's intelligence, literacy, experience, and general familiarity with or ability to understand the document he/she eventually signed—things like the age of each party at the time of the agreement, his and her specific level of education or specialization, previous marital experience with legal documents (or with attorneys), the extent, if any, to which a party (or both) has been a business person and dealt with the business world and valuation of property and investment, and the like.)

13. The agreement itself should not only appear to be, but should, in fact, be generally fair, free of fraud, and even-handed to both sides, and more especially to the general welfare and security of the minor child(ren), if there are any. This is the so-called "fairness" issue of pre-marital agreements generally, which is a prime element closely scrutinized by most courts confronted with making a ruling on property settlement and settlement agreements.

14. The agreement may not provide for the parties to engage in unlawful activities, or in any act that is against "public policy" (e.g., prostitution, spouse-swapping, bigamy, remarriage while still married to the present spouse, sexual relations with a third party, non-support of the couple's children, and the like). In brief, a provision is deemed to be against public policy if it attempts by it provisions to change the normal duties and responsibilities which arise by virtue of the marital status.

    No provision specifically promoting divorce or providing to secure a divorce, to commit a crime or otherwise engage in anything illegal, may be included in the agreement.

15. The parties entering into the agreement must both have been "competent" to do so—that is, each must have been sane, not underage, and generally in full control of his or her mind **at the time** of the negotiations and signing of the agreement.

16. Each side should make certain that he or she provides something of value—"consideration", in legal jargon—to the other side. That is, each person who promises to do or give something in the relationship, should also get something in return, though not necessarily something identical or nominally equal in value. (A "consideration" might be something as simple as a promise to share the living-together expenses, say 50-50; or a promise by one party to pay off a common debt in return for a promise by the other party not to sue in the future over past acts or obligations; or one partner might promise to give up his or her job to care for the household, in return for the promise by the other to pay the household expenses for a certain period of time.) With respect to a prenuptial agreement, generally the entering into marriage constitutes sufficient consideration to make such an agreement enforceable.

17. A couple's agreement (which, presumably, is otherwise fair and equitable) may provide that the wife (or husband, as the case may be) promises not to sue for increases in the amount of alimony or child support already provided for in the agreement. However, when the agreement does not expressly make such a provision, the wife (or husband, as applicable) is not relieved of the right to ask for increments, especially when she can show that the terms of the agreement were not fair or equitable, in the first place. (NOTE: In at least one state, the state of New York, the courts have ruled in a case involving a separation agreement, that where such an agreement does not *specifically* provide that a "substantial change in financial circumstances"[2] of the husband may entitle him to a modification of an alimony or a child support obligation, the husband is not relieved of such obligation to the extent provided for in the agreement.[3]

18. A clause should be included in the agreement whereby each party waves the right to be financially supported by the other in the event, and as of the time, of any separation or termination of the relationship.

19. A confidentiality clause might also be included in the agreement to protect the privacy of each party in the event there were to be termination of the relationship.

---

[2] Events such as these would be examples of a substantial change in financial circumstances: Retirement or loss of job, cut in pay, disability, major illness, a large inheritance or an increase in responsibility.

[3] The general rule, however, is that in cases of serious change in the circumstance of the husband, the amounts set for child support or alimony payment may be modified, and the separation agreement which so provides is generally not invalid. Furthermore, a separation agreement may also provide that in case of any disagreement on whether a change in condition has, in fact, occurred, or on the amount by which child support or alimony is to be reduced or increased, the dispute may be submitted to a designated person or institution for settlement by a binding arbitration, and that the cost of litigating the agreement in court shall be borne by the party who is found to be at fault.

20. Give the names, ages, and addresses of all living children, natural or adopted, for which **both** partners are currently the parents or are otherwise responsible, if any; and state whether the woman partner is currently pregnant and by whom. If the couple do not have any children together and are not expecting one, expressly say so in the document.

21. If you already have children together in your relationship, or plan on having some in the future, specify the terms you have worked out as to who should have custody (which could be either "sole" or "joint" custody) in the event of a future breakup, who should pay child support and at what intervals and in what amounts, and who should have visitation rights and how often. If any alimony or separate maintenance allowance is to be paid by one spouse or partner in support of the other, specify the details—who should make the payments, how much and at which intervals. Do not lump child support and alimony payments together. Also, make the payments periodic rather than lump-sum. (NOTE: Under the provisions of the Uniform Pre-Marital Agreement Act, while the parties to an agreement are somewhat limited in the nature of the child support provisions they can make, the Act only requires that "the right of a child to support may not be *adversely affected* by a pre-marital agreement.")

22. Give details of the agreements (or merely the understanding) reached on allocating the monies, earnings, properties and assets in the future marriage or relationship, if any, including who should have ownership or use or inheritance of what specific assets or property. (Clearly specify and enumerate the property involved, and which party it is to go to under what circumstances, including who is to be responsible for any outstanding debts owed on them).

23. The agreement must be entered into and signed voluntarily, freely, without duress, coercion, and overreaching or undue advantage by either party—absolutely by the free will of each individual.

24. Provide a means for third-party arbitration, rather than the courts, in the event of a disagreement concerning the enforcement or interpretation of the terms of the agreement.

25. In general, though not favored or recommended as a general rule, this is one place you may seriously—and beneficially—consider including a cause concerning payment of attorney's fees by a party who breaches the contract or causes the other to have to resort to litigation. This provision is helpful in certain states (e.g., California) where the prevailing party in a lawsuit is not otherwise automatically entitled to an award of attorney's fee.

26. Above all, each sentence, paragraph, or provision you make in your agreement must be clear, precise, simple and unambiguous as to what it says or means to say, and not open to more than one interpretation or meaning under the most ordinary and reasonable reading of the contract. (Just keep it simple and uncomplicated!)

SUMMARY: By way of a summary, all other things being equal, the courts will generally find your agreement valid and enforceable if, at the time it was signed by the parties, the agreement meets these basic tests:
   (1) It was entered into by the free will and consent of the parties, without fraud, duress, coercion, or overreaching;
   (2) The agreement makes no provisions that could be deemed to be against public policy, such as promotion of divorce or profiteering by divorce;

(3) A full and reasonable disclosure was made, and a fair understanding had, by the parties concerning the value and extent of the parties' property and financial circumstances at the time.

In a word, what is of the utmost interest to the court in such a situation, is the apparent "fairness" of the agreement to both parties—did each party seem to know what he/she was signing at the time he/she did; was each party given all the facts and information necessary to make an informed decision at the time he/she signed the agreement; does the agreement appear to be basically fair, reasonable, balanced and evenhanded to both sides; and did each party sign the agreement freely by his/her own free will, and the like?

So long as your agreement can boast of these basic elements, then you are home free, the chances are overwhelming that the courts will generally uphold your agreement in almost every jurisdiction and direct its enforcement.

CHAPTER 7

LET'S NEGOTIATE AND DRAFT THE PRE-NUPTIAL AGREEMENT BETWEEN YOU AND YOUR PARTNER:
The Step-By-Step Procedures

A. SOME HELPFUL PRACTICAL PROCEDURES FOR NEGOTIATING AND WORKING OUT A GOOD AGREEMENT

Follow these procedures and formalities in negotiating and working out the terms of your agreement:

1. Each partner should first hold preliminary "rap session" type discussions with a trusted confidant(s) or advisor(s) (they could be one's parents or relatives or trusted friends) about what the couple is contemplating doing. Run down, in general terms, the whole range of the issues, and concerns and conditions that persons in your particular circumstances might consider incorporating into an agreement. [Refer to Chapter 3 as your primary guide for the typical issues, and thoroughly go through Chapters 2 & 6, as well, for the basic elements and requirements that make for a sound couples' agreement. With a good comprehension of the two or three chapters you shall have had a fair familiarity with your rights under your particular state's divorce laws and how you'll need to write your agreement to make it legally valid and solid. Don't forget as well, Appendix B on the grounds for a divorce.][1]

2. Be brutally frank and objective with yourself (yourselves)! Be realistic. Put aside the emotions and idealism of marriage or future marriage, for the moment. Recognize that, like it or not, the stark reality is that in today's social climate marriage and marital relationship are often viewed simply as an economic partnership where often the central, underlying issue, as well as concern, is essentially the "practical" and "economic" aspects of marriage and breakup—that is, MONEY, in a word![2]

   To put it brutally, but honestly, the point simply is that in today's social climate the whole business of negotiating and hammering out a pre-marital contract between parties, is as much a business and financial matter as it is a romantic and social or family matter, pure and simple! And you had better approached it in exactly that same spirit here in attempting to work out the provisions for your own agreement—a balanced but realistic approach.

---

[1] It might well be advisable for you to give a copy of this book to your lay relatives and advisers and ask that they be sure to read it before hand in advance of your engaging in substantive discussion with them. Point, specifically, to a thorough reading—and mastery—of Chapters 2,3,5 and 6 at least, among others.

[2] One observer, an experienced New York divorce lawyer, put it bluntly it this way: "The rules of divorce [as well as of marriage, have] changed…and the emphasis has shifted from sin to economics. In today's climate, with marriage viewed as an economic parternship…[consequently , being] familiar with the practical aspects of divorce is necessary…Instead of hiring detectives to raid motel rooms in search of adulterous behavior, today's attorneys [or divorce filers] must often be prepared to trace monetary transactions, locate and determine the value of certain assets, and work closely with accountants and appraisers". (Koff, in *"Love and The Law*," p.166)

NOTE: *Experts experienced in the matter, who have participated in the making of several pre-nuptial agreements, advise that work on the agreements shall have been done at least two months before the actual marriage. This is necessary, they advise, because parties might often find that there are some difficult issues which take time to resolve.*

3. Alright, over the course of your courtship and the promises of your future marriage to each other, you and your partner shall have talked about a whole range of issues that are particular to your situations and circumstances—the extent of property owned, if any; your jobs and careers and the demands on your time and resources, any prior marriages or commitments to children; any outstanding commitments and financial obligations you have to others; your current financial position and income and networth and future expectations; the extent of existing debts owed, if any; your physical and health conditions; sexual proclivities, if any; what each of you expects of the other, or out of the relationship in a married life; your respective likes and dislikes, and so on. ***Absolutely nothing should be taboo or out of bounds to discuss!*** Any and everything conceivable must be discussed and thoroughly gone over, anything presently relevant or potentially relevant in the future to your lives together. FULL, FAIR, AN HONEST DISCLOSURE ON IMPORTANT FACTS ABOUT YOURSELVES TO EACH OTHER, IS THE RULE!

   Among other things, both parties (you and your partner) are to complete, in full (or should already have completed by now) a separate list of each person's assets and liabilities—called STATEMENT OF ACCOUNT or a NETWORTH. [See copy of a STATEMENT OF NETWORTH reproduced on pp. 104-6, for a sample]

   Have each partner swear to (notarize) his/her networth statement and then exchange them, preferably a week or more before the day of formal meeting or face-to-face pre-agreement negotiations. This way, when the actual pre-drafting discussions start, each party would have fully studied the statements (and other information) and made relevant comments or judgements. In any case, it should be well understood that a written statement of each party's assets and liabilities is an essential part of any good pre-nuptial Agreement, and must usually be attached as an appendix to the actual agreement.

4. This point cannot be emphasized enough: It's most important that you BE THOROUGHLY PREPARED BEFORE HAND. As one veteran marital settlement negotiator, a lawyer, put it, "A well-prepared client makes for a well prepared attorney, which helps to achieve the best possible result." You should be certain to come to the negotiations fully armed with certain essential information on the "facts" as well as the "law" about your rights, entitlements and obligations [Refer principally to Chapter 3 at pp. 15-30 for the basic law and your rights.]

   Here are, in brief, the kinds of essential information you and your partner may seek to assemble, to the extent relevant to your circumstances, and share with your partner and/or bring to the formal negotiations:

   - A copy of any pre-existing property settlement or marital agreements involving a party, if any.
   - A detailed inventory of all property in your home (including antiques, furniture, works of art, jewelry, and even appliances).
   - A listing of your marital property, including real estate, automobiles, furniture, appliances, artwork, collections, computers, electronic equipment.
   - A complete list, with account numbers, of joint bank accounts, certificates of deposit, stocks and bonds, retirement accounts, money-market funds, etc.

- A listing of your separate property, including jewelry, bank accounts, investments, real estate, etc.
- A list of all joint debts you owe with other persons, if any, as well as any individually owed ones, including mortgages, credit-card balances, car loans, etc.
- Copies of your tax returns for the past two or three years; and of your business returns, if applicable.
- A list of health, life, disability, homeowners, automobile, and other insurance policies.
- Copies of all pertinent financial records: tax returns, recent pay stubs, bank accounts, insurance documents, deeds, statements and records regarding items such as fringe benefits, pensions, personal expenses paid for by a business, tax-exempt investment income, etc. etc.

Be aware that often not all (or most) of the items mentioned above (or contained in the various sample agreements used in this guidebook) may necessarily or specifically be relevant or applicable to your particular case. In general, however, much of the relevant information of financial nature that may be needed for effective negotiations on an average case, is summed up in the STATEMENT OF NETWORTH on page 104 just in case you should need it.

5. Get into discussions and actual negotiations with your partner on the various issues of relevance in your situation. [See Chapter 3 for an idea about the typical issues; and review the three different versions of the sample Pre-marital Agreements set forth on pp.56-64, 65-75, & 76-8, for an idea of the outlines of a possible agreement plan.] In such negotiations, both parties should actively vent out your stands and desires fully; each of you must participate actively and freely in hammering out the terms that need to be provided in the agreement.

The negotiations with your partner do not necessarily have to be face-to-face between the two of you. You may, if that's the parties' preference, do the negotiations from a distance—by phone, fax, letters, exchange of draft agreements. However, in the case of pre-marital agreements, it's probably better recommended to do the discussions and negotiations for it face-to-face, preferably over a period of time over several informal meetings in different settings. Why? The reason is simple. Unlike the situation in a divorce case where the interpersonal relationship between the parties is contentious and distant, the relationship between parties involved in a pre-marital agreement situation is expectedly friendly and enthusiastic, and a good prenuptial agreement is supposed to serve, among other things, as a constructive force for developing a stronger future relationship based on marital trust and honesty. It is supposed to be a force to help the two partners learn more about their mates, and to avoid undue misunderstandings about and disagreements between themselves. Hence, what better way to get to evaluate someone and try to "read" him and his good faith and depth of sincerity about issues of some sensitivity, than to confront him or her head-on, on an eye-ball-to-eye-ball, face-to-face, but friendly and cordial discussion!? By doing it in person, face-to-face, you get to observe the body language, and physical reactions of your partner to issues discussed (as well as your reaction to him or her, in turn). And what a more effective way of communication, or more powerful way of fleshing out the issues and revealing a person's true character!

6. Eventually, after you and your partner shall have had several discussions and exchange of views on the various issues of your concern over a period of time, there now comes a time when you'll have to get together to negotiate more directly in a kind of final, more formal negotiation session. You and your partner may each write a first draft of the proposed agreement and bring it along when getting together. [Use the sample, PREMARITAL AGREEMENT forms on pp.56-78, as an aid and sample in helping you draft the terms].

You will, in general, merely be summing up the general areas where you and your mate have already had an agreement; and in the areas where there is yet no agreement between you, you can simply put down what you want on the various issues, or the alternatives; and then come prepared to work from there. When the actual negotiations start, you may simply run through the various issues and together discuss the alternatives and make genuine, good faith efforts, to try to come to some reasonable, sane compromises over matters that still remain unresolved. In any case, a good approach generally will be to use the sample agreements provided in the manual (pp.56-78) as a model, a basis for discussion and negotiation and raising pertinent issues between the parties, then composing your own draft that suits your particular facts and circumstances out of all that.

NOTE: *Whatever you do, though, try your darnest (both of you) to avoid ever having to bring in the lawyers in these negotiations—at least at this stage! It could be the most deadly thing you ever did <u>against</u> yourselves, against being able to work out a level-headed, balanced compromise agreement. [Refer, especially, to Chapter 2, Sections E,G & H thereof, at pp. 6-11, for some of the reasons why not to.] Bring in a lawyer (let alone two of them!) into the picture early on, and there comes contentiousness and "me first" selfishness amidst you and your partner; do that, and there goes right out of the window that element of residual trust and light spirit of good will and personal sacrifice you'd still need to exist between the partners if you are to go on to a loving, amicable married life even after the prenuptial agreement document shall have long been signed and put away!*

Lawyers simply being the lawyer they are, would tell you just to rush right out and get the first lawyer you can find to represent you (each party), and to have them negotiate and draw up the agreement. But, a more constructive and better approach of greater advantage to YOUR own interest, is for both you and your future spouse to work out the terms of the agreement yourselves before either of you should ever involve or consult with a lawyer, if ever at all. For, the truth that the both of you must first contend with, is that invariably lawyers will only make it more difficult, not easier, for parties to reach an agreement! Now, after both parties shall have reached an agreement, it would not hurt any, or ruin anything for each to consult with an attorney at that point, if you so desire[3]. The lawyers' primary role under those circumstances, would be merely to go along with the provisions already agreed to in the parties' agreement (and not to try to change them or introduce radically different ones), except that he/she may suggest language or phrasing by which to make clearer or stronger the same points already contained in the agreement, or to point out provisions that could be illegal or against public policy, if any.

B. THE ACTUAL DRAFTING OF THE AGREEMENT

Once a general agreement or understanding is arrived at between you and your partner (whether it is by phone or mail or direct negotiations, or through a mediator or even a lawyer), the way is now cleared for you to commence the actual, formal final drafting of the Prenuptial Agreement. **THIS IS WHERE THIS DO-IT-**

---

[3] The primary object why each person may consult legal counsel before they sign the agreement, would be, of course, so as to make it further less likely that any possible court challenge to the agreement would be successful. However, that potential problem has already been more than adequately taken care of for anyone who draws up the agreement with close adherence to the rules and guidelines set forth in this manual. If you closely follow the rules addressed in this manual, anyway, and negotiate and prepare and sign your agreement (with two or more live witnesses to the signing) exactly as recommended, you can just about go home and be assured that your agreement is as solid as a rock—challenge proof! And consulting a lawyer or not consulting one in such instance just wouldn't matter much!!

YOURSELF MANUAL KIT COMES IN HANDY. USING THE STEP-BY-STEP INSTRUCTIONS PROVIDED BELOW IN THIS SECTION AS YOUR AID AND GUIDE, YOU WILL THEN DRAW UP AN AGREEMENT GENERALLY AGREEABLE TO BOTH OF YOU—*i.e., you simply write what and what you have both agreed to into an agreement.*** As you go through the process of drawing up the agreement, bear in mind the major incidental issues that generally need to be worked out and resolved by such an agreement—property division, division of marital debts and bills, alimony, custody of children, child visitation rights, child support, etc., as it might apply to you. [Refer to Chapter 3, at pp. 15-30 for elaborate listing of the various typical issues, and the general legal principals (generally "community property" or "equitable distribution" rules) which govern their respective determinations]

Now, we come to the actual mechanical drafting of the written agreement. To begin the process, in the passages below (pp. 56-78), you'll find three different samples of a prenuptial agreement, each involving a particular situation or circumstance:

> **Sample 1:** For a couple with substantial (or anticipated substantial) marital property, and no provision for minor children (pp. 56-64).
>
> **Sample 2:** For a couple with substantial (or anticipated substantial) marital property, and Provision for the support, custody and maintenance of anticipated children by the couple (pp. 65-75).
>
> **Sample 3:** A shorter, simpler, more general version that is written in a less impersonal or threatening legal language that is traditional with contract law agreements (pp. 76-8).

Now, you may select either Sample #1, or 2 or 3, representing that sample form that is more appropriate for your particular situation, and complete it by filling in the necessary information or optional range of information in the blank spaces in each paragraph. For any articles, paragraphs (or contents, or provisions) which may not be applicable in your case, simply cross that out and mark it so that it will not be included in your final drafted copy. In short, the sample agreements can serve as a foundation or starting point for writing your own. You may adapt, and change and personalize them to fit your particular needs and circumstances.

C. YOU MUST GO STEP-BY-STEP, STRICTLY IN ORDER

THIS IS VERY IMPORTANT: in preparing the final draft agreement form, take it one (and only ONE) step at a time, following the items in the sample agreement **EXACTLY** in the same numerical order in which they are listed in the manual. In each clause or paragraph you come to, first read it to understand what is called for. Then, go one step (and only one step) at a time according to the order of the numbering. ***Do not skip around from step to step or from page to page***.

Make Photocopies & Use them As Your "Practice" Worksheets

A good practice in preparing the drafts, is to make some photocopies of the sample form (just a photocopy, please, do not tear up the book!), and use that photocopy as a "practice" worksheet. Fill in the appropriate information in all the photocopy Practice Sheets, from the first page to the last, and as you go along, if there are any paragraphs or provisions which do not apply to your particular situation, cross them out. You'll simply "pencil in" on the sample practice form, in the blank spaces, the appropriate words and statements for a given entry. In each instance, be sure that the words or statements you fill in or enter do clearly state exactly what you want to convey to yourselves and to everybody who reads them.

CLUE: Ask yourself this question: "Would a stranger reading these words or statements readily know what I'm trying to say? Would they make simple sense to him or her? Are my intentions clear, straightforward and unambiguous?" Then, after checking to make sure you have everything pretty much in order, type out the form, with all information fully filled in, on a separate final true sheet.

What To Do When You've Completed Making Up The Draft Copy Of Your Agreement

Let's assume you've finished writing up the initial practice drafts. There are a few things left before you are done: TYPING OUT A FINAL PERFECT COPY OF THE AGREEMENT. Here's what to do. Now, run through the initial draft copy of your agreement, from its first page down; and, carefully and in order, type (or print) out on clear separate sheets of paper, the complete Agreement with the contents of each and every clause or paragraph that you filled in or checked off now included. Type (or print) out everything onto separate sheets of white paper to make out a final, true copy of your agreement. (Number the pages of your completed agreement at the top of each page and be sure to provide at the bottom left corner of each page, a space for you to initial and date the agreement.) You should make two (and only two) final copies of the Agreement; you may use carbon paper, but make sure that each copy is *exactly* the same in contents.)

Avoid erasing, crossing out or other corrections in your final draft to avoid suspicions that might arise later that someone might have slipped in such changes other than you. (Note: if your final agreement contains any substantial errors, always retype completely that entire page.)

When you run down the contents of your final draft and carefully compare the items to be sure that the contents reflect exactly what both parties intend to provide, ask yourselves (both of you) these questions: Did we get everything? Is there anything we might like to adjust or add in the final draft? Is my intent and my partner's and the language of the Agreement—every sentence, paragraph—clear and unambiguous? Counter-check and make the necessary adjustments, accordingly. And if there had been any further corrections, then type (or write) out a final, perfect copy.

IT'S NOW DONE. The next order of business is the " execution" phase—the SIGNING AND WITNESSING of the Agreement you've just finished drafting. For that, turn to Chapter 8 at p. 79 for the procedures.

Copyright © 1998, by Do-It-Yourself Legal Publishers, Newark, NJ

Sample I: *For A Couple With Substantial Property, With NO Provisions For Minor Children*

PRENUPTIAL AGREEMENT [Sample #1]

This AGREEMENT is made between Mr/Ms _____, presently residing at _____ hereinafter called (1st party's first name) and Mr/Ms _____ presently residing at _____, hereinafter called (2nd party's first name), both of whom together are hereinafter called the Parties.

WITNESSETH

WHEREAS the Parties intend to marry each other in the State of _____, and to reside in the City of _____, and desire, in anticipation of their marriage, to settle certain financial questions which might otherwise arise during and/or as a consequence of their marriage; and

WHEREAS the Parties each desire to maintain his or her financial independence from the other, except as the Parties shall otherwise mutually agree; accordingly, the Parties hereby make the following stipulations and representations:

(A) The Parties have made full and complete disclosure to each other of their respective financial positions, including the net worth and income of each of them and their expectancies, including, but not limited to future inheritances.

(B) The Parties have each submitted to the other a financial Statement of Net Worth as of the _____ day of _____ 19___, and each party herewith acknowledges receipt of same; and each represents to the other that the assets and liabilities reflected on the said statements are an accurate true picture of his or her own financial condition. The said net worth statement is attached hereto as Exhibit "A", and each is counter-signed and dated by the other to indicate acknowledgment of receipt of same. [*]

(C) Each of the Parties represents that presently, prior to the date of their marriage, he or she owns, possesses or has title to certain property of significant value, which property is to remain his or her sole, separate property in the future as evidenced either by title to such property or ownership.

(D) JOHN represents that the items of property listed in Schedule B, which is attached hereto, is his sole and separate property. The said property constitutes the total assets of JOHN which shall remain his separate property as designated in this Agreement, unless changed in accordance with the terms specified herein.

(E) JANET represents that the items of property listed in Schedule C, which is attached hereto, is her sole and separate property. The said property constitutes the total assets of JANET which shall remain her separate property as designated in this Agreement, unless changed in accordance with the terms specified herein.

_____

[*] [NOTE: Parties must be sure to actually exchange and attach this statement before or at the actual execution date, and to countersign each statement with date of the exchange]

(F) Each of the Parties acknowledges that he or she is fully acquainted with the business and resources of the other, that the other has answered any and all questions that he or she may have asked of the other concerning his or her business and resources; each Party acknowledges and understands that by the execution of this Agreement he or she is waiving any and all other rights of any kind to any payment of any kind or nature at the death of the other or upon dissolution of the marriage, and that in the absence of this Agreement he or she might be entitled to receive a substantial portion of the estate of the other.

(G) Each Party expressly acknowledges that he/she has been advised of and knows it, that he/she has the right to obtain his/her own individual legal counsel for this Agreement, but that each has either received such counsel or has, in the exercise of his/her adult right to choose, chosen by his/her own free will to act for and by himself or herself in the drafting and signing of this Agreement without legal counsel.

(H) Each Party represents that he or she has considered all of the facts and circumstances involved herein, that each believes this Agreement to be fair and reasonable in the light of all the facts and circumstances, and each acknowledges that in entering into this Agreement he or she has done so absolutely freely, voluntarily, and with full knowledge.

SAMPLE SHEET

NOW, THEREFORE, it is mutually agreed between the parties as follows:

1. **Consideration.** The consideration for this agreement is the marriage of the parties, the mutual promises, covenants, and agreements contained herein, and other good and valuable considerations, receipt of which are hereby mutually acknowledged.

2. **Separately Owned and Joint Marital Property.**
   a) Each Party shall keep and retain sole ownership and control and enjoyment of all separate property, real and personal, that are now owned by him or her in any manner whatsoever, and do so as if the parties had remained unmarried, and each shall have the absolute and unrestricted right to dispose of such property, free from any claim that may be made by the other by reason of their marriage.

   b) Wherever a separate property is a source of income or generates other assets, any such income shall remain the sole separate property of the Party holding the property, and shall be placed in the sole name of that Party.

   c) In the event that the nature or character of any separate property of either Party shall change, the legal title, as evidenced by an instrument of writing, shall reflect the intent of the parties as to whether the new property shall be considered as separate property or as joint property.

   d) The Parties anticipate that they will be purchasing a home or apartment in the future, such home or apartment to be their marital residence. It is the plan of the Parties that the down payment for such purchase shall come from the sale of JOHN'S Apartment, Apt No_____ at this address: _____. In such event, JOHN shall be credited for the full amount of such down payment in the new acquisition. However, title in the new anticipated acquisition shall he held in joint ownership and each Party shall be entitled to full rights as equal owners, once John is credited as above. This shall be the case regardless of the respective contributions of either Party to the payment of mortgage, maintenance or other expenses related thereto.

e)   The Parties agree that all real and personal property already acquired to this date, or those acquired during the course of the marriage, shall not constitute marital property unless title to such property is placed in both the name of JOHN and JANET. All property acquired hereafter shall be the sole and separate property of the party who purchased said property or otherwise acquired it, free and clear of any claim or demand of or by the other party, unless such property is specifically titled in the name of both JOHN or JANET or is listed on a schedule of jointly owned property and kept as part of this agreement.

f)   *In determining whether real or personal property acquired during the marriage is to be titled to JOHN or JANET, the parties agree to be governed by the following rules*:

i.   All real or personal property acquired by a party by gift, including gifts from the other party, inheritance, or any death benefit under an insurance policy, shall be the separate property of the spouse acquiring such property. In the event such property is acquired jointly by both parties, such property shall be marital property to be held and divided in accordance with this agreement.

ii.   All earnings by JOHN shall be the separate property of JOHN, and all earnings by JANET shall be the separate property of JANET. All earnings from jointly held property of JOHN and JANET shall be marital property to be held and divided in accordance with the terms of this agreement. Earnings for purposes of this agreement shall include wages, salaries, bonuses, interest income, pensions, profit sharing, rents, disability income, social security income, and any other income which would be reportable on the parties' income tax return.

iii.   All professional licenses, business licenses, partnership interests, joint venture interests, sole proprietorship interests, or other business interests, shall be the separate property of the spouse who owns or operates such business interest, and the other spouse shall make no claim to such interest owned by the other unless the parties have agreed in writing that the business interest is jointly owned or is being operated as a partnership between the parties.

iv.   All income or proceeds received in exchange for separate property shall be separate property, and all income or proceeds received in exchange for jointly held property, shall be marital property.

v.   All appreciation, either active or passive, in the value of a separate property shall be separate property, and all appreciation, either active or passive, in the value of jointly held property shall be marital property.

vi.   All claims for personal injury, pain, and suffering, shall be the separate property of the spouse making the claim. Any claim for a child of the marriage shall belong to the child, except that a spouse or both spouses may be reimbursed to the extent of expenditures for the medical care made on behalf of the child.

vii.   All claims for loss of consortium shall be the separate property of the party making such claim.

viii.   Each party shall maintain separate checking and savings accounts as may be necessary for conducting his or her own separate business, and such accounts shall be the separate property of the spouse in whose name the account is maintained. In addition, the parties shall establish a joint checking account for the maintenance of jointly held property and household expenses. The joint account or accounts shall be deemed marital property to be held and divided in accordance with the terms of this agreement. Neither party shall make any expenditure from a joint account without the express permission or joinder of the other party. The parties agree to establish a family budget on July 1st of each year for the payment of all joint expenses and household expenses, including, but not limited to groceries, utilities, lawn care, garbage pick-up, newspaper delivery, and cable television. The family budget expenses shall be paid from the joint account, the parties shall compute the percentage that each spouse contributes to the total net income of the parties, and contribute such percentage of income as is necessary to establish the family budget based upon their respective net incomes from the previous year. For purposes of this paragraph, "net income" shall be the total take home pay of a party.

ix. It is understood that as the parties acquire and dispose of items of personal property, they may add or delete items from Schedules B, C, or other Schedules as they from time to time mutually agree and in accordance with this agreement, but no later than thirty (30) days after the acquisition or disposal of any such item. John and Janet acknowledge that certain household goods listed on Schedules B and C as separate property of one party or the other are necessary for the maintenance, use, and enjoyment of the parties' family residence, and so long as the parties should live together in marriage, each party is entitled to use, possess, and enjoy any of the said items without the exclusion of the other.

x. JOHN and JANET agree that the title to all real property acquired during the course of the marriage shall be placed solely in the name of either JOHN or JANET, or in the name of both JOHN and JANET in accordance with the rules set forth in this agreement. Such property as is placed solely in the name of JOHN shall be JOHN'S sole and separate property, and such property as is placed in the name of JANET shall be JANET'S sole and separate property. Such property as is placed in the name of both JOHN and JANET shall be marital property to be held and divided in accordance with this agreement.

3. *Mutual Release and Waiver Of Rights in Each Other's Estate.*

a) Except as otherwise provided herein, JOHN and JANET do hereby waive, release, discharge, quitclaim, and renounce to each other and to their respective heirs and assigns, all rights to claim an equal or equitable distribution of property or distributive shares of intestate succession, of community property, of dower, courtesy, or homestead rights. And further, the parties do hereby waive and renounce all such rights under or by virtue of the laws of any state or country, to elect to take a life estate upon the death of the other, all rights to dissent from the other's will and any and all other rights which either party may now have or may hereinafter acquire under the present or future laws of any jurisdiction arising out of the marital relationship.

b) Except as otherwise provided in this Agreement, each party grants, releases and forever quitclaims to the other, all right, title, interest, claim, and demand whatsoever in the real and personal property which he or she now owns or may hereafter acquire, and each party may hereafter acquire, own, possess, encumber, dispose of, and convey any and all kinds of real and personal property, free from the consent, joinder, and interference of the other party. Each party agrees that hereafter in the sale, transfer, and conveyance of any property, real or personal, it shall not be necessary that the other party sign the deed, and any and all future documents necessary for the grantee or purchaser to have a good title. If the laws of a state or a third party requires the release of a spouse's rights or interests, the other spouse agrees to execute whatever documents that are necessary to give such release in the separate property of the other spouse.

c) Except as otherwise provided in this agreement, each party waives and releases any right or claim to receive any benefit under Sections 401(a)(11)(A) of the Internal Revenue Code from a qualified plan (or any similarly substituted law), it being intended that this provision shall constitute a waiver of all such benefits under Section 417(a)(2) of the Internal Revenue Code, and waives and releases any right he or she may have to serve as administrator of the estate of the other.

4. *Reservation of Rights.* Except as expressly provided in this agreement, all other rights and obligations accruing to either party by virtue of the marriage relationship shall remain in full force and effect, each party agreeing to give his or her best efforts toward fulfilling all marital duties and obligations.

5. *Execution of Wills.* Each party agrees that each reserves the right to manage, control, and dispose of his or her respective separate property independently as each alone may freely choose, either by deed, will or otherwise. The parties agree that they may hereafter execute any will or trust agreement without making any provisions therein for the other, and this agreement shall in no way affect or invalidate any provisions which either party may purely on his or her own make for the other in any will, trust agreement, contract, or other document hereafter executed.

Nothing contained in this Agreement, however, shall be deemed to constitute by either Party a waiver of any bequest or of fiduciary appointment that one Party may choose to make to the other party, by Will or other means, nor a waiver of any transfer by either Party to the other, either by gift or by placing property in joint names or in both Parties' names as tenants by the entirely. The Parties acknowledge, however, that they are otherwise not obligated to do so and that no promises of any kind whatsoever have been made by either of them to the other with respect to any such bequest, appointment, or transfer.

6. *Additional Instruments.* Each Party shall, upon the request, take any and all steps to execute, acknowledge, and deliver to the other Party any and all future instruments that may be reasonably necessary or expedient to carry out the purposes of this Agreement.

7. *Income Tax Returns.* The parties agree to execute and file joint tax returns for all calendar years during their marriage as long as permitted by law. The Parties shall be liable for all taxes, penalties, fines, and other assessments in an amount equal to a proportion of the total tax, penalty, fine, or assessment as the case may be, for which he or she would be responsible if he or she had filed a separate return. The parties agree that any income tax refunds shall be divided between them upon receipt in accordance with their respective contributions to the tax payments.

8. *Debts and Obligations.* Each Party represents and warrants to the other that he or she has not heretofore incurred any debt or obligation for which the other may be liable, and each Party agrees that he or she shall not hereafter, without the expressed written consent of the other, incur any such debt or obligation for which the other may be liable. Each Party agrees to indemnify the other against any loss, expense (including reasonable attorney's fees) and damage in connection with or arising out of a breach of the foregoing mutual representation and covenants. From and after the date of this agreement, each party shall be responsible for all bills incurred by him or her. If the parties incur joint debts, joint debts shall be paid from the joint accounts of the parties.

9. *Waiver of equitable distribution and maintenance:* In the event of the separation of the Parties or the dissolution of the marriage, each Party waives any right he or she might otherwise have to equitable distribution, or to a distributive award or to maintenance or alimony under the laws of the State of _____, or of the laws of any other jurisdiction wherein a party may be residing at the time or which may otherwise be applicable. This provision is intended to constitute a waiver of any right to equitable distribution or maintenance, as authorized by the provisions of the applicable law of the State of _____ or of the same or similar law of any jurisdiction which may be applicable. This provision, however, is not intended to be, and shall not be construed as, a waiver of the right of either Party to claim payments of child support, if the Parties shall hereafter become parents.

10. Notwithstanding any provision or interpretation herein to the contrary, or any applicable law of this or other state to the contrary, distribution of marital property or assets between the parties shall under any and all circumstances whatsoever be made without regard to marital behavior or conduct, and under no condition shall the conduct of either party be considered or addressed in any property division issues between the parties by any judge or tribunal.

11. *Full Disclosure.* The Parties acknowledge that each has made a full, fair and reasonable disclosure to the other of all property and interests in property owned by each of them. However, the parties agree that any failure (in part or in whole) to disclose shall not be a basis for setting aside this agreement.

12. (a) *Competence, voluntary execution & acceptance of the parties in entering this agreement.* The parties acknowledge that the provisions of this agreement are equitable, adequate, and satisfactory to each of them, and shall be so deemed both now and at such time as either party shall seek to enforce this agreement; and they further acknowledge, each and both, that they have entered into this agreement completely of their own free will and volition, and that no undue influence, coercion, pressure, or force, directly or indirectly, has been used against them in the making, signing and acceptance of this agreement, either by the other party or by any other persons.

(b) Each party stipulates, under the penalty of perjury, that he or she is of full age, sufficient education and intelligence, and is of sufficient experience, knowledge and familiarity with legal documents and his/her rights in the world of business; that each has fully read and considered the provisions of this agreement and completely understands and agrees with the same.

(c) Each party has either consulted legal counsel of his/her own choice or has otherwise educated himself or herself in, and is fully advised and knowledgable about his or her legal rights and the effects and ramifications of this agreement relative to their property rights and to each other. Furthermore, each party has familiarized himself or herself with what his/her property rights and obligations would be in the absence of this contractual agreement, as well as with what they would be under this contractual agreement, and each party hereby expressly declares under the penalty of perjury, that he or she completely agrees with the said legal effects and implications.

13. *Modification and Waiver.* A modification and waiver of any of the provisions of this agreement shall be legal and authorized only if made in writing and is executed with the same formality as this agreement. The failure of either party to insist upon strict performance of any of the provisions of this agreement shall not be construed as a waiver of any subsequent default of the same or similar nature. All provisions of this agreement are deemed executed by the parties; however, should any provision be determined to be executory, such provision shall be valid and binding on the parties unless modified in writing as provided herein.

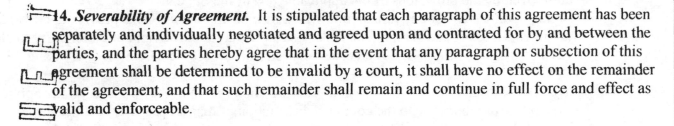

14. *Severability of Agreement.* It is stipulated that each paragraph of this agreement has been separately and individually negotiated and agreed upon and contracted for by and between the parties, and the parties hereby agree that in the event that any paragraph or subsection of this agreement shall be determined to be invalid by a court, it shall have no effect on the remainder of the agreement, and that such remainder shall remain and continue in full force and effect as valid and enforceable.

15. *Binding Effect and Entire Agreement.* This agreement represents the entire understanding of the parties, and there are no representations, warranties, covenants, claims or allegations, or understanding between the parties other than those expressed and set forth herein. And except as otherwise stated herein, all the provisions herein shall be binding upon the respective heirs, next of kin, executor, administrator and legal representatives of the parties.

16. *Termination of Agreement.* If the marriage anticipated by this agreement does not occur within six (6) months from its execution, this Agreement shall be null and void.

17. *Arbitration of Dispute.* In the event that a dispute or disagreement should arise over the interpretation or fulfillment of any clauses in this agreement, or over any or other matter or cause whatsoever except for the custody of children, the matter shall be submitted to arbitration to be resolved, and the following person(s) and or institution(s) are hereby appointed to act as the arbitrator(s) in such matters: .

Any decisions made on the disputed issues by such arbitrators shall be binding upon and final for both parties. The costs and expenses, including any legal fees, incurred for such arbitration, or otherwise incurred for enforcing or litigating the disputed matters in a court of law, shall be charged to and be borne solely by the party who is found to be substantially at fault on the disputed matters

---

* Enter the names of the appointed persons and/or institutions, as agreed, including their addresses. Include how they are to be appointed and the process of final selection of a particular arbitrator in the event of a deadlock by the two parties

18. *Construction of Agreement.* Both parties together assume joint and equal responsibility for the form, content, and composition of this Agreement. No provision of this agreement shall be interpreted or construed for or against either party because that party, or the party's legal representative, drafted this agreement. Both parties acknowledge and stipulate that they are completely aware that they have the right to, and are given the opportunity to, seek individual legal counsel or representation of their choice in the making of this Agreement, if they so choose or prefer, but the parties, in the exercise of their adult right to choose, have by their own free will chosen to act for and by themselves herein.

19. *Governing Law.* This agreement shall be construed in accordance with and governed by the provisions of the UNIFORM PRE-MARITAL AGREEMENT ACT, regardless of the forum where it may come up for construction. However, no matter where construed, no interpretation or construction of this Agreement shall conflict with or be inconsistent with the terms and provisions herein.

IN WITNESS WHEREOF, the parties have signed, sealed, and acknowledged this agreement in duplicate originals, one of which is retained by each of the parties hereto, this the day and year first below written.

SIGNED: _____   _____
(Husband)   (Date of Signing)

Present Address: _____

_____

SIGNED: _____   _____
(Wife)   (Date of Signing)

Present Address: _____

ACKNOWLEDGEMENT/VERIFICATION

STATE OF_____

COUNTY OF_____, ss:

I, a Notary Public in and for the State and County captioned above,

HEREBY CERTIFY that on the _____ day of _____ 19____, the following person(s), _____

_____ and _____, known to me or made known to me to be the individual(s) described

in, and who executed the foregoing agreement, came before me, and that thereupon, the said person(s) severally acknowledged

to me under oath and under the penalty of perjury, that they signed the within document and that the facts and statements

contained in the said agreement are true and accurate.

WITNESS my hand and notarial seal, the day and year last written above.

_____
(Notary Public)

CERTIFICATION BY SUBSCRIBING WITNESSES TO AGREEMENT

We, the undersigned witness(es) whose names are hereunto subscribed, **DO HEREBY CERTIFY** under the penalty of perjury, that on the _____ day of _____ 19__, both of the parties above named, respectively signed their names to this instrument in our presence and in the presence of each of us and at the same time, in our presence and to our hearing, the said persons declared the same to be their Written Agreement, made by and freely agreed to by them, and requested us and each of us, to sign our names thereto as witnesses to the execution thereof, which we hereby do in the presence of the parties and of each other, on the day of the date of the said execution. The said parties appeared to be under no duress, force, compulsion or constraint of any kind when they signed the said agreement.

SIGNED: SAMPLE SHEET

(1) _____ of _____
       (Signature and Name)   (Address)

(2) _____ of _____
       (Signature and Name)   (Address)

(3) _____ of _____
       (Signature and Name)   (Address)

Copyright © 1998. By Do-It-Yourself Legal Publishers
Newark, N.J.

Sample 2: For a couple with substantial marital property, with provisions for minor children.

PRE-MARITAL PROPERTY AGREEMENT [Sample #2]

THIS AGREEMENT is made between _____(his full name)_____ ("Husband") of ____(City)____, in the State of
_____; and _____(her full name)_____ ("Wife"); of ____(city)____, in the state of _____;
alternatively referred to as the "Parties" to this agreement.

RECITALS:

WHEREAS the Parties to this Agreement intend to marry one another and are making this Agreement in contemplation of becoming Husband and Wife; and

WHEREAS the Parties desire to contract with each other concerning ownership and control and management of their incomes, assets, expenses and liabilities during and as a consequence of their marriage; accordingly the parties hereby make the following stipulations and representations:

(A) Joseph has previously been married to another person and has a child by that person who is his presumptive heir-at-law;

(B) Joseph and Monica intend that the terms and provisions of this Agreement shall apply to property and/or property interests currently owned by either of them, and also to property and/or property interests which they or either of them may hereafter acquire;

(C) Each Party is fully aware and understands that in the absence of this Agreement, the law would confer upon him/her certain property rights in the present or future property of the other, and, except as expressly set forth in this Agreement, it is the intent of each Party by this Agreement to completely relinquish all rights in such property; and

(D) Except as expressly provided in this Agreement, it is the intent of the Parties to alter the applicability to them of the laws of any state or jurisdiction to which the parties are or may be subject relating to their marital property rights and financial interests, as well as any other marital property law or community property law which may at any time be applied or applicable to the Parties and the various property rights, obligations, remedies and economic incidents, which have arisen or will arise during their marriage;

NOW, THEREFORE, with the express intention that this Agreement be legally binding, the Parties revoke all prior agreements and hereby mutually agree as follows:

1. **Effective Date and Duration of Agreement**

    This agreement shall take effect as of the date of the marriage of the Parties, and shall subject to the terms of this agreement, remain in effect until final disposition of all property upon termination of the marriage of the Parties by death or dissolution.

    In the event that the marriage anticipated by this agreement does not occur within six (6) months from its execution, this Agreement terminates and shall be null and void.

2. Consideration

The sole consideration for this Agreement shall be the mutual promises and covenants contained in this Agreement.

3. Financial Disclosure

Both Parties affirm that they have, in negotiating this Agreement, fairly and reasonably disclosed to the other their respective incomes, assets, expenses, and liabilities, and each further represents that he/she has received any and every information and records requested and complete answers to every question asked, and that he/she is completely satisfied thereto that a fair and reasonable disclosure has been made. Each Party further waives the right he/she currently has to information about the other's incomes, assets, expenses, and liabilities, beyond that already provided, and agrees that he/she enters into this Agreement with sufficient knowledge of the financial affairs of the other. However, neither Party waives the right to future information about the other's incomes, assets, expenses and liabilities, all of which the Parties agree to exchange upon reasonable request of one to the other in the future.

*[The Parties have exchanged financial statements showing their assets and liabilities and the approximate values thereof.] While neither Party represents his/her respective financial statement to be a precise statement of his/her assets and liabilities, it constitutes a fair and reasonable and adequate approximation of such assets and liabilities for the purposes of this agreement and the health of the parties' future marital relationship.

4. Classification and Ownership of Assets

(a) General Rule. The Parties agree that all of their assets now owned or hereafter acquired by them, shall be classified in accordance with the manner in which such assets are "titled." Assets or interests in assets titled or deemed to be titled in the name of one Party, shall be classified as the individual property of that named Party under the rules described in sub-paragraph (b) below. Assets titled in the names of both Parties and property defined as "household property", shall be classified and owned according to paragraph 5. Earned income shall be classified and owned according to paragraph 6.

(b) The Parties agree that assets of particular kinds shall be "titled", and, therefore classified, in accordance with the following general conventions:

(1) *Real Estate*, including improvements thereon, shall be titled to the Party named as owner on the Deed, Land Contract, or other instrument of conveyance.

(2) *Bank Accounts* (including Certificates of Deposit) shall be titled to the Party named as owner on the passbook or records of the entity holding the account.

(3) *Stocks and Bonds* shall be titled to the Party named as owner on the certificate.

(4) *Tangible Personal Property* for which a certificate of title is issued shall be titled to the Party named as owner on the certificate of title. Except as provided in paragraph 5 (relating to household furniture and furnishings and antiques, collections and personal effects), tangible personal property for which a certificate of title is not issued, shall be deemed titles to the Party who would be the owner of the asset as determined by the common law system of property ownership in effect in the State of _____ on (Date)_____.

---

* Include this statement [the one enclosed within the bracket], <u>ONLY</u> <u>IF</u> the parties actually exchange the financial statement, otherwise include it.

(5) All assets acquired by gift or inheritance of any kind or lottery, regardless of date of acquisition, shall be deemed a separate property of the recipient.

(6) Retirement, pension accounts and IRAs will remain individual property.

5. Property Titled in Both Names; Household Property

(a) Property Titled in Both Names. The Parties may acquire property with joint funds, and such property shall be held, owned, or titled in both their names with or without further designation of such property as to status or classification. In the event that the Parties designate the form of ownership of such property in writing, such designation shall control the classification of, and the parties' rights with respect to such property, including but not limited to, the rights defined under common law forms of property ownership. In the event that no designation is made in writing, such property shall be deemed owned by the Parties as survivorship marital property.

(b) Any untitled household furniture and furnishings and antiques, collections and personal effects, owned by either Party, shall be classified and owned as follows:

(1) Untitled Household Furniture and Furnishings. Any untitled household furniture and furnishings owned by either Joseph or Monica before the date of their marriage, shall be classified as his/her individual property; any untitled household furniture and furnishings acquired by either Joseph or Monica on or after the date of their marriage, shall be classified and deemed owned as survivorship marital property, unless such property is acquired by either Party alone or as a gift or inheritance received from a third party, in which event such gifted or inherited property shall be classified and deemed owned as individual property of the party receiving such gift or inheritance. As used herein, the term "untitled household furniture and furnishings" shall include household furniture, furnishings, silverware, equipment, supplies, china, books, and other similar property of household use or decoration, provided, however, that such household furniture and furnishings are not antiques, collections, or personal effects, all of which are classified pursuant to (2) below.

(2) Antiques, Collections, and Personal Effects. The antiques, collections and personal effects of either party, whether acquired before or after the marriage of the Parties, shall at all times be classified and owned as individual property of the Party who originally furnished monetary consideration in money or money's worth for the property, unless such antiques, collections and personal effects are acquired by either party as a gift or inheritance received from a third party or as a gift received from the other party, in which event such gifted property shall be classified and deemed owned as the individual property of the party receiving such gift or inheritance. As used herein, the term "antiques, collections and personal effects" shall include all antiques, all collections (coin, stamp, art, etc.), clothing, jewelry, family memorabilia and other similar property of personal use or decoration.

(c) In the event that the classification of property as survivorship marital property in this section is invalid or ineffective for any reason, such property shall be classified and deemed owned as marital property.

(d) If the homestead is in the name of only one party, the other party hereby grants a waiver to the titled party to sell the homestead without a signature from the other party.

6. Classification of Earned Income

The earned income of either Party shall be classified and deemed owned as his/her individual property. As used herein, the term "earned income" includes all wages, salaries, commissions, bonuses, and gratuities or payments in kind, generated by a Party through the application of services, labor, effort, inventiveness, physical or intellectual skill, creativity or managerial activity.

SAMPLE

7. Income, Additions, Mixing, Appreciation

The classification and ownership of property as the individual property of a Party, shall extend:

(a) To income from the property;

(b) To improvements and additions to the property, regardless of the source of the funds or property used to make or acquire the addition;

(c) To property of other classifications mixed or comingled with the property;

(d) To realized or unrealized appreciation in the value of the property, regardless of whether that application occurred through general market conditions, or through the application of labor, efforts, inventiveness, physical or intellectual skills, creativity or managerial activity, to the property by either of the Parties without receiving reasonable compensation therefor; and

(e) To property received in exchange for, or with the proceeds of sale or financing of such property.

8. Management and Control of Individual Property

Each Party shall have the absolute and unrestricted right of management and control of his/her individual separate property, free from any claim or interest that might otherwise be made by the other Party by reason of their marriage; and the other Party on his/her own part hereby ratifies and consents to the right of the other Party to have such unrestricted management and control, and waives any right he/she may otherwise have to challenge that or to otherwise pursue any remedy, statutory or otherwise, with respect to such management and control. As used herein, the term "management and control" shall include all common law rights of management and control, including without limitation, the right to buy, sell, use, transfer (with or without consideration), exchange, abandon, lease, consume, expend, assign, create a security interest in, mortgage, encumber, dispose of, institute or defend a civil action regarding or otherwise dealing with property as if it were property of an unmarried person. Each party hereby grants the other a waiver for the other party to sell a homestead titled in only one party's name.

9. Separate, Individual Liabilities and Obligations

With respect to all liabilities and obligations of either or both Parties, the Parties agree as follows:

(a) Except as specifically provided otherwise in this Agreement, each Party agrees to, and shall bear and pay out of his/her individual property and his/her interest in any marital property or survivorship marital property, all of his/her individual liabilities and obligations, including, without limitation, the following:

(1) All of the liabilities and obligations which either Party has incurred or may hereafter incur in his/her sole name, including, without limitation, liabilities arising from tort, obligations arising from contract, punitive damages, penalties, fines and forfeitures.

(2) Each Party's respective share of all liabilities and obligations which have been or may be incurred jointly, either with the other Party or with third persons.

(3) All expenditures of each Party for his/her gifts and contributions to third persons.

(b) Except with respect to any liability or obligation which may be incurred by both parties jointly, all obligations of a Party shall be satisfied from property in the following order:

(1) From the incurring Party's interest in his/her individual property.

(2) When such individual property has been exhausted, then from the incurring Party's interest in property which is owned by the Parties as marital property or as survivorship marital property, if any.

(c) Each Party agrees to, and shall give notice, and a copy of this Agreement, to all of his/her own creditors prior to incurring, renewing, extending or modifying any liability or obligation to such creditor. Such notice shall be in writing and shall be delivered to the creditor by personal delivery or certified mail.

(d) If either Party fails to provide effective notice to any creditors as required pursuant to sub-paragraph (C) above, and if the said creditor thereby acquires and exercises rights in any property of the non-obligated Party, then the non-obligated Party shall be entitled to recover from the obligated Party, in addition to all other rights and remedies provided by law, an amount or property or assets equal in value to the loss suffered by the non-obligated Party in satisfying the liability or obligation of the obligated Party, together with all reasonable attorney's fees and costs incurred by the non-obligated Party in pursuing a recovery for such loss.

(e) Notwithstanding the foregoing paragraphs, either Party may, at his/her sole option, voluntarily contribute toward the payment of any liability and obligation of the other Party. However, such payment shall in no way be deemed to constitute an admission or assumption of such liability and obligation by the contributing Party.

10. Preparation and Filing of Income Tax Returns

The Parties may file a joint income tax return for any calendar year in which they so agree. The Federal income tax liability and any state income tax liability due with respect to any such joint returns shall be allocated between the Parties and be paid and payable by each of them out of his or her own individual property, or out of their joint account, if so agreed by the Parties. The ratio between the amount payable by a Party and the total payable by the Parties filing jointly, shall be the same as the ratio between the amount payable by that Party and the total payable by the Parties filing separately. Neither Party shall have, and each Party waives and releases the other from, any claim against the other Party for any reimbursement if the filing of a joint return and the application of the foregoing formula results in no tax due from one Party and a tax savings to the other Party. If an item of income, or deduction or exemption, or a credit, is not clearly allocable to one Party or the other, it shall be divided equally between the Parties. Any additional assessments or costs of taxation by audit or other adjustments, including interest, shall be allocated between the Parties as provided in this paragraph. Any tax refunds from jointly filed tax returns shall be deemed marital property. A Party shall not be responsible for any tax, interest, or penalty for liabilities occurring as a result of an audit with regards to past tax years of the other Party prior to the marriage. Such premarital liabilities would be paid solely from the individual property of the incurring Party. The Parties' election to file joint, rather than separate federal or state income tax returns, shall not create any marital property interests or reclassification of interests in property.

11. Common Household Expenses

The Parties agree to establish a common checking account to pay common household expenses, such as rent or mortgage, utilities, food, joint travel expenses, and joint entertainment. The Parties will contribute to this common checking account in such amounts as they hereafter agree from time to time. The Parties will each receives a monthly statement from the joint account for their personal expenses.

12. In the Event of Dissolution of Marriage—Property Division

In the event of a divorce, annulment, or legal separation by the Parties, the Parties agree as follows:

(a) It is the express intention of both Parties that this Agreement shall be binding on the issue of property division. The Parties herewith agree and stipulate that this Agreement shall in such an event constitute the parties' agreement and intent which shall be binding upon the Parties, and that it be strictly respected and honored by the courts of any state having jurisdiction. The Parties further acknowledge that this Agreement is equitable to both Parties.

(b) Any property which is classified as marital property or survivorship marital property, shall be divided equally between the Parties.

(c) Any property which is classified as individual property shall be retained by that Party.

(d) At the time this Agreement is executed, the Parties acknowledge and agree that the property division set forth above is equitable to both of them. The Parties expressly acknowledge and agree that the value of the Husband's and Wife's individual property may significantly increase or decrease in the future and that such increase or decrease standing alone, shall not be deemed sufficient to affect the equitableness of this Agreement. The Parties further expressly acknowledge that such future increase or decrease has been foreseen by them and considered in the negotiation and preparation of this Agreement.

(e) Neither Party shall have any obligation to the other for property division except as provided herein.

(f) Spousal maintenance remains open as to both Parties.

13. Death—Disposition of Property

(a) *Survivorship Marital Property.* In the event of death by either Party, with the other Party surviving, any property which is classified and deemed owned by the Parties as survivorship marital property or joint property, shall pass outright to the surviving Party, by right by survivorship.

(b) In the event of death by either Party, with the other Party surviving, any property which is classified as individual or personal, shall follow the terms of their Last Will and Testament.

14. Interspousal Transfers

Notwithstanding any other provision of this Agreement, either Party may, by will or other appropriate written instrument, and at his or her sole and free discretion, transfer, give, convey, devise or bequeath any property to the other. Neither Party intends by this Agreement to limit or restrict the right, if made by one, to receive any such transfer, gift, conveyance, devise, or bequest from the other.

15. *No consideration of spousal conduct in property division.*

Notwithstanding any provision or interpretation to the contrary herein, or any applicable law of this state or any other state to the contrary, distribution of marital property or assets shall be made without regard to marital behavior or conduct of a Party under any and all circumstances whatsoever, and under no condition shall the conduct of either Party be considered or addressed in any property division issue between the Parties.

16. Social Security Benefits

Notwithstanding anything to the contrary contained herein, neither Party intends to limit, or in any other way restrict, the right of either Party to receive Social Security benefits after the death of either Party. The surviving Party shall be entitled to apply for, and to receive, all such benefits to the maximum extent provided by law.

17. Prenuptial Custody Agreement

We soon intend to enter into marriage out of love for one another and consequently may bring forth children as a celebration of our love; but if our union would unfortunately result in separation or divorce, we agree that the within Article 17 of this Agreement with its conditions will govern any custody settlement so as to avoid conflict and further pain and trauma to ourselves and to out children. We believe that this will be in the best interest of our children. We recognize that not all of this section is legally binding on the court, but it represents our true, genuine, good faith wishes while in a mutual state of good will. For this reason, we exhort the court to accept this agreement.

(a) We mutually believe and agree that it is in the best interest of children for them, at all times and under any circumstances, to continue to have a continual substantial loving relationship with both their mother and father, equally. We believe that not to have a substantial involvement of both a mother and father in a child's life would be detrimental to healthy psychological and spiritual growth in the child, hence it is our honest and dedicated intention hereby to foster such a cooperative relationship between the children and both parents at all times and at all costs. We recognize that while divorce between parents may terminate the marriage relationship for the parents, it does not ever diminish a mother's or father's parental relationship or responsibilities. Consequently, we stipulate the following:

(1) We stipulate to a joint legal custody and that each parent shall have physical placement of the children 50 percent of the time.

(2) Each parent will, thus, be paying one-half the child support costs since the children would be spending one-half of their time with their mother and father. Each Party shall pay the said support until each child reaches the age of majority (or finishes college). This Agreement to provide support shall remain binding whether or not we (the parents) live together with the children.

(3) Each parent will be responsible for one-half of all medical and dental costs. Each parent will have the right to authorize medical care. Major medical decisions will be made mutually. Both parents must give their consent to psychological counseling for the children.

(4) Each parent will be responsible for one-half of all child care responsibilities in time spent (parental child care), duties (taking to lessons, doctors, school, etc.), and financial (daycare costs, clothes, etc.).

(5) Both parents will have access to school, medical and legal records.

(6) Each parent agrees to live within a sufficiently close distance so that 50/50 physical placement is practicable.

(b) In the event of a court contest by reason of a custody disagreement between the Parties, each Party will be responsible for its own legal fees, and 50 percent of any other legal fees (court, filing, GAL, etc.).

(c) Neither Party will leave the state to live, and/or do so in such a way as to disrupt the other parent's right to the child and the children's right to the other parent. If both parents are deemed fit and one parent insists on moving, it shall be presumed that the parent moving or leaving the state so that physical placement is not possible, will have diminished physical placement with the children.

(d) In the event that the court would order child support, the Parties agree that those funds will be spent exclusively for the children, and that the receiving parent would provide a quarterly financial report to the paying parent giving an accounting for the use made of the paying parent's child support.

(e) This stipulation has been entered into voluntarily and without coercion. We have mutually and enthusiastically agreed to this approach because each of us recognizes as realists' and parents (or would-be parents), that voluntary stipulation is by far preferable to court fights and extended litigation, and that extended litigation usually harms the children, and is deemed not in their best interests. Neither Party considers this stipulation unfair, selfish, unreasonable or unconscionable.

(f) If a disagreement should arise over the terms of this stipulation concerning your child(ren), we agree that a third party agreeable to both of us be chosen to mediate the difference in good faith. However, the conclusions of a mediator, which shall be in writing, should attempt to stay as close to the terms of this agreement as possible, and shall be deemed evidence to be considered in any subsequent legal proceedings that may arise, if any.

(g) In any or all events, in marriage or otherwise, we will always do our best to see that our child(ren) maintain a close and loving relationship with each of us; we will share jointly and cooperatively in the children's upbringing, support and discipline, and we will make good faith effort to make all major decisions concerning our children's health, education, and welfare, in a joint and cooperative manner. In everything we do concerning the children, our overriding consideration shall not be selfish or self-centered, but shall be what is in the best interest of the children.

(h) We declare that we are in a state of good will and the best of best wishes toward each other, and that the terms of this stipulation are most likely to conform to our unselfish view of the legal standard of what is in the "best interests of the children."

18. Governing Law

At the time of the execution of this Agreement, the Parties are domiciled in the State of _____. However, the Parties agree that this Agreement shall at all times be construed in accordance with the provisions of the The Uniform Pre-Marital Agreement Act, notwithstanding the establishment of a domicile elsewhere by either or both of the Parties at any time subsequent to the execution of this Agreement.

Hence, pursuant to this, the Parties agree that the enforceability of this agreement shall be judged pursuant to the standards set forth in the said Act. To the extent, however, that the said Act imposes more stringent standards than stipulated herein on the issues of property division or custody stipulation, the Parties agree that the said Act shall be inapplicable in governing the enforceability of this Agreement and that the stipulations of this agreement shall then govern.

19. Good Faith Duty

Each of the Parties agrees to act unselfishly and in good faith toward the other in the interpretation or fulfillment of this agreement.

20. Binding Effect

It is the express intention of both Parties that they shall be bound by this Agreement regardless of the occurrence of unanticipated events in the future. To the fullest extent permitted by law, the Parties expressly waive all common law contract defenses, and agree to be bound by the standards of enforceability set forth in The Uniform Pre-Marital Agreement Act. The Parties believe that each of them is more advantaged by the ability to rely absolutely on this Agreement than by the availability of common law contract defenses.

This agreement shall be binding upon, and ensure to, the benefit of the Parties and their respective heirs, executor, Personal Representatives, successors and assigns.

21. Voluntariness

Each of the Parties solemnly acknowledges, under the penalty of perjury, that he/she has voluntarily and freely executed this Agreement, with full knowledge and information of the contents and provisions thereof, and that no coercion or pressure or undue influence, has been used by or against either Party in making or signing this Agreement.

22. Amendment
This Agreement may be amended or revoked only by a written Agreement signed by both Parties with the complete and exact procedures used in the execution of this original Agreement.

23. Entire Agreement
This Agreement represents the entire agreement of the Parties with respect to the subject matter hereof. All agreements, covenants, representations, and warranties of the parties, whether express or implied, oral or written, with regard of the subject matter hereof, are contained completely in this agreement. No other agreements, covenants, representations or warranties, express or implied, oral or written, have been made to either Party by the other with respect to the subject matter of this Agreement. All prior and contemporaneous conversations, if any, or negotiations, possible and alleged agreements and representations, covenants and warranties with respect to the subject matter hereof, are waived, merged herein, superseded hereby, and otherwise hereby adjudged nonexistent.

24. Construction of Agreement
Both Parties assume joint responsibility for the form, content and composition of this Agreement. No provision of this Agreement shall be interpreted or construed for or against either party because that party, or that party's legal representative, drafted this Agreement.

25. Severability
In the event that any of the provisions of this agreement are deemed to be invalid, inequitable or unconscionable, the same shall be severed from this Agreement and shall not affect the enforceability of the remainder of this Agreement. If such provision shall be deemed invalid, inequitable or unconscionable under The Uniform Pre-Marital Agreement Act, or under any other law of construction, or due to its scope or breath, such provision shall be deemed valid to the extent of the scope or breadth permitted by law.

26. Execution, Signing of Documents
Each Party shall, upon the request of the other or of the other's personal representative, sign, acknowledge, and deliver to the other party any instruments appropriate or necessary to effectuate the intent and provisions of this Agreement.

In particular, if required by this Agreement, a Party shall execute any spousal waivers and consents to take any other action necessary under the provisions of the Employee Retirement Income Security Act of 1974, the Retirement Equity Act of 1984, or any similar law, to relinquish any right, claim, or property interest existing under or created by such law in any deferred employment benefit that is classified and deemed owned as the other Party's individual property. And he/she shall also allow such Party to name any beneficiary and to elect any settlement of payment option under such deferred employment benefit and to otherwise freely dispose of it as if the Parties were unmarried persons.

27. Consultation with Attorney
Each Party hereby stipulates and represents that by choice and personal preference, prior to signing this Agreement each party either consulted with an attorney of his or her own choice and/or otherwise informed and educated himself/herself on the law and legal imports about this agreement. Each Party is satisfied that he/she has received from such attorney, and/or other sources an adequate explanation of the provisions of this Agreement and their legal significance, and the effect which this Agreement has upon any interest which each Party might acquire in the property of the other and an explanation of the legal

rights that exist for each Party in the absence of this Agreement. Each Party acknowledges that he/she understands the Agreement and the said legal effects and that he/she completely agrees with such effects; and that with this in mind he/she is signing the Agreement freely and voluntarily. Neither Party has any reason to believe that the other did not understand the terms and effects of the Agreement or that he/she did not freely and voluntarily execute said Agreement.

28. Arbitration of Dispute
In the event that a dispute or disagreement should arise over the interpretation or fulfillment of any clauses in this agreement, or over any other matter or cause whatsoever except for the custody or support of children, the matter shall be submitted to arbitration to be resolved, and the following person(s) or institution(s) are hereby appointed to act as the arbitrator(s) in such matters: [*]_____
_____ Any decisions made on the disputed issues by such arbitrators shall be binding upon and final for both parties, except, however, that no decision rendered by the arbitrator shall, in any way, directly contradict or be inconsistent with, the explicit provisions of this Agreement. In rendering his/her determination, the arbitrator shall adhere strictly to, and make only direct, literal, logical interpretation of, the provisions of this Agreement, or it shall otherwise be deemed, at law and equity, a miscarriage of justice but strictly under such circumstances only. The Parties shall not be obligated to, but may at their sole discretion, be represented in arbitration proceedings by an attorney and/or any other third party of any kind or profession of their choice. The costs and expenses incurred for arbitration, including without limitation any attorney or legal fees, if any, or those otherwise incurred for enforcing or litigating the disputed matter in a court of law, shall be charged to and be borne solely by the party who is found to be substantially at fault on the disputed matters. The arbitrator shall render his decision in writing within 30 days of the final hearing.

IN WITNESS WHEREOF, this Agreement is signed on the _____ day of 19____ .

Signed:
1. _____
    (Husband)

Name _____
    (Print Same Name)

2. _____
    (Wife)

Name _____
    (Print Same Name)

Financial disclosure statements, dated ____(enter this)____ for both parties, hereby attached, are hereby acknowledged as received by:

_____
(Husband)

_____
(Wife)

_____
[*] Enter the names of the preferred persons and/or institutions, as agreed, including their addresses. Include how they are to be appointed and the process of final selection of a particular arbitrator when there is a deadlock by the two parties.

ACKNOWLEDGEMENT/VERIFICATION

STATE OF_____

COUNTY OF_____, ss:

I, a Notary Public in and for the State and County captioned above,

HEREBY CERTIFY that on the _____ day of _____ 19____, the following person(s), _____

_____and_____, known to me or made known to me to be the individual(s) described

in, and who executed the foregoing agreement, came before me, and that thereupon, the said person(s) severally acknowledged

to me under oath and under the penalty of perjury, that they signed the within document and that the facts and statements

contained in the said agreement are true and accurate.

WITNESS my hand and notarial seal, the day and year last written above.

_____

(Notary Public)

CERTIFICATION BY SUBSCRIBING WITNESSES TO AGREEMENT

We, the undersigned witness(es) whose names are hereunto subscribed, **DO HEREBY CERTIFY** under the penalty of perjury, that on the _____ day of _____ 19__, both of the parties above named, respectively signed their names to this instrument in our presence and in the presence of each of us and at the same time, in our presence and to our hearing, the said persons declared the same to be their Written Agreement, made by and freely agreed to by them, and requested us and each of us, to sign our names thereto as witnesses to the execution thereof, which we hereby do in the presence of the parties and of each other, on the day of the date of the said execution. The said parties appeared to be under no duress, force, compulsion or constraint of any kind when they signed the said agreement.

SIGNED:

(1) _____ of _____
　　　(Signature and Name)　　　　　　　　　(Address)

(2) _____ of _____
　　　(Signature and Name)　　　　　　　　　(Address)

(3) _____ of _____
　　　(Signature and Name)　　　　　　　　　(Address)

SAMPLE SHEET

Sample 3: Shorter, Simpler, Less Formal, General Version

Copyright © 1998, by Do-It-Yourself
Legal Publishers, Newark, N.J.

PRE-MARITAL AGREEMENT [Sample #3]

THIS AGREEMENT is made in this City and State of _____, between (John Doe) _____ and (Jane Edwards)_____. The parties are engaged to be married and in anticipation of their marriage, now scheduled to take place on or about _____, 19____, they agree as follows:

1. The parties have advised each other that they own separate property as follows: That John owns the apartment house where he now lives at Sutton Place Manhattan; holds a controlling interest in the XYZ Corporation, and has substantial indebtedness to various creditors. And Jane owns two pieces of real estate on 4th Avenue in Brooklyn, New York, and maintains a savings account with a substantial balance at the Bowery Savings Bank on 42nd Street. She also has a 1996 Mercedes Benz, and has no major indebtedness.

2. The property and indebtedness of each person will remain separate throughout the duration of their prospective marriage, and each will retain sole control, ownership, responsibility for, and management of his or her assets and liabilities, and may sell, pledge or otherwise dispose of the separate assets as they wish without the consent or interference of the other. The parties will maintain separate books of account on their separate assets or funds, but will open a joint checking account for household expenses and obligations.

3. The parties agree to contribute equally for the maintenance cost of the new family. Jane desires to go back to college, however, to complete the nursing training she had interrupted years ago. This will necessitate her giving up her present job as a secretary. In sympathy for that, John accepts to assume the sole responsibility for the rent, mortgage, utilities and medical expenses of the new marital household immediately after the marriage of the parties, and to continue same during the pendency of the marriage so long as they live together, but in no case should it be for more than four (4) years. Jane will only be responsible for the food eaten by the household, which she would pay from the income from her separate holdings, until such a reasonable time that she graduates and resumes an employment. Thereafter, the parties may share the household expenses evenly, or, at their discretion, as they see fit.

4. John and Jane have children each from a previous marriage from which they are both divorced and widowed, respectively. John is aware of Jane's desire to raise her children in the Catholic religious faith, in accordance with her prior understanding with the deceased father of her children. And likewise, Jane is aware of John's desire to raise his children in the orthodox Jewish faith. Both parties will respect each other's desires in this regard.

5. If the parties bear any children together, they agree that they may be raised in the Orthodox Jewish faith, and in any and all event the parties shall have joint rights, role and legal authority to raise and to discipline the children.

6.   The source of the major part of Jane's separate holdings is the inheritance from her deceased husband's estate, and John willingly accepts to respect the feeling previously expressed to him by Jane that these separate holdings from her inheritance should go to her children by her deceased husband (or their offspring) upon her death. In like manner, John's separate property will go to his separate children by previous marriage. John and Jane agree not to assert any marital or inheritance rights of any kind whatsoever which either one will otherwise have on these separate properties under the laws of this or any other state.

7.   Both parties are confident that they will live together in love and harmony, treating each other with fairness, equity and utmost consideration in matters financial and otherwise.   They therefore wish to leave it to the good judgement of each party to make an equitable and suitable provision by will, trust, life insurance, or otherwise for each other in the event of the death of one or the other. Provided this simple rule of reasonableness is observed by both parties, neither party will assert the marital, dower or inheritance rights he/she may otherwise have on their separate property under the laws of this or any other state.

8.   The laws of the state of _____ shall govern in any interpretation of this agreement.

9.   Both parties hereby acknowledge and stipulate that they are fully aware that they have the right to, and do have the opportunity, to seek individual legal counsel or representation of their choice in the making making of this agreement, if they so choose or prefer, but the parties in the exercise of their adult right to choose, have by their own free will to chosen to act for and by themselves herein. Each party is satisfied that he/she is fully advised or otherwise well informed of and knowledgeable about the provisions of this agreement and their legal implications and significance, and the effect which this agreement has upon any interest which each party might acquire in the property of the other, as well as what his/her property rights and obligations would be in the absence of this agreement, and each party hereby expressly declares that he/she completely agrees with the said legal effects and implications.

10.   *Arbitration of the dispute.* In the event that a dispute or disagreement should arise over the interpretation or fulfillment of any clause in this agreement, or over any matter or cause whatsoever, the matter shall be submitted to arbitration to be resolved, and the following persons and/or institutions are hereby appointed to act as the arbitrators in such matters:[*] _____.
Any decisions made on the disputed issue by such arbitrators, shall be binding upon and final for both parties. The costs and expenses, including without any limitations, any attorney or legal fees incurred for arbitration, or otherwise incurred for enforcing or litigating the disputed matters in a court of law, shall be charged to and be borne solely by the party who is found to be substantially at fault on the disputed matters.

11.   This agreement may be amended or modified but only in writing and with the same formalities as in the making and signing of the within agreement.

12.   This agreement will take effect as of the date of the marriage of the parties, and shall remain in effect during the entire marriage. Should the marriage be, for whatever reason, uncontracted six (6)

---

[*] Enter the names of the preferred persons and/or institutions, as agreed, including their addresses. Include how they are to be appointed and the process of final selection of a particular arbitrary in the event of a deadlock by the two parties.

months after the date of signing below, this agreement shall lapse and terminate, unless revived or extended by both parties in writing.

IN WITNESS WHEREOF, this agreement is signed on the _____ day of _____ 19_____.

Signed: _____

            John Doe (man)   Date

            _____

            Jane Edwards (woman)   Date

<u>ACKNOWLEDGEMENT/VERIFICATION</u>

STATE OF _____

COUNTY OF _____, ss:

I, a Notary Public in and for the State and County captioned above,

    HEREBY CERTIFY that on the _____ day of _____ 19_____, the following person(s), _____

_____ and _____, known to me or made known to me to be the individual(s) described

in, and who executed the foregoing agreement, came before me, and that thereupon, the said person(s) severally acknowledged

to me under oath and under the penalty of perjury, that they signed the within document and that the facts and statements

contained in the said agreement are true and accurate.

    WITNESS my hand and notarial seal, the day and year last written above.

                                          _____

                                                (Notary Public)

CERTIFICATION BY SUBSCRIBING WITNESSES TO AGREEMENT

    We, the undersigned witness(es) whose names are hereunto subscribed, DO HEREBY CERTIFY under the penalty of perjury, that on the _____ day of _____ 19__, both of the parties above named, respectively signed their names to this instrument in our presence and in the presence of each of us and at the same time, in our presence and to our hearing, the said persons declared the same to be their Written Agreement, made by and freely agreed to by them, and requested us and each of us, to sign our names thereto as witnesses to the execution thereof, which we hereby do in the presence of the parties and of each other, on the day of the date of the said execution. The said parties appeared to be under no duress, force, compulsion or constraint of any kind when they signed the said agreement.

SIGNED:

(1) _____ of _____
       (Signature and Name)   (Address)

(2) _____ of _____
       (Signature and Name)   (Address)

(3) _____ of _____
       (Signature and Name)   (Address)

THE SAMPLE SHEET — SAMPLE SHEET

CHAPTER 8
LET'S SIGN THE WRITTEN AGREEMENT: FOLLOW THESE PROCEDURES FOR THE ALL-IMPORTANT "EXECUTION" OF THE AGREEMENT

A. This Execution Phase Is Of The Utmost Importance

After an agreement is drawn up (the subject matter of the proceeding Chapter 7), the next order of business is the "*Execution*" phase (the signing) of the document by the two principal partners. Technically speaking, *the execution phase of the making of an agreement is probably the most critical part of the whole process.* Indeed, to sum it up **IN ONE WORD, SUFFICE IT SIMPLY TO SAY THIS: THE SIGNING EVENT IN THE MAKING OF THE AGREEMENT IS THE KEY ITEM, EASILY THE MOST VITAL EVENT IN THE MAKING OF A LEGALLY VALID AGREEMENT.** This is so for the simple reason that, over and above the issue of the content of the agreement, the execution act is the key piece of event the courts look to in determining whether an agreement is, indeed, the free, informed, consensual act of the parties. *Therefore, this is an extremely important and most serious business and should be treated with the utmost care and attention to every detail by the agreement makers.*

B. Some Recommended Practical "Ceremonies" For a Valid Signing

The relevant rules of each state stipulate certain basic procedures or requirements for a valid "execution" (signing) of the agreement. *It's to ensure that the requirements of almost every state whatsoever are met, and to ensure the most effective "execution" of the agreement, that we suggest this:* **YOU (BOTH PARTIES) MUST STRICTLY FOLLOW THESE STEP-BY-STEP "CEREMONIES" OR PROCEDURES TO SIGN YOUR AGREEMENT.**

FIRST: Let's say that you and your partner (spouse) have set a date when the signing event is to take place. Thereafter, it is highly advised that you look for at least two adult persons (one person chosen from each party's side) who you are to invite to the signing event who are to act as witnesses to the signing.[1]

At least one, but preferably two witnesses (one person from each party's side) will usually suffice. And they could be anybody (parents of either of the parties, your adult children, relatives, friends, neighbors, etc.), providing they are over 18 years of age and generally of sound mind and character. *Note that it is not necessary—indeed, it is not usually advisable—that the witness (es) (or Notary Public) should read or know the specific contents of the agreement at the time of the agreement signing.* It is sufficient if the would-be spouses should merely tell the witness (es) at the time, that the document presented before

---

[1] In actuality, not all states require (in fact, only one or two actually do require) that the agreement be specifically signed before witnesses. However, this is highly advised herein, because as a practical matter, the use of witnesses is almost always beneficial and advisable in this type of event in that it can only enhance, not detract from, the legitimacy of the agreement before any court of law, making it much harder for one spouse or the other to come up with a claim that he or she was somehow forced into signing an agreement against his/her will, or that he/she did it under less than normal conditions. An important prerequisite in proving the validity of an agreement of this sort between marital parties, is evidence that the parties dealt at an "arm's length" with each other—i.e., genuine, business like, bonafide dealings that were neither "forced" nor rushed or based on obviously favored or unreasonable terms.

them is the couple's ante-nuptial (or separation settlement) agreement and that the couple merely request that they bear personal witnesses to the signing event.

Get a colored ink pen ready, also, to be taken to the signing event for use in signing the agreement.

SECOND: O.K. Let's assume that on the appointed date, you and your spouse (or partner) have now gathered at the designated place for the signing affair, along with the invited witnesses. You and your spouse (or partner) should excuse yourselves from the rest in the house and get into a separate room to privately read the agreement. Or merely go to a separate desk apart from the rest to do so.

Using the two final copies of the agreement you prepared, each partner should read out the contents of the agreement to the other, going clause by clause, and asking questions of each other to make sure the provisions are fully understood and taken notice of by both parties.

THIRD: Next, you both should then rejoin your witnesses, after you have both finished reading the contents to each other. Briefly inform the witnesses present of the following:
1) that the document you and your partner have in front of you, about to sign, is a pre-marital agreement with each other (or a settlement or living together agreement, as the case may be); **2)** that both of you have just fully read the contents and are about to sign this agreement with full comprehension of the provisions and with free and voluntary consent to its provisions; and **3)** that you invite them to sign their own names after you as witnesses to the signing.

(You may just say something like: ***"Gentlemen (and/or ladies), this document is our pre-marital Agreement [or, a settlement or living together agreement, as the case may be]. Both of us, Mary and John, have read it, and completely comprehend the provisions and implications. We freely and voluntarily consent to its provisions, and ask you to witness our signatures, and to sign your names after us as witnesses"***. If this statement is made by one spouse (or partner), at the end of the statement the speaking spouse, say the Husband, will add: **"And Mary, just for the record, is everything I just said correct and true?" Mary: "YES!"**

FOURTH: With that statement made (and the other partner's response), as the witnesses attentively watch you, <u>each</u> partner should take turn to sign. One party will, first, initial and date each and every page of the agreement (just the two originals) at the bottom left-hand margin space, and then only sign it on the last page where the agreement ends, in the appropriate space provided for "Husband" or "Wife." **SIGN IN COLORED INK ONLY.** (This way, the original document could be differentiated.) Then, print your name just below your signature (at the end of the agreement). Fill in the date of the signing at the last page. Then, the other party will do exactly the same. [Each party should examine the documents and counter check to be sure that each page of all two copies are initialed, dated and signed by <u>both</u> parties at the spots required].

FIFTH: It will now be the turn of the witnesses to sign. Ask each of the witnesses to read the paragraph just following the last page of the Agreement under the caption **"Certification By Witnesses"** – the one just coming after or below your own signatures. (Note that it is not necessary that the contents of the agreement be read by or made known to the witnesses; in fact, it is advised against!)

Then, as you watch each of the witnesses, they would take turns to sign their names and enter their individual addresses in the spaces provided for them. Only after that—after all of the witnesses have signed their own names—should anybody in the group leave the room, or be joined by anybody else not in the signing group. [The role of the witnesses is over, and they may now leave if they wish].

NOTE: The central point of engaging in the formalities ("ceremonies") of Agreement-signing should be clearly borne in mine. The idea is to make the event MEMORABLE to those who participated, especially to the witnesses—to make the event "stick out" in their minds, so that they'll always recall the event , however remotely or vaguely, if or when it should ever become necessary that they be called upon to do so.

SIXTH: In all you do, whether in the negotiations or in the actual signing of the agreement, avoid the appearance of haste or hush. Even though you and your partner may have been in accord on all the terms of the agreement, don't sign the documents hurriedly after the start of negotiations. Events not only have to actually be, but have to appear to be as though everybody has been given every opportunity and an ample time for thinking things over.

SEVENTH: YOU & YOUR PARTNER SHOULD NOW HAVE THE AGREEMENT NOTARIZED. There's one more important thing for you to do before you're done. You and your spouse (or partner) should take the Agreement (all two originals) with you to have them notarized in the presence of a Notary public. Under the laws of most states, for the purpose of using the agreement as a "stipulation" or "petition" in a future divorce or other court action, it is required that the agreements be "acknowledged" before a Notary Public.

It's simple! Simply take the document (both parties) to a Notary Public and there, have the agreements and your own signatures "notarized" and "acknowledged" by the notary. (Ordinarily, under most states rules, except when title to real property is involved, an agreement which is not notarized or acknowledged, however, does not necessarily become invalid just on account of that. It will still remain legally valid, in such an instance. Nevertheless, it does add to the strength of the agreement to always have it notarized, regardless.)

EIGHTH: *What To Do With The Finished Signed Agreements.* What do you do with the signed and completed agreements? Simply, the wife (or one partner) safely keeps a copy, and the husband (or the other partner) safely keeps one.

C. Filing of the Agreement With the County Clerk's Office May be Requires in Certain States

Under the laws of certain states, upon completion of a separation or property settlement agreement, a true copy of the agreement—or a Memorandum of that agreement—is required to be promptly filed with the County Clerk's office (or a recorder of deed's office). Such public filing or recordation is hardly ever required in any state for a cohabitation or premarital type of agreement, however, as this is deemed a private document between the parties. New York is one state which has the filing requirement for separation or property settlement agreements. North Carolina and some other states also requires filing of the settlement agreement. *The overwhelming majority of states do not require a court filing even of the separation or property settlement agreements between married parties, however.* Parties in other states may ascertain whether filing is required in their states (for separation or property settlement types of agreements, primarily) by simply calling the office of their local county court's clerk in charge of matrimonial and domestic relations matters. (See Appendix B for the name of the appropriate matrimonial court to call for your state.)

Under New York State's rules, for example, the procedures for filing are simple. You'll merely submit the Memorandum of Agreement to the office of the County Clerk of the State Supreme Court in the specific county in which either you or your spouse lives. (There's a filing fee charge for this—$170 in New York as of this writing). The county clerk will assign you an "index number" which you will then affix to the Memorandum Form and then have it filed away with the clerk, along with a copy of the agreement. Now, make sure you also enter this number on your own respective copies of the Agreement as this is the court's official identifying number by which your case would be traced at any time in the future. NOW IT IS FINALLY DONE!

D. Some Few Final Words On Post-Agreement Matters

Your Pre-marital agreement is now concluded. You may now go home and rest assured. But while you do that, it would be helpful to **have a few more final facts in mind as you put your separation document away:**

FIRST: You must bear in mind that unless your proposed or intended marriage is consummated as anticipated within a reasonable time from the signing date, the pre-marital agreement may lapse and become void (unless of course, revived by the parties by written amendment or otherwise).

SECOND: Bear in mind that a pre-marital agreement becomes effective as of and from the date of marriage, and that its provisions remain in force (except as may otherwise be modified or amended by the parties by subsequent agreement) during the duration of the marriage, usually terminating only by divorce or death.

THIRD: Retain and *securely put away* your own original copy of the agreement. Put it away in a separate, safe location away from your marital residence and other personal papers—say, in a bank safe deposit box to which only YOU have access, or in your parent's or brethren's homes, and the like. Make several photocopies of it and use just those copies for any immediate interim needs you may have to consult with the contents in the meantime.

FOURTH: Remember that, for most practical purposes, a premarital agreement is more or less the same thing as a marital property settlement agreement. Hence, the terms of this kind of agreement, (with some modification, perhaps, to take account of an update in time and circumstances), would generally and gladly be acceptable to just about every divorce court in settling the disposition of a couple's property and their maintenance, and a reasonable provision on the support, custody and visitation of their children, and the like.

CHAPTER 9

COURTSHIP GIFTS, ENGAGEMENT CONTRACTS AND RELATED ISSUES: SOME QUESTIONS & ANSWERS

Question 1: Is an engagement a lawful contract?

Answer: Generally, yes. When a man proposes marriage to a woman who then proceeds to accept the proposal, the arrangements which follow between them in relation to that "engagement" is considered a binding contract. Ordinarily, what this means is that, except with the mutual consent of both, one party can't jump up at will and break the engagement without a reasonable basis. One current rule common to most states, however, is that the promise of marriage made by or to a person who, to the knowledge of the parties concerned, has a living spouse at the time, is against morality and public policy, and is therefore absolutely invalid from the beginning. And this is true, even if the promise is not to be performed until the death of, or divorce of the partner from the present spouse.

Question 2: What happens if I break the promise or engagement to marry someone?

Answer: The person whom you had engaged but did not marry may take you to court for "breach of contract" — that is, for breaking or not fulfilling your obligations under a contract. This kind of case is more commonly known as a **"heart balm"** suit, in legal circles. Now, if she is able to prove to the court's satisfaction that you had no genuine basis for breaking off the engagement, the court may award her some damages for any social, emotional, and especially *material,* damages she may have suffered on account of that disengagement.

Question 3: What would the woman have to prove before she may possibly win in court?

Answer: Basically, the woman (or man, as the case may be) would need to prove two things: 1) that you had no legitimate grounds for breaking off the engagement; and 2) that she suffered a material or monetary loss (not just the humiliation and mental anguish) directly as a result of her reliance on your promise to marry her.

Question 4: What are some examples of the kind of material losses the courts are likely to uphold?

Answer: Say, for example, that the woman sold, gave away or auctioned off her house or property at a loss in the hope of moving in with the prospective husband, or that she gave up a promising career or a job with seniority, or that the mental anguish of the disengagement caused her to be hospitalized and to lose her job or some time from job. Other examples, would be the loss of another opportunity to marry, investment losses, say from a hasty sale of one's business, the giving up of a potential opportunity for a higher job or for inheriting an estate.

Question 5: What kind of reasons could be considered legitimate for breaking off an engagement.

Answer: One or more of these could be considered good enough by the court: a fundamental lack of affection or inability to get along with each other; underage; pre-existing marriage or engagement to another person; a history of chronic illness or insanity in the family of the other party which came to light later; major physical infirmities or ill-health conditions, such as impotency; the existence of blood relationship; discovery of fraud or lack of full disclosure on important facts on which the man had relied in making his promise to marry.

Question 6: Does every state in the union permit persons to bring "heart balm" suits?

Answer: No. In about 10 states (Alabama, California, Florida, Indiana, Massachusetts Michigan, New Hampshire, New Jersey, New York and Pennsylvania), such suits are entirely prohibited; while in a few others (such as Colorado, Connecticut, Louisiana, Maryland, Nevada, Wyoming and Washington), the conditions under which the award of damages may be made, and the amount of damages that may be awarded for merely breaking a pledge to marry another person, have been greatly curtailed by law. These limiting laws are, of course, known as **"heart balm"** laws.

Question 7: What happens to the gifts? Do the "heart balm" laws also prohibit engaged parties from recovering engagement gifts?

Answer: Generally, no. The policy with respect to property given as engagement gifts, in contrast merely to the engagement or promise to marry, is quite different; in general, even in the so-called "heart balm" law states, court actions to recover gifts in anticipation of a marriage (or their equivalent value) are not prohibited.

THE GENERAL PRINCIPLES WHICH GOVERN COURT DECISIONS IN ENGAGEMENT GIFT DISPUTES

The following are the broad general principles by which legal determinations are made regarding gifts given in engagement situations:

1. Gifts made between engaged persons who later had to break off the engagement, cannot be reclaimed where either the donor (the one who made the gift) or the donee was married to another person at the time the gift was made, at least where the parties were aware of the existing marriage.[*]

2. With respect to minors, the view that now generally prevails, is that an engagement gift made to a minor who broke her promise to marry, may be recovered, in kind, if the minor still has possession of the gift at the time of the court action. However, if the minor has, in honest good faith, sold or given away the gift, recovery of damages for the gift's value will not be granted.

3. Gifts can generally be recovered by the donor in cases where the termination of an engagement is by mutual agreement of the parties, or in cases where an engagement is justifiably broken off by the donee. In a case, however, where an engagement is unilaterally broken by the donor, especially where this is done without good justification, the donor cannot usually recover.

4. Engagement gifts may generally be retained by the donee who breaks an engagement *with* legal justification.

---

[*] This is because getting engaged to another person while one is still involved in an existing marriage, is said to violate the "public policy" against undermining an existing family unit.

5. Engagement gifts given in anticipation of a marriage have, in several cases tried in many states, been held *not* recoverable by the donor or his estate, where the reason for which the anticipated marriage did not materialize was the subsequent death of the donor or the donee.

6. In situations where recovery of engagement gifts is otherwise considered appropriate, the general line of reasoning followed by the courts is that engagement gifts are not immediately absolute or final once they are given but are **"conditional"** — meaning that a donee does not necessarily become entitled to retain a gift made to her, *unless* she (the donee) has either fulfilled her lawful obligations under the engagement "contract", or at least, unless there still exists certain other material conditions which are the basis for the gifts.

7. In determining which particular gifts are *"conditional"* (meaning, still recoverable by the donor), and which ones are **"absolute"** (meaning not recoverable), most courts have made distinctions based on the so-called "nature" of the gift item given. Wedding gifts (such as an engagement ring or wedding gown) are often classified as "conditional" gifts that should be recovered, since the courts reason that if the anticipated marriage does not take place, the basis for a gift of that nature is gone and the gift should therefore be returned to the donor. Most other gifts (such as jewelry, birthday or graduation presents), gifts that might have been given anyway if no engagement had been entered into, are considered "absolute" gifts that may be retained by the recipient.

8. Fraud on the part of the donee may be grounds for a donor to recover his (her) gift — that is, if, at the time of receiving the gift, the recipient had actually intended not to marry the donor.

9. Gifts which are merely "courtship" gifts, as opposed to genuine engagement gifts, are ordinarily regarded as "absolute" and not usually subject to recovery. Courtship gifts are gifts which are not made in connection with an agreement or understanding between the donor and the donee to marry, but are made primarily for the purpose of promoting the donor's proposal or endearing him to the donee.

10. What about third-party gifts —gifts made by persons other than the engaged parties to the engaged persons? Such gifts would generally be recoverable if the expected marriage should fail to materialize.

Summary Rule of Gift-making: To briefly summarize, *in general, if the gift is made "in specific contemplation of marriage" (and not, say, just for a partner's birthday, graduation, or Christmas present and the like), and if the disengagement has come about through no fault or misbehavior of yours, you stand on a fairly solid legal ground to recover, regardless of the fact of who actually broke off the engagement.*

CHAPTER 10

EVERY QUESTION YOU MAY WANT ANSWERED ABOUT HETEROSEXUAL/HOMOSEXUAL COHABITATION, THE "MARVIN CASE," AND PROPERTY RIGHTS OF NON-MARITAL COUPLES

A. WHAT IS THE PRESENT STATE OF THE LAW IN REGARD TO NON-MARITAL COHABITATION?

By and large, the law governing relations between unmarried or non-marital ("cohabiting") partners still remains an uncharted legal jungle in which anything may still turn out one way or the other. For the most part, it is yet a murky legal — or even social — area to be fully developed in the years ahead. True, it is still rare to find any state which has enacted any specific laws in this area. However, the courts of many states, notably those of California, Washington, New York and others, have taken it upon themselves to hand down some decisions concerning such relationships, especially with respect to the division or allocation of property. In deed, it is rare to find a knowledgeable legal expert or observer in the matrimonial relations scene who does not now predict that the famous California (Marvin) decision, the pioneering decision in the nation on the matter, is a legal "precedent" soon to be duplicated in the rest of the country.

There has been, in recent times, a dramatic and still growing increase in the number of adult Americans who simply choose to cohabit with each other without the benefit of a marriage. And the same thing has also been true of the number of marriage-age young Americans who have either never married at all, or have not bothered to marry after being divorced.[*] *All in all, the growing significance of this area in family law courtrooms, make it necessary that persons involved in any sort of living-together arrangements be familiar with some basics on this.*

B. ANSWERS TO EVERYTHING YOU PROBABLY WANT TO KNOW ON COHABITATION LAW

What follows, in question and answer format, may answer some of the questions that have, so far, been answered by the courts in the so-called "cohabitation law issues," especially by the nationally influential state courts of California, Washington State, New Jersey and New York, among others.

QUESTION 1: Is cohabitation legally permissible in every state?

ANSWER: No. Many states have laws prohibiting persons of opposite sex (or the same sex) from living together without being married with various penalties attached for violation of that rule. It is basically a carry over from the

---

[*] According to a U.S. Census Bureau report released in April 1978, the number of Americans, most of whom were under the age of 25, who were cohabiting in March of 1977 was 1,508,000, up 14% from the 1976 level, and over 130% from 1970: the proportion of all women aged 20-24 who had never been married, rose from 28% in 1960 to 45% in 1977, and from 53% to 64% for men during the same period. The number of divorces from 1970-1977 increased 79% with 8 million divorced persons choosing not to remarry. Overall, the number of couples who were living together without being married in 1974 was about 8 times what it was 10 years earlier. It should be pointed out, though that although the number of nonmarital-couple households has more than doubled since 1970, such households still make up only 3 percent of all couples living together in the United States.

common law where open and notorious sexual conduct outside of marriage was deemed offensive by and to the public.

As of this writing, some laws against non-marital cohabitation still exist in the following states: Arizona, Florida, Idaho, Illinois, Michigan, Mississippi, New Mexico, North Carolina, North Dakota, Virginia, and West Virginia.

To be sure, as a practical matter these laws are rarely enforced though sometimes they are.

QUESTION 2: What about living together among gay or lesbian couples? Are there any states in which this is recognized as a legal marital relationship of some kind?

ANSWER. To our knowledge, no state has yet accorded legal validity or recognition (by way, that is, of enacted statute) to gay/lesbian couples' relationships. While "cohabitation" between unmarried persons of opposite sex is still not exactly viewed with favor in much of the country, cohabitation relationships among persons of the same sex are by and large viewed as immoral, sinful and illegal in virtually every state, subject to state sanctions of varying degrees. However, all indications are that such state of affairs notwithstanding, in practice the practice of living together by gay and lesbian couples is widely tolerated by the authorities in most states, and that an otherwise valid property settlement agreement, even among homosexual couples, would enjoy the same kind of recognition and legality generally accorded non-marital agreements, as outlined below elsewhere in this chapter.

QUESTION 3 where do we stand with the law, today, on homosexuality and sodomy?

ANSWER: As of this writing in 1994, it is safe to say that in many states, though by no means all, homosexuality per se still remains strictly against the law. And so is the homosexual act of sodomy — defined by law as "any sex act involving the sex organs of one person and the mouth or anus of another."

The landmark ruling on the matter to date, is the 5-4 decision by the U.S. Supreme Court in June 1986, involving a sodomy charge against Michael Hardwick, an Atlanta Georgia man.

Hardwick had been observed by a police office performing oral sex on another man. A Federal district judge initially dismissed the case on procedural grounds, but a three-judge panel of the United States Court of Appeals subsequently ruled in May 1985 that the Georgia anti-sodomy law was unconstitutional in that it unduly interfered with "certain individual decisions critical to personal autonomy because those decisions are essentially private."

The state of Georgia appealed arguing that sodomy is an unnatural act and a crime against the laws of God and man. The Supreme Court, in its decision, ruled that the constitution does not protect homosexual relations between consenting adults even in the privacy of their own homes and that the Georgia law could be used to prosecute homosexual and other persons who engage in oral and anal sex. Writing for the Court, Justice Byron White rejected the view "that any kind of private sexual conduct between consenting adults is constitutionally insulated from state proscription." Quite to the contrary, he stated, the Federal Constitution does not "confer a fundamental right upon homosexuals to engage in sodomy and hence [does not] invalidate the laws of many states that still make such conduct illegal and have done so for a very long time." In short, any state, if it chooses, may prohibit the act of homosexuality, and it would presumably be within its constitutional sphere of authority to do so.

Today, there are twenty-six states that have decriminalized sodomy, and five of the twenty-four that still make homosexual sodomy a crime have decriminalized heterosexual sodomy at least in some contexts.

The following are the states without a sodomy law: Alaska, California, Colorado, Connecticut, Delaware, Hawaii, Illinois, Indiana, Iowa, Maine, Massachusetts, Nebraska, New Hampshire, New Jersey, New Mexico, New York, North Dakota, Ohio, Oregon, Pennsylvania, South Dakota, Vermont, Washington, West Virginia, Wisconsin, and Wyoming.

The following are the states that have heterosexual and homosexual sodomy laws: Alabama, Arizona, Florida, Georgia, Idaho, Kentucky, Louisiana, Maryland, Michigan, Minnesota, Mississippi, Missouri, North Carolina, Oklahoma, Rhode Island, South Carolina, Tennessee, Utah, Virginia, and Washington, D.C.

States with a homosexual sodomy law only are: Arkansas, Kansas, Montana, Nevada, and Texas.

Many cities and communities across the country, however, have attempted to balance the scales somewhat by passing homosexual rights laws. In New York City, for example, the city council, after rejecting a homosexual rights bill for fifteen years, finally enacted Local Law 2 on March 20, 1986, banning discrimination on the basis of sexual orientation in housing, employment, and public accommodations.

QUESTION 4: In a state where, as is frequently the case, the legislature has not enacted any laws to govern the distribution of property acquired by cohabiting persons during their relationship, by what "law" would the courts go in deciding a property settlement dispute between such persons?

ANSWER: The courts would rely solely on their "judicial judgment" in deciding such cases, since there's no body of statutes to go by.

QUESTION 5: Are there any general principles which the courts would employ in deciding such cases?

ANSWER: Yes, in the famous "Marvin case" of California, the California Supreme Court, a leader in matrimonial law innovation, seemed to have set forth another precedent which many other states have to varying degrees copied on this question. In that case, decided in 1976, the California high court laid down the following rules as "the principles which should govern distribution of property acquired in a non-marital relationship":
        "1) The courts should enforce express contracts between non-marital partners except to the extent that the contract is explicitly founded on the consideration of meretricious sexual services; and 2) in the absence of an **express contract ****, the courts should inquire into the conduct of the parties to determine whether that conduct demonstrates an **implied contract****, agreement of partnership or joint venture, or some other tacit understanding between the parties. The courts may also employ the doctrine of **quantum meruit****, or equitable remedies such as **constructive or resulting trusts****, when warranted by the facts of the case."

QUESTION 6: What does this really mean in simple layman's language?

ANSWER: These are what the California court is saying:

i.) that persons who are just cohabiting or having sexual relations but are not married to each other, have just as much legal right to enter into a lawful contract as any other persons, just like persons who are either married to each other, or are unmarried to any one, in ordinary contractual business relations.

ii.) that where there's any contract between two (or more) non-marital partners that is of "express" (i.e. spoken or written) type, the courts would enforce the provisions of that express contract *except* those provisions that are "explicitly founded on the consideration of meretricious sexual services" — that is, those provisions which *explicitly*

** See Glossary of Legal Terms (Appendix B) for definition.

say, in effect, 'I owe or give you this or that property or income, in return for your owing or giving me your sexual services'.

iii.) that where, on the other hand, there's *no* "express" contract between the non-marital partners, in such a situation, says the California high court, the courts would enforce any apparent understanding or "implied contract" between the parties — that is, any understanding the courts can infer or "imply" from the conducts or circumstances of the parties as indicative of what they meant to do, if any.

iv.) that, depending on the facts of a particular case, the Court may, among other remedies, allocate the property of the parties to one or the other partner on the following basis: a) on the principle of "according to what he or she deserves" (the legal doctrine of quantum meruit); or b) the Court could use its "independent judicial judgment" to determine that one or the other partner should really have been entitled to a certain property, even though it may not have been so expressly stated by the parties, or even if the property may have been held in "trust" in the other partner's name ("constructive" or "resulting" trust).

QUESTION 7: What is a "meretricious sexual" service or consideration?

ANSWER: Basically, this is an explicit pledge or promise of a sexual service by one unmarried person to another (or between two persons who are not married to each other), as a condition for entering into a relationship or for doing or getting something. The reason that such a conduct is "meretricious", is because it is immoral and illicit, by society's standards, and against the generally accepted "public policy" of promoting the institution of marriage.

For example, if a woman *expressly* says to a man to whom she is not married: 'Let's make an agreement. I'll just live with you as your wife and bear you children.' And the man says, 'O.K. And I'll provide for you and give you my home.' This is a contract or understanding that is based on "meretricious" (i.e., immoral and illicit) consideration, because the woman is offering adultery, or, at least, fornication, prostitution and illegitimacy, in return for the man's material support. Another example might be where a contract requires that one or both parties would divorce their spouses, or rewards them for doing so, since it's considered to be in the public policy that marriage and the stability of the institution be promoted, not undermined.

QUESTION 8: Since it is still generally considered illicit and immoral (or, at least, not the model behavior) for persons who are not married to each other to live together and engage in sexual relations, does the mere living together by such persons automatically disqualify an agreement between them or automatically make it unlawful?

ANSWER: No. The courts have ruled that while such a relationship may be immoral alright, it does not, in and of itself, disqualify the partners from entering into a lawful agreement with each other. It does not make an agreement between them automatically unlawful, *as long as the (immoral) relationship itself was not made a consideration of their agreement* — i.e., so long as the immoral relationship was not the thing that was promised or pledged to induce either of them to enter into the agreement. Where, for example, the conveyance or transfer of a property from one non-marital partner to another was not made for the purpose of inducing or prolonging illicit cohabitation, a resulting trust or agreement between the parties involved in the illicit cohabitation does not necessarily become automatically illegal.

QUESTION 9: What if only some parts of a contract, but not the whole contract, made between cohabiting partners is "explicitly founded upon immoral and illicit consideration of meretricious sexual services", does that mean that the entire contract is doomed?

ANSWER: No. In all cases, the court is required to examine each contract on a case-by-case basis, and if it can determine that there is a "separable" portion of a contract which was not based on a meretricious sexual consideration, it would separate out that portion and enforce that portion *only*.

QUESTION 10: What is the courts' attitude towards the property rights of partners who are involved in a putative marriage or relationship?

ANSWER: In general, property acquired during such a relationship is considered as "quasi-marital" property, and may therefore be divided between the partners in accord with the same laws governing division of property in regular dissolution of marriages. In California, for example the courts have ruled that putative spouses may recover for the reasonable value of the service they rendered to the putative household, less the value of the support they had received up until the time of the discovery of the invalidity of the marriage. It has also been ruled that both the "guilty" spouse (i.e., the one who was aware all along that the marriage was not valid), and the "innocent" spouse (i.e., the one who was not), are entitled to one-half of the property acquired during the relationship under the California Community property rule.

QUESTION 11: What if I had merely promised my non-marital partner that I would perform homemaking service for him and went ahead and did just that , is that a lawful and sufficient "consideration" for a contract?

ANSWER: Yes, nowadays it is. You don't have to pay back in money. Your household services are just as valuable.

QUESTION 12: What sort of things or factors do the courts look for to determine whether or not a non-marital relationship qualifies for property division or compensation rights under the principles we've been discussing?

ANSWER: They include factors like one or more of the following:
Did the parties live together, especially for several years (in a stable, long-term relationship), rather than just being engaged in a casual relationship from time to time; and did they "hold themselves out" to friends, associates or relatives as husband and wife — in terms, for example, of say rearing children together, purchasing a home or other property together, obtaining credit or maintaining bank accounts jointly, filing joint income tax returns, introducing each other as a "husband" or "wife" to the public, or otherwise conducting themselves as if they were married?

Did the parties have an agreement or a reasonable understanding of some sort (oral or written or implied) to live together and combine or pull their efforts, earnings, or assets; or, was there a reasonable expectation or understanding by one or both of them that each would share in any property accumulated by the parties?

Did each of the parties contribute some service or income to the relationship (e.g., as a companion, caretaker of the house or children, homemaker, cook or provider for the household, etc.)? Did one (or both) of the parties give up or sacrifice something of value just on account of the non-marital relationship, or because of an understanding or arrangement made because of the relationship (e.g., giving up a career, especially if it can be shown that it was a promising or flourishing one before the party was compelled to abandon it in order to devote time to the non-marital relationship)?

Is there a reasonable indication (either written, oral, or implied from the conduct of the parties) that one or both of the parties reasonably expected to be provided for or to be supported financially by the other?

In general, the test is whether the general relationship between the parties and the way they conducted themselves towards each other reasonably indicate an intention to establish a long-term relationship and joint activities — the sort of relationship that is ordinarily associated with "married" couples.

QUESTION 13: If the parties in a non-marital relationship had lived together for a long time but still did not take that final step of getting married, wouldn't the Court interpret that as a strong indication that they never planned or intended to share their earnings or property, in the first place?

ANSWER: Not necessarily. The rule established by the California Supreme Court in the Marvin case, is that it is unwise to jump to the assumption or conclusion that the parties intended to keep their earnings and property separate and independent merely because they lived together for a long time and did not get married. The court said that "the parties' intention can only be ascertained by more searching inquiry (by the courts) into the nature of their relationship." That:

> Some non-marital couples may wish to avoid the permanent commitment that marriage implies, but still be willing to share any property acquired during their relationship.
> Some may not want to get married because they entertain some fears of losing a pension, welfare or tax benefits, etc.
> Some may engage in a non-marital relationship as a "test period" before deciding on getting married.
> Some may just not be able, at the moment, to afford the difficulties or expenses involved in getting a former marriage dissolved to allow for a remarriage.
> Some may believe (correctly or incorrectly) that a common-law marriage is valid in the particular state.

QUESTION 14: You hear so much about the "Marvin Case" lately. What was the case all about?

ANSWER: This was, in a word, the famous "landmark" California case that has just about revolutionized all the traditional concepts and practices in the country regarding cohabitation between unmarried persons.

Michelle Marvin (she had changed her last name legally from Triola to Marvin just before her relationship with Mr. Marvin ended), had lived for nearly 7 years with Lee Marvin, an Academy award-winning actor, without being married to him—from October 1964 through May 1970. During this period, a lot of property was acquired, including real estate, personal property and motion picture rights said to be worth over $3 million, but all were in Mr. Marvin's name. Then in May 1970, Mr. Marvin asked Ms. Marvin to move out of the couple's household. Mr. Marvin continued to support her, though, until November 1971 when he stopped doing so. Ms. Marvin sued Mr. Marvin to court. In court, Ms. Marvin claimed that the couple had made an oral "contract" under which she was to get one-half of all the property accumulated by the couple during their relationship, as well as support for life in return for her companionship; and that she had given up a singing career on the strength of this promise just to serve as his cook, companion and confidante.

The lower court (the Superior Court) denied Ms. Marvin's suit, on the ground that such a contract between two unmarried persons was an agreement for prostitution. The decision against Ms. Marvin was further upheld on an appeal. Again, however, Ms. Marvin appealed to the Supreme Court of California. And, in its decision, handed down on December 27, 1976, the State's Supreme Court reversed the decision of the two lower courts. The court then went ahead and set down some general "principles" which it said should govern judicial decisions in all future similar cases. It then ordered the Marvin case sent back to the original (superior) court for a new trial.

Thus, a new precedent with potentially far and wide implications, was set for deciding disputes involving property rights among persons engaged in cohabitation situations.

QUESTION 15: What happened when the Marvin case was retried in the lower court?

ANSWER: The case was retried before Judge Arthur Marshall of the Los Angeles Superior Court. And in its new decision in April of 1979, the court said it found no basis or proof that Ms. Marvin had either an "express" or "implicit" contract with Mr. Marvin calling for the two to share Mr. Marvin's assets and earnings (which was now estimated to be $3.6 million.) Therefore, said the court, Ms. Marvin was not entitled to share the Marvin assets because to authorize that " would mean that the court would recognize each unmarried person living together to be automatically entitled by such living together and performing spouse-like functions to half of the property bought with the earnings of the other non-marital partner." This would in effect mean, Judge Marshall said, recognizing the concept of common-law marriages which had been abolished by law in California since 1895.

QUESTION 16: But wasn't Ms. Marvin awarded some money by Judge Marshall?

ANSWER: Yes, she was. She was awarded only $104,000 (not the one-half of $3.6 million she sought). But, more important, look at the reason on which the Judge based the award. It was made only for reasons of "rehabilitation purposes"— the so-called **"rehabilitative alimony"**. In other words, the reason that any money at all was awarded to Ms. Marvin in this case, was *not* because the court agreed that she had any contract with Mr. Marvin which entitled her to compensation for her live-in time, but because the court felt that it was only fair that she be given something— "so that she may have the economic means to re-educate herself and to learn new employable skills." *

   On a subsequent appeal of the amount of the award by Ms. Marvin, however, the California Court of Appeal ruled in August 1981 that not even the $104,000 award to her ought to be paid to Ms. Marvin, "since the award itself is without support in either equity or law." This ruling stood and became the final word on the case to date when, in October 1981, the California Supreme Court — the State's highest — refused to review the Court of Appeal's decision.

QUESTION 17: What, in the final analysis, could be said to be the ultimate message and significance that came out of this whole famous, landmark Marvin case in the field of matrimonial law in America?

ANSWER: The fundamental, lasting significance about the Marvin decision was that it was a step in the direction of giving legal protection to cohabiting parties who do not have the benefit of marriage. The court's decision was that if in its determination Marvin and Triola had, in fact, had an agreement, it would have been enforceable. *Hence, growing out of the Marvin case, it became clear that if you are an unmarried partner and want the court to give you some of the same rights to which a married person is entitled, you had better be sure to meet certain criteria; more particularly, you had better be able to show that there is some kind of contractual obligation on the part of your partner to give you what you are asking for.*

   Thus, if for example, you seek support from your partner and you are unmarried to him (or her), you had better be prepared to establish that that demand is based on some kind of a contractual agreement made between the two of you. In essence, in the absence of a written agreement or some proof of an oral agreement, the unmarried man or woman who makes some kind of financial claim on his partner would likely wind up getting nothing! So, you can begin to see why many lawyers knowledgeable in the field generally advise on the need for a written agreement by cohabiting non-marital partners.

QUESTION 18: What are the various kinds of financial arrangements which non-marital partners may lawfully consider or make, by contract or otherwise?

ANSWER: They vary from case to case, depending on a couples' preference. However, here are some of the forms the arrangements might take:

> Parties may choose to keep their separate earnings and property separate, but agree to compensate one party for service which benefits the other.
> They may choose to pool only a part of their earnings and property together.
> They may choose to form a partnership or joint venture.
> They may choose to hold any property acquired in the relationship as "joint tenants" or as "tenants in common".

---

* Note the further implication of this decision. This new concept of "rehabilitative alimony" implies, perhaps for the first time, that even where there's no legal or contractual basis to award alimony or property settlement to a live-along partner, the court may, on occasion at least, still find reason or legal justification (such as the legal practice of "equitable remedy") to make an award for the "rehabilitation" needs of one or the other partner.

QUESTION 19: Some states, including California, do not recognize or permit common law marriages. Doesn't these recent Marvin-case-type decisions in California, Washington, and other states on property rights for non-marital partners really amount to a recognition of such marriages?

ANSWER: No. In the Marvin case, for example, the court made it clear that in accordance with the California statute abolishing common law marriages, it's decision was not intended to legalize common law marriages. Persons involved in such relationships would still not be entitled to the rights and privileges (e.g., inheritance rights or the widow's share of Social Security) ordinarily enjoyed by valid or even putative spouses. "We held only that she (a non-marital partner)
has the same rights to enforce contracts and to assert her equitable interest in property acquired through her effort as does any other unmarried person," the court said.

QUESTION 20: Which other states, beside California, have had similar cases involving partners who were not legally married to each other?

ANSWER: Quite a few states. One 1979 report put the number of such states then at 15, among which were the states of Washington, New Jersey, New York, Connecticut, Illinois and Oregon. And a more recent report in May 1981 put the number of states at 28, indicating the ever increasing trend.

QUESTION 21: What legal principles, if any, were established in the New Jersey case as governing non-marital cohabitants?

ANSWER: Basically, the governing principle handed down by the New Jersey Supreme Court is that promises made between two (or more) adults living together, whether married to each other or not, can constitute a legal and binding contract between the parties. This principle was laid down in the Koslowski case decided upon in June 1979.
In that case, Ms. Irma Koslowski, who had lived with Mr. Thaddeus Koslowski for 15 years without marriage, had sued Mr. Koslowski for compensation, claiming that she went to live with him because he made a verbal promise to support her for the rest of her life. The court emphasized that it was not reviving the concept of common-law marriage which had been abolished in New Jersey since 1939. However, the court added, the evidence showed that Mr. Koslowski had lured the woman away from her former husband in 1962, and had again persuaded her to return to him in 1968 when she left him after a quarrel, by promising to support her forever. That, the court said, was a valid contract.[*] The court awarded Ms. Koslowski a compensation of $55,000 to be paid by the man.

QUESTION 22: How about New York--what legal principles, if any, were established as governing non-marital cohabitants?

ANSWER: Basically, the governing principle handed down by New York's Court of Appeals is that a woman living with a man to whom she is not married (or a man living with a woman to whom he is not married) may be entitled to a share of his assets — providing she can prove three basic things: 1) that the parties had an "express" oral or written agreement to that effect; 2) that the complaining partner had a continuing relationship with the other partner; and 3) that the complaining partner contributed measurably to the domestic and business lives of the couple.
This principle was laid down in the Morone case decided upon in June 1980. In that case, Ms. Frances Morone, who had lived with Mr. Frank Morone for 25 years without marriage, had sued Mr. Morone for compensation, claiming that she had an (unwritten) agreement for her to provide domestic service to the man in exchange for his financial support of her and their two children. The court reasoned as follows: "(that) the difficulties attendant upon establishing property and financial rights between unmarried couples under available theories of law other than contract warrant application of

---

[*] The key paragraph of the New Jersey ruling, which had a somewhat close counterpart to the California ruling, is this: "We do no more than to recognize that society's mores have changed and that an agreement between adult parties living together is enforceable to the extent that it is not based on a relationship proscribed by law, or on a promise to marry."

the recognition of express contract even through the services rendered be limited to those generally characterized as 'housewifely'." Hence, the court ruled, Ms. Morone would be entitled to receive payment from her live-in companion only if she could prove to a judge or jury that there was such an "express" agreement to share in Mr. Morone's assets or earnings.

QUESTION 23: I heard that unmarried persons who live together automatically have a legal marriage after they have lived together for some period of time, say 7 years. Is this correct?

ANSWER: No. That's the "common-law marriage" myth to which there's no truth or validity whatsoever. Quite to
the contrary, what is true is that the length of a living together relationship has nothing whatsoever to do with making that relationship a legal marriage. There are only about 16 states (plus the District of Columbia) where common-law marriages are recognized as a valid marriage. Now, unless a couple lives in one of these states — and conducts itself totally in the usual husband-and-wife tradition — a living together relationship may not be recognized as a valid marital relationship, no matter how long the parties lived together.

QUESTION 24: Are there any disadvantages in having a common-law marriage rather than a legal marriage?

ANSWER: Yes. If you move out of a common-law marriage state, you automatically become unmarried, and if you move from a state which prohibits it to one which recognizes it, you'll find yourself automatically married, whether or not you want to be. Furthermore, with a common-law marriage, it may be harder to prove that a marriage existed — e.g., when you want to claim a widow's (or widower's) share of Social Security, Workman's Compensation, inheritance or alimony.

Lee Marvin Told to Pay $104,000 But Judge Prohibits Property Split

Lee Marvin   Michelle Triola Marvin

Associated Press

Lee Marvin and Michelle Triola Marvin, his former live-in mate, both of whose now famous "Marvin case" in California revolutionized cohabitation law in the nation, as they appeared in an April 1979 photo in The N.Y. Times.

CHAPTER 11

TAX CONSIDERATIONS IN SEPARATION AND PROPERTY SETTLEMENT AGREEMENTS

A. Some Realities About Tax Consequences In Marital Agreements

Income tax implications of provisions made in separation and settlement agreements (the same as in divorce decrees) could be very important to the contracting persons. The whole subject matter, itself, is one which, because of its sheer complexity and ever-changing nature, would take a separate volume of its own to treat, and is in fact a subject often better handled by tax accountants than by lawyers. However, there's one cheerful note concerning this matter for users of this manual, namely: *for the vast majority of couples who would be involved in divorce or matrimonial settlement agreements, no significant "tax consequence" would probably ever arise,* anyway. *Except for the category of relatively few couples who are fortunate enough to fall under the upper echelons of the society's income earners or property owners, significant knowledge of tax laws and record-keeping would not be necessary.*[*]

Nevertheless, it would be useful for you to be aware of a few main tips and pointers on taxes for divorced or separated persons. There's some truth in the statement of one New York city matrimonial lawyer that, "no (matrimonial) agreement may be intelligently arrived at without consideration of the tax impact." This may be true in light of the fact that, nowadays, most settlement agreements wind up being used as a framework on which divorce terms are eventually based. We highlight below, therefore, a few (and only a few) significant general principles of income taxation normally applicable in divorce and legal separation cases.

B. Some Major Critical Tax Considerations

The Tax Reform Act of 1984 [P.L. 98-369, 98th Cong. ζ422 (a), (b)] made sweeping changes in the tax laws relating to domestic relations. And in that context, among the major critical tax considerations that are important, are the following:

1) Whether alimony payments will be deductible by the party obligated to pay them and taxable to the other party, and to what extent?
2) Whether certain other payments made for the other party's benefit (e.g., insurance premiums) are deductible as alimony?
3) Whether and to what extent there should be a differentiation between alimony to a spouse and child support?
4) Which party is eligible to claim a child dependency exemption?
5) Whether a transfer of property between the parties is a taxable transaction? And,
6) Under what conditions the parties are eligible to file a joint tax return.

---

[*] Never mind the occasional television and motion picture dramatization of couples locked in dramatic "property fights." The fact is this: studies on the matter show that it is the rare exception, not the rule, to find the divorcing couple with that much income or property to fight over. Usually, by the time of separation, or divorce especially, couples are already financially drained from such expenditures like legal costs and the costs of maintaining two household budgets in rents, food, housekeeping services, children's toys and clothing, medical coverage, utilities, transportation, magazines or newspapers, etc. As one New York Times investigator reported, "even for a moderate income divorced family... such a split can virtually overnight transform the family into two low-income households." (N.Y. Times, July 5, 1973 p. 43).

C. Tax Consequences In Matrimonial Decrees And Settlements Made <u>Before</u> January 1, 1985

1. Under the old previous law, marital support payments (alimony and maintenance) to be acceptable, had to be "periodic" payments — that is, they had to be paid in fixed amounts per week or month. And lump-sum payments were generally not acceptable. Furthermore, under the old law it was required that the payment made must be on account of a marital obligation imposed under local law. And only if these requirements were met, did the Internal Revenue Code (the tax law) allow such payments made in settlement of marital and support obligations to be a deductible expenditure in the payer's (mostly the husband's then as now) income tax returns, and similarly considered taxable income to the receiving spouse (generally the wife).

Under the old law, if a spouse (say the husband) makes *support payments to the other spouse* (say the wife), the payments will be generally deductible to him in his separate tax return and included within the gross income of the recipient spouse under these three conditions:

(a) That the payments he made are specifically required by a court decree of divorce, separation or separate maintenance, or by a written separation or settlement agreement.

(b) That the payments are made in relation to a legal marital relationship; and

(c) That the payments are "periodic" (or "semi-periodic"), as defined by the Internal Revenue Code.*

In brief, generally speaking alimony payments made either terminable or subject to change in the case of death, remarriage, or change in the economic structure of either party, were deemed "periodic". The contingent event may be provided either by the court decree or agreement or by state law. It is not essential that the "periodic" alimony be paid in equal amounts or at regular intervals.

There is one exception where, by a special provision of the Internal Revenue Code, even if the amount paid is not an "indefinite amount" (i.e., even if it is a lump sum payment), the payment may still be allowed as a deductible item by the payer: where the amount, though not an indefinite sum, is to be paid in "installments" over a period of <u>more than</u> 10 years from the date of the agreement or court decree. Such payments are said to be "quasi periodic" payments which would therefore qualify as a deductible expenditure by the paying spouse.

Thus, an agreement between a husband and wife whereby the husband is to pay the wife a fixed sum, say $100,000, in monthly equal installments but through a period of just 9 years and 11 months from the date of the agreement, will not qualify as a **"periodic" or "quasi-periodic" payment** — it will not be tax deductible by the husband (which also means that it would not be a taxable income to the wife who receives the payment). However, if the $100,000 were to have been similarly paid to the wife in fixed installments *but* OVER a period of 10 years and 1 month (more than 10 years), the payments would have fully qualified for tax deduction by the husband (and will also be taxable as income to the wife).

In this case, though, there is one qualification: the alimony payments will be deemed "periodic" alright, but deductions are limited in this case to a maximum of 10 percent of the principal sum each year, and applies only to advance alimony payment but does not include arrearages.

2. Payments made (whether over a 10 year period or otherwise) which are not in satisfaction of the *obligated party's* marital obligations, but rather are in settlement of the *recipient* party's marital obligations, are not considered "alimony" and are not deductible. Also, advance payments of periodic alimony made voluntarily by a party — that is, payments made which are informally arranged between the wife and the husband, but had not been specifically ordered by a court or required by a separation or settlement agreement — may be considered as not in discharge of a legal obligation and, therefore, as not being a deductible expense for tax purposes under Section 71 and 215 of the Internal Revenue Code.

---

*   Periodic payments are of two basic types: 1) payments of specific amounts from time to time over an "indefinite period of time" with payments stopping only when a specified contingency, such as a spousal death or remarriage, occurs (i.e., fixed amounts for indefinite period based on the happening or non-happening of an indefinite future event); or 2) payments of indefinite amounts, such as a specific percentage of the husband's salary, from time to time over a specific period, say 5, 10, or 15 years (an indefinite or changeable amount for a fixed period of time). For a payment to qualify as "periodic," it must be payable: (1) for an indefinite period of time; or (2) in an indefinite amount; or (3) over a period of more than 10 years.

Likewise, such "voluntary" alimony payments made by the obligated party after the recipient party has remarried, are not deductible by the payer, nor are they considered as income to the recipient party, since under the laws of most states the spouse's legal obligation to pay alimony automatically terminates upon the remarriage of the spouse unless otherwise provided in the divorce decree. However, if the obligated party continues to make payments by reason of the ignorance of the recipient party's remarriage, the payments may be taxable to the recipient party.

Payments to recipient party in satisfaction of marital obligation.

In addition to qualifying as "periodic," all deductible alimony payments must be paid as a result of the marital relationship according to one of the following forms:

(1) A decree of divorce, regardless of the date entered, which may include a written agreement incidental to such decree; or

(2) A written separation agreement executed after August 16, 1954 (no date on the agreement is required, and an oral agreement stipulated to in open court proceedings will satisfy a "written requirement"); or

(3) A decree for separate maintenance (including temporary orders) entered after March 1, 1954.

In each of the above instances, the couple must be living in a state of separation (where the husband and wife are residing in the same household, they are not considered to be living in a state of separation) and filing separate returns for the year in which the deduction is claimed. If a joint return is filed, the alimony is not deductible by the obligated party, and the payments will not be income to the recipient party. The written agreement, however, is not required to be legally enforceable.

Temporary alimony payments required by court order are deductible under the same rules as permanent alimony. However, payments made pursuant to an oral agreement before the divorce, not required by order of the court, are not deductible.

Effective for taxable years beginning after December 31, 1976, alimony payments will be treated as a deduction from gross income rather than as an itemized deduction.

D. Tax Consequences In Matrimonial Decrees & Agreements Made <u>After</u> December 31, 1984

Under the new law (Tax Reform Act of 1984), the requirement that the alimony and separate maintenance payments must be made on account of a marital obligation imposed under local law has been repealed, and the requirement that the payment be "periodic" has been eliminated. The parties may designate in the instrument that otherwise qualifying alimony payments are to be nondeductible by the payor and excludable by the payee. The alimony and separate maintenance rules apply to divorce or separation instruments executed after December 31, 1984. The law also applies to any divorce or separation instrument executed before January 1, 1985, but modified on or after that date if the modification expressly provides that the provisions of the Act are to apply. The Tax Reform Act of 1986 amendments apply generally to instruments executed after December 31, 1986. It also applies to any divorce or separation instrument executed before January 1, 1987, but modified on or after that date, if the modification expressly provides that the provisions of the law are to apply.

Alimony and separate maintenance payments are deductible by the payor and are included within the gross income of the payee under the following conditions:

a) The payments must be made in cash;[1]

---

[1] I.R.C.ξ 71 (b) (1). Only cash payments, including checks and money orders payable on demand, qualify as alimony payments. Transfers of property, services, a debt instrument of a third party, an annuity contract, or use of property of the payor, etc., do not qualify. Thus, a party who transfers property, such as a vehicle, in satisfaction of alimony, would receive no deduction. Payments of rent, mortgage, liabilities, taxes, medical expenses, school tuition, or other expenses, qualify as alimony, provided payment is made pursuant to a divorce or separation instrument. See ξ 16-3, infra.

b) the payments must be made to the payee (or a third party for the payee's benefit) under a divorce or separation instrument;

c) Liability for payments must terminate at the death of the payee spouse;[2]

d) The divorce or separation instrument must state that there is no liability to make payments for any period after the death of the payee spouse;[3]

e) the parties, where separated under a decree of divorce or of separate maintenance (as distinguished from a separation agreement or decree for support), must not be members of the same household at the time of payment; the parties must not designate the payment as not being alimony, such as designating it as support for the children; and if any amount specified in the instrument will be reduced on the happening of a contingency relating to a child (e.g., reaching a specified age, marrying, dying, leaving school, or a similar contingency), then an equal amount will be treated as child support rather than alimony. (Example: if the divorce decree provides that payments will be reduced by $100 per month when a child reached age 18, then $100 of each monthly payment will be treated as fixed for child support).

In addition to the foregoing requirements, under the Tax Reform Act of 1986, any payments in excess of $15,000 during any calendar year will be deductible only if the divorce or separation instrument provides that the payor is required to make alimony payments for at least three consecutive calendar years beginning with the year a payment is first made (assuming neither spouse dies during that period and that the payee does not remarry); and the payments may not vary by more than $15,000 a year, or the excess payments (i.e., those earlier year payments in excess of the sum of the later year payments plus $15,000) will be includeable in the income of the payor and deductible by the payee in the subsequent year.[4]

There is no alimony income or deduction if the parties choose to file a joint return. The payee must furnish the payor with his or her social security number and the payer must furnish the name and social security number of the payee to the Internal Revenue Service.

E. Alimony: Indirect Payments

One area where the Tax Reform Act of 1984 (TRA '84) completely rewrote the tax laws relating to alimony and separate maintenance payments, is with respect to *indirect* alimony payments.

benefit and it will qualify as deductible so long as the other conditions[5] for the payments to qualify as deductible are met. Thus, assuming all other conditions are met, payments of the following to third persons for the benefit of the

---

[2] There must be no liability to make any payment in cash or property as a substitute for such payments. I.R.C.ξ 71 (b) (1) (D); Treas. Reg ξ 1.71-1T (b)(A-10)

Under the Tax Reform Act of 1986, ξ 1981, payments must still be terminable upon the death of the dependent spouse. However, it is no longer necessary to make an explicit statement that the payments are terminable on death. If the payments are terminable by reason of state law (as they are, for example, in a state like North Carolina), they are deductible to the payor and taxable to the payee even though no explicit statement is made. This change is retroactive to the date of enactment of the Tax Reform Act of 1984. It is now appropriate for taxpayers to file amended returns claiming the deductions for 1985 or 1986 if the deductions were disallowed for failure to make an explicit statement. It is also necessary for the dependent spouse to file an amended return including the payments in income.

[3] I.R.C.ξ 71 (b) (1) (D). The 1986 Tax Reform Act has modified this requirement so that although it is still necessary that the payments actually terminate at the payee's death, it is not necessary for the document to state such. But a good prudent practice is still to state in the document the intention of the parties as to taxability and deductibility.

[4] The recapture provisions of the 1984 Act were altered by the Tax Reform Act of 1986, ξ1843. The new law (the 1986 law) applies to instruments executed on or after January 1, 1987, and reduces recapture only to three years instead of six under the previous Tax Reform Act of 1984; recapture occurs only in the three post-separation years; and there is a $15,000 cushion instead of a $10,000 cushion. The recapture rules under the 1986 Act are illustrated as follows:

(1) If payments for the second year exceed payments for the third year by more than $15,000, the excess is recaptured in the third year. For example, under a 1987 agreement, husband made payments to the wife in 1987 and 1988 of $30,000, and payments in 1989 are $10,000. Since the 1988 payments exceeded 1989 payments by $ 20,000 , the excess over $15,000 (or $5,000) is ordinary income to the husband in 1989 and not income to wife in 1989.

(2) If payments for the first year exceed the average of payments for the second and third year by more than $15,000, the excess over $15,000 is recaptured in the third year. For example, under a 1987 agreement, husband makes payments to wife in 1987 of $50,000, payments of $22,000 in 1988 and of $14,000 in 1989. The average payments for the second and third years is $18,000. Since 1989 payments exceed the average of 1988 and 1989 payments by $32,000, the excess over $15,000 ($17,000) is ordinary income to husband in 1989 and not income to the wife in 1989.

(3) If both of the rules above apply, the amount recaptured under the first rule is subtracted from second year payments for purposes of applying the second rule. For example, under a 1989 instrument, husband makes payments to wife in 1987 of $50,000 in 1988 of $40,000, and 1989 of $20,000. Under the first rule, second-year payments exceed third-year payments by $20,000, thus the excess over $15,000 ($5,000) is recaptured. To apply the second rule, the $5,000 recaptured under the first rule is subtracted from 1988 payments. Therefore, the average of 1988 and 1989 payments is $27,500. Payments in 1987 exceed the average of 1988 and 1989 payments by $22,500; thus the excess over $15,000 (7,500) is recaptured under the second rule. Therefore the total recapture is $12,500 — $5,000 under the first rule and $7,500 under the second rule.

The tax reform Act of 1986 allows parties to modify instruments executed in 1985 and 1986 that the recapture provisions of the new law, rather than that of the 1984 law, will be applicable.

[5] See Sections C.&D above.

payee spouse (or ex-spouse) would be deductible: medical expenses, house or rental payments, real estate taxes, insurance and home improvements, utilities, life insurance premiums, school tuition, the recipient spouse's income tax on alimony payments, and under certain limited conditions, attorney's fee.[6]

Apparently, life insurance proceeds, payments of trust corpus (but not the trust income), annuity payments, and payments made to maintain property owned by the payor spouse and used by the payee spouse, will not be subject to alimony treatment.[7]

F. Tax Treatment of Child Support

As explained in the preceding sections of this chapter, the tax Reform Act of 1984 (TRA '84) completely rewrote the tax laws relating to *alimony and separate maintenance payments*. The story, however, is totally different with respect to the tax treatment of *child support* payments: here, there's no change in the law, with the exception of the overruling of the decision in Commissioner v. Lester [366 U.S. 299, 81 S. Ct. 1343, 6L. Ed.2d 306 (1961)], as discussed below.

With respect to **child support,** payments made for child support which are the terms of a divorce decree or separation agreement, are treated exactly in the opposite way from payments made for the support of a spouse. Child support expenditures by the spouse or parent are *not* a tax deductible expense by the payor, and are *not* taxable income to the payee spouse — that is, the spouse or party (or even the child himself) who collects such payments does not pay tax on such receipts; they are not deductible by the payer, nor are they includable in the gross income of the payee (the party collecting it on behalf of the child). In such cases, if and when a payment is less than the amount specified in the divorce or separation instrument, it will be applied first to the required child support, and then any remainder to alimony; i.e., there is no pro rata division between child support and alimony.

On the other hand, suppose the payor makes a lump-sum payment for alimony and child support and does not specify what portion of the support payment is "child support"? In that event, the entire amount will be treated as alimony, assuming it otherwise qualifies, unless the parties have designated otherwise by written agreement. For example, the parties to an agreement may designate in the instrument that the alimony payments are to be non-deductible by the payor and excludable by the payee. However, if any amount specified in the instrument will be reduced on the happening of a contingency event relating to a child (e.g., the attainment of a specified age, marrying, dying, leaving school, etc.), then an equal amount will be treated as child support rather than alimony.[8] For example, if the divorce instrument provides that payments will be reduced by $100 per month when a child reaches age 18, then $100 of each monthly payment will be treated as fixed for child support and thus not deductible by the payer nor treated as income to the payee.

> **NOTE:** To be absolutely on the safe side, it is advised that the provisions of a settlement or separation agreement, or of a court decree, always clearly identify and ***differentiate*** any payments which are meant for child support, from those that are for the wife's support (alimony), if any. Support provisions should *not* be lumped together in a clause like: "The husband shall pay the sum of $200 per month for alimony and child support." Rather, a specific breakdown of how much is meant for the children's support and what part is meant for alimony, if applicable, should be exactly given. Lumping the payments together has had a long history of causing a lot of complications for both spouses with the Internal Revenue Service. [In one case, for example, the tax court

---

[6] The general rule is that attorney's fees are not deductible by either party, since they are considered to be personal expense. I.R.C. § 262. However, there are few well-defined exceptions. A recipient party may deduct expenses for attorney's fees incurred for the "production or collection of alimony." I.R.C. 212 (1). However, the recipient party must be prepared to show what proportion of the attorney's fees is attributable to the collection of alimony. In Re: Mirsky, 56T.C. 664. Both parties may deduct any portion of their attorney's fees attributable to tax advise. I.R.C. 212 (3). Adequate records must be kept showing what part of attorney's fees are attributable to tax advice. Hall v. U.S., 78-1 U.S.T.C. para. 9126 (Ct. Cl. 1977). However, except as provided above, the legal costs of prosecution or defending a divorce action are not deductible by either party, since it is presumed that the litigation arose from a personal as opposed to a business relationship. U.S. v. Gilmore, 372 U.S. 39, 83 S. Ct. 623, 9 L. Ed. 2d 577) (1963); U.S. v. Patrick, 372 U.S. 53, 83 S. Ct. 618, 9 L. Ed. 2nd 580 (1963). The obligated party's payment of the recipient party's attorney's fees is not deductible, unless it can otherwise qualify.

[7] See TRA '84 §421 (B) (2), repealed I.R.C. §101 (e), which made life insurance proceeds taxable to the payee spouse (or ex-spouse) as alimony. I.R.C. §682 and H.Rpt. 98-432 (Part 3) at p. 1492; TRA '84, §421 (b) (1), repealed I.R.C. §72 (k), which made annuity payments subject to alimony treatment; and Treas. Reg. §1.71 (b) (A-6).

[8] This derives from Tax Reform Act of 1984 422 (a) [I.R.C. S. 71 (c)(2)], overruling Commissioner v. Lester, 366 U.S. 299, 81 S. Ct.1343, 6L. Ed.306 (1961).

ruled that a wife who used payments designated as "alimony" to support the children in their custody, was entitled to claim them as her dependents for tax purposes.]

Historically, tax laws have made it advantageous for the parties to allow all or a major part of support payment to be treated as alimony, since the recipient party was typically in a lower income tax bracket than the obligated party. Due to the tax savings, the obligated party could afford to pay a larger sum as alimony, and the recipient party's higher income tax would normally be more than offset by the increase in alimony payments. Generally, careful planning can obtain these same advantages under the new laws. However, any such planning must take into consideration the strict requirements of the new tax laws (see Sections D & E above). Any such planning should also take into consideration which party will claim the child dependency exemption for each of the minor children.

Apparently there is nothing in the new tax law which would prevent the parties from modifying the divorce or separation instrument in order to effect a more advantageous tax treatment, but based on past rulings, the change will apply only to prospective (future) payments.

G. Treatment With Respect To Dependency Exemptions For Children

Tax Laws relating to dependency for children is another aspect that was completely rewritten by the Tax Reform Act of 1984 (TRA of 1984). Under the prior Law, while payments specifically designated as *"Child Support"* were, then as now, neither a taxable income to the payee-spouse nor a deductible expenditure to the paying spouse, the paying spouse may, however, be entitled to claim the children as his *"dependents"*, which would then entitle him to take the $1,000 per dependent child "exemption" credit in his income tax return. A paying spouse did not, however, automatically qualify to take this dependency exemption; rather, the qualifying spouse entitled to claim a child as a dependent was the one who met the following requirements:

    (a) If the child received the greater part of his support (over 50%) from his divorced or separated parents, then the child will be considered the dependent of that particular parent who has custody of him for *more than* 6 months of the calendar year.

    (b) If the parties had a court order or a separation agreement which expressly provides, however, that the non-custodial parent (the one who does not have custody) would be entitled to the dependency exemption if he should contribute at least $600 towards the support of the child per year, then the provision or the court ,order or agreement would prevail. A spouse (say the father) would, in such a case be entitled to the exemption *providing* he paid $600 (or more) per child in child support for the year.

    (c) If there was no court order or a valid agreement, or if the court order or agreement said nothing about the $600 provision mentioned above, then the non-custodial parent was nevertheless entitled to the exemption if he provided at least $1,200 in child support per child in a given year. The only way the custodial mother, rather than the non-custodial father, would be entitled to the exemption under such a circumstance, would be by showing a "clear evidence" that she contributed more than the husband did in support of the child for that year.

In short, under the prior law, to qualify for the $1,000-per-dependent child-exemption, the parent had to provide over one-half of the dependent's support, and there were special rules where the parents were divorced or separated.

Under the new law, however, beginning January 1, 1985, the new law provides that the "custodial parent"(defined as that parent who has custody for the greater portion of the calendar year), will be entitled to the exemption in all cases unless he or she waives the exemption by written declaration and the non-custodial parent attaches the declaration (I.R.S. Form 8332) to his or her tax return. In certain cases, pre-1985 decrees and agreements (unless amended) will continue under the same rules as prior law.

(1) Qualified pre-1985 decrees and agreements. Any "qualified" pre-1985 instrument (defined as any decree of divorce or separation maintenance or written agreement signed before 1/1/85, which provides that the non-custodial parent is entitled to claim the dependency exemption, and is not modified to provide that this exemption will not apply to it) will continue under the prior law whereby the non-custodial parent will be entitled to claim the $1,000

dependency exemption[9] (i) if he or she contributes at least $600.00 to the support of the child during the calendar year; (ii) if the
"qualified" instrument proves that the non-custodial parent will be entitled to this exemption; (iii) if the child receives over half of his support during the calendar year from the parents; (iv) if the child is in the custody of one or both of his parents for more than one-half of the calendar year; and (v) if the parents are divorced or legally separated under a decree of divorce or separate maintenance, or are separated under a written separation agreement, or have lived apart at all times during the last six months of the calendar year.

(2) Taxable years beginning AFTER December 31, 1984. Except for "qualified" pre-1985 instruments (see definition above) for taxable years after December 31, 1984, in all cases the custodial parent (that parent who has custody for the greater part of the calendar year) will be entitled to the $1,000 dependency exemption[10] unless he or she signs a written declaration (IRS Form 8332) that such custodial parent will not claim the child as a dependent for any taxable year beginning in such calendar year and the non-custodial parent attaches the declaration to his or her tax return for the taxable year beginning during such calendar year. Furthermore, for the exemption to be available to either parent, the child must receive over half of his support during a calendar year from the parents; the child must be in the custody of one or both of his parents for more than one-half of the calendar year; and the parents must be either divorced or legally separated under a divorce decree or separate maintenance, or written agreement, or lived apart at all times during the last six months of the calendar year.

Since the Internal Revenue Code now requires an express waiver of the dependency exemption by the custodial parent, there is conflicting authority as to whether the court has the authority to allocate the dependency exemption to a parent. The court has three basic options: it may allocate the exemption, order the custodial spouse to execute a written declaration waiving the exemption, or refuse to do either. Public policy in creating more income to pay support would, however, support the court's allocation to the payor spouse. The exemption may also be a property right to be allocated by equitable distribution.

(3) Miscellaneous. As under present law, the foregoing rules will not apply in the case of multiple support agreements under the new tax law. For purposes of the medical expenses deduction, a child who is subject to the above rules will be treated as a dependent of both parents. By waiving the right to claim the dependent exemption, the custodial parent does not lose eligibility for head of household status, child care credit, nor earned income credit.

H. Transfers Of Property

The Tax Reform Act of 1984 [I.R.C. ξ1015; ξ104; ξ1239], completely rewrote the tax laws relating to transfers of property incident to a divorce. Generally, after July 18, 1984, property transfers between the parties because of a divorce will no longer be a taxable event (repealing U.S. v. Davis, 370 U.S. 65, 82 S. Ct. 1190, 8 L. Ed. 2d 335 [1962]). The transfer will be treated for income tax purposes in the same manner as a gift. The transferor will have no recognized gain or loss, and the transferee will receive the property at the transferor's basis. However, prior law will continue to apply to transfers pursuant to a divorce decree or separation agreement in effect on the date of enactment of the new law (July 18, 1984), unless both parties elect to have the rules apply to such transfers.

(1) Transfers of property pursuant to instruments in effect PRIOR TO July 18, 2984. Unless both parties elect to have the new rules apply, prior law will continue to apply to transfers made pursuant to divorce decree or separation agreement in effect prior to July 18, 1984. [Note that the Tax Reform Act of 1986 eliminated the capital gains rates]. Accordingly, if the transferor transfers appreciated property to the transferee as alimony, or otherwise transfers it in discharge of marital rights, the transferor will realize a gain subject to taxation under the usual rules. Whether the gain will be taxed as ordinary income or capital gain depends upon the character of the property

---

[9] The $1,000 is subject to a cost-of-living adjustment. The Tax Reform Act of 1986 increased the dependency exemptions to $1,900 in 1987, $1,950 in 1988, and $2,000 in 1989 and subsequent years. If the spouse paying child support has taxable income which exceeds $149,250 on a joint return, $89,560 on a single return, and $123,790 on a head of household return, it may be advisable to allocate the dependency exemption to the recipient spouse, since the 1989 Tax Reform Act ξ1(g), recaptures the entire benefits of the exemptions at such income levels.

[10] The dependent is the parent's "child" as defined in I.R.C. ξ151 (e) (3) (biological child, stepchild, legally adopted child) where the child has not reached age 19 before the close of the taxable year. Note that where there is no award of legal custody, physical custody is the determining factor. See Treas. Reg. ξ1-152-4(b)

transferred. The amount of the gain is the difference between the transferor's adjusted basis for the property and the fair market value at the time of the transfer.

A clear distinction should be drawn between a property settlement, whereby the parties simply divide their jointly owned property, and a transfer in satisfaction of the transferee's inchoate marital rights. In the case of a strict property division, there is no taxable event and no tax. On the other hand, where the transferor transfers property to the transferee in consideration of the latter's claim for alimony, any gain realized by the transferor is subject to taxation. In other words, in such a situation the controlling criterion is the intent of the parties rather than the designation placed on the transfer.

The transferee is not considered to have realized a gain in the release of his or her claim for alimony, and any assets which he or she receives in the transaction will have the current fair market value as a basis for future transfers.

(2) **Transfers of property subject to the law.** Under I.R.C §47 (e), there are three types of transfers between spouses or incident to a divorce subject to the 1984 law: (i) transfers made after the Law's date of enactment (July 18, 1984) (other than transfers pursuant to an instrument in effect prior thereto); (ii) transfers after the law's date of enactment (July 18, 1984) pursuant to an instrument then in effect, if both parties elect to have the new rules apply to the transfer; and (iii) transfers after December 31, 1983, if both parties elect to have the new rules apply to the transfer, per new IRS regulations.

The 1984 law overrules United States v. Davis, and provides that no gain or loss will be recognized on a transfer of property between spouses or between former spouses if the transfer is incident to a divorce. The property transferred will be treated as acquired by the transferee by gift, and the basis of the transferee in the property will be the adjusted basis of the transferor. A transfer of property is incident to a divorce if such transfer (1) occurs within one year after the date on which the marriage ceases or (2) is related to the cessation of the marriage.

The new rules also apply to transfer in trust, transfers of annuities, transfers of life insurance contracts, and transfers of installment obligations.

As a general rule, benefits under a tax deferred retirement plan cannot be assigned or alienated without the possible loss of deferred tax benefits. Because of the need to transfer retirement benefits incident to divorce, the Internal Revenue Service created an exception to the general rule. This rule continued until the passage of the Retirement Equity Act of 1984. The 1984 law allows the transfer of retirement benefits, provided the parties meet the requirements for a *Qualified Domestic Relations Order (QDRO)*. When the requirements are met, the benefits are afforded favorable tax treatment, and the plan remains tax deferred.

I. Miscellaneous Provisions

The Tax Reform Act of 1984, made many miscellaneous changes to the tax laws relating to married persons and divorced persons. Generally, these rules were effective after December 31, 1984.

(1) Head of household status. A party may qualify for a lower income tax rate as a "head of household" if he is not married at the end of a taxable year and maintains a household within the meaning of I.R.C. §2 (b). For tax years prior to 1985, the taxpayer's household must be the residence of the child for the entire taxable year for the taxpayer to qualify as head of the household. Beginning with the taxable year 1985, the new law requires only that the household be the child's principal residence only for more than one-half of the taxable year.

(2) Joint return. A joint return may not be filed by parties who are divorced or separated under a decree of separate maintenance, since they would be considered for tax purposes as unmarried. Neither may a husband or wife file joint returns while one spouse claims alimony payments as deductions. Of course, the filing of a joint return renders both spouses jointly and severely liable for all due taxes, but the 1984 law liberalized the *"innocent spouse rule"* in that, under certain conditions, a spouse may be relieved of liability for a substantial understatement of tax on a joint return that is attributable to the grossly erroneously items of the other spouse.

(3) Individual retirement accounts. Under the 1984 tax law, alimony or separate maintenance payments qualify for purposes of computing contributions to an individual retirement account (IRA).

(4) Federal estate tax. For estates of persons dying after July 18, 1984, the obligation to transfer property to a former spouse of the deceased will be deductible as a claim against the estate if the transfer is pursuant to an agreement which satisfies certain conditions.

(5) Federal gift tax. For transfers of property to a former spouse in consideration of the release of that spouse's marital rights, prior law provided that if certain conditions were met, there would be no taxable gift. For gifts made after July 18, 1984, to a former spouse, the new law liberalizes the conditions under which a transfer would not be a taxable gift.

(6) Attorney's fees. Generally, legal services rendered in connection with divorce and other marital issues are deemed to be "personal" rather than business-related, and are therefore not deductible. However, an individual is allowed to deduct all the ordinary and necessary expenses paid or incurred:

(1) for the production or collection of income;

(2) for the management, conservation, or maintenance of property held for the production of income; or

(3) in connection with the determination, collection, or refund of any tax. Thus, legal expenses attributable to the production or collection of taxable alimony are deductible by the recipient of the alimony. (IRS ξ31.262-1). Legal fees for the conservation or maintenance of property held for the production of income in the divorce setting have generally failed.[11] Legal fees incurred for tax research and advice in connection with a divorce and property settlement are deductible.[12] Beginning in 1987, otherwise deductible legal fees will be deductible as "any other miscellaneous itemized deduction" only to the extent that they exceed two percent of the adjusted gross income of the taxpayer.

[11] See U.S. v. Gilmore, 372 U.S. 39, 83 S. Ct. 623, 9L. Ed. 2d 570 (1963)

[12] Carpenter v. U.S., 338 F. 2d 366 (Ct. Cl. 1964); Rev Rul. 72-545, 1972-2 C.B. 179; U.S. v. Davis, 370 U.S. 65, 82, S. Ct. 1190, 8 L. Ed. 2d 335, reh. den., 371 U.S. 854, 83 S. Ct. 14, 9 L. Ed. 2d 92 (1962).

Copyright© 1996 by Do-It-Yourself Legal Publishers

APPENDIX A

FINANCIAL STATEMENT OF NET WORTH   Date Made: _____

   Made by Mr/Mrs _____

A. *List Your Assets*

Real Estate (land, home, business property, condos, co-ops, etc.)

Description or address	Type of ownership (sole, joint, etc)	Market Value Equity

Cash or Equivalent Funds (checking accounts, savings accounts money market accounts, certificates of deposit, etc.)

Bank	Account Type & Number	Balance

Investments (stocks, bonds, mutual fund shares, CD's other securities, etc.)

Type	Company	Number of shares	Market Value

Personal Property

List major items of personal property owned (including furs, jewelry, art, cash on hand, all items of substantial value):

_____
_____

Other Personal Property—whatever you own (furniture's, clothes, etc.) that are not major. (You need not list individual items unless of significant value)

Description	Approx. Value

MARKED: EXHIBIT _____

Automobiles — List all interests in automobiles

Type   License Number   Insurance Company

_____

_____

_____

Retirement Plans (IRS's profit sharing, pension plans, Keoghs, etc.)

Type   Name of Plan   Beneficiary   Current Value

_____

_____

_____

Life Insurance (also note the policy number and type of insurance coverage, such as "whole" or "term")

Insured Person   Company   1st Beneficiary   2nd Beneficiary   Death Benefit

_____

_____

_____

Accounts/Notes Receivable & Debts owed you (include name, address and phone number)

Who owes   Amount owed you

_____

_____

_____

Special items of value (items of substantial value, e.g., coin collections, antiques, jewelry, art, etc.)

Description   Approx. value

_____

_____

_____

B. List Your Liabilities

Type   Company/Persons owed   Amount owed   When due   Secured by

Mortgages _____

Installment Loans (credit cards, etc.) _____

Education Loans _____

Personal Loans _____

_____

_____

_____

Taxes owed _____

Other debts _____

_____

C. Figuring Out Your Net Worth

AMOUNTS

Yours   Joint (if any)

ASSETS

Real Estate   _____

Cash or Equivalent Funds _____

Investments _____

Personal Property _____

Other Personal Property _____

Automobiles _____

Retirement Plans _____

Life Insurance _____

Accounts Rec./Debts owed to you _____

Special items of value _____

Deferred compensation(income earned but not received) _____

Total Assets ....(A) _____

LIABILITIES

Mortgages _____

Installment Loans _____

Education Loans _____

Personal Loans _____

Taxes owed _____

Other debts _____

Total Liabilities ....(B) _____

NET ESTATE .... _____
        (assets minus liabilities)
        (A) — (B)

Submitted By: **X**_____
                            (signature of maker)

A Copy is Hereby Acknowledged Received By: **X**_____ on _____
                                                            (signature of partner)   (date)

APPENDIX B

GROUNDS AND OTHER RELEVANT INFORMATION FOR OBTAINING A DIVORCE IN ALL 50 STATES & D.C.

As of the time of this writing, all 50 states in the nation have now adopted some form of "no-fault" law or procedure for dissolving marital relationships. This relatively recent development in matrimonial law administration has, in turn, translated into a big practical difference for the average divorce seeker across the nation.

The big difference is this: for *the first time in the nation's history, the standards and requirements for getting a divorce (the so-called "grounds") are now more or less uniform and standardized across the country!* Now, for the most part at least, all you'll practically need in order to file or be granted a divorce in just about any state, is to submit some form of a written statement* to your state's court making the claim that both spouses are in agreement that your marital relationship has absolutely failed or broken down. And hardly any judge or court official necessarily needs concern himself any more with whose "fault" it is, before you could be granted a divorce under such circumstances!

In view of this new reality, most Separation or Settlement agreements nowadays are ultimately used as a basis for final settlement in a divorce action [see Chapter 4   for a fuller treatment of this]. Hence, it is hoped that couples or persons in every state would find the contents of this Appendix both relevant and helpful in educating eir themselves about the nature of separation or divorce, and some of the basic rules and requirements.

Included in this chapter, are the following information: the statutory "grounds" (reasons) for which divorce is allowed in each state; the court which handles divorce matters in each state; the title by which the state statutes (or laws) governing divorce is cited in each state; some clarifications or court interpretations of the laws in certain states; the principles by which marital property is allocated upon divorce** ; the state residency requirement for filing in each state, and identification of the 'no-fault' grounds for each state.

The actual procedures for filing for divorce are, of course, beyond the scope of this manual, and those interested in this may consult the volumes by the publisher, *How To Do Your Own Divorce Without A Lawyer*, authored by Benji O. Anosike. But, in general the procedures, especially for an "uncontested" divorce, are basically identical from state to state. It often boils down to one rather simple routine: securing a set of simple forms prescribed by the local court, filling them out, and submitting them to the appropriate state court for approval and the judge's signature.

NOTE: The companion manual, the 10-Volume *"How To Do Your Own Divorce Without A Lawyer"* series, published by The Selfhelper Law Press of America, a subsidiary of this publisher, provides the interested reader with the same facility to enable you undertake the procedures for actually filing for a divorce yourself. Included in each regional edition, which covers all the 50 states, are details of the actual procedures and sample forms for filing for divorce in each state, information on how to obtain the necessary filing forms, and other relevant details. Readers may write to the present Publisher for availability and price information.

---

*
It doesn't matter whether your local court calls it a "petition," a "stipulation," a "verified complaint," or whatever. They're all generally one and the same thing.

**
The rules by which marital property is divided up on divorce, fall into three different basic categories: 1) The "community property" states, in which spouses split *equally* all assets acquired by either or both parties (usually excluding those acquired before marriage, or by gift or inheritance); 2) the "equitable property" states, which make marital assets distributable to the spouses on the basis of justice and fair play determined on a case-by-case manner; and 3) the "common law" states, where ownership of property goes to the spouse who has legal title or his/her name to it at the time of divorce. Most states (as of this writing 48 of the 50 states) are now either community property or equitable property-based. [See Chapter 3 of the guidebook for more on this]

THE GROUNDS FOR A DIVORCE IN EACH STATE NOW FOLLOW.

ALABAMA
Grounds:

*1.) Voluntary separation for over 1 year; *2) Incompatibility of temperament so that parties can no longer live together; *3. Irretrievable breakdown of the marriage so that further attempts at reconciliation are impractical or unproductive; 4) Incurable physical incapacity to enter into the marital state at the time of the marriage; 5) Adultery; 6) Imprisonment (actual confinement) in a penitentiary for two years, under sentence for seven years or more; 7) Commission of a crime against nature before or after marriage; 8) Drug addiction or habitual drunkenness; 9) Confinement in an insane asylum for five successive years after marriage; 10) Pregnancy (by wife) caused by another man at the time of marriage; 11) living apart and non-support of wife by husband for two years (wife has to file).

Incompatibility is defined by court decisions as conflicts in personality and disposition that render it impossible for the parties to continue a normal marital relationship with each other. Lipham v. Lipham, 281 So. 2d 437.

Court: Circuit Court
Statute: Code of Alabama, Title 30
Residence: 1 year

ALASKA
Grounds:

*1. Incompatibility of temperament; *2. Failure to consummate the marriage at the time of marriage, and up to the time of the commencement of the divorce action; 3) Adultery; 4) Conviction of a felony; 5) Desertion for one year; 6) cruel and inhuman treatment; indignities against the other spouse; 7) Habitual drunkenness for one year prior to commencement of divorce action; 8) insanity or mental illness for which the spouse is confined to an institution for a period of at least eighteen months prior to commencement of the action; 9) Narcotic addiction.

Court: Superior Court
Statute: Alaska Statutes Annotated 09.55.110.
Residence: 1 year

ARIZONA
Grounds:

*1. A finding that the marriage is irretrievably broken (Defined as where there is no reasonable prospect of reconciliation).

Arizona Revised Statutes 25-314, states as follows, in part:

"The verified petition in a proceeding for dissolution of marriage or legal separation shall allege that the marriage is irretrievably broken or [that] one or both of the parties desire to live separate and apart, whichever is appropriate, and shall set forth:

"The verified petition in a proceeding for dissolution of marriage or legal separation shall allege that the marriage is irretrievably broken or one or both of the parties desire to live separate and apart, whichever is appropriate, an shall set forth:

1. The age, occupation and address of each party and the length of domicile in this state;
2. The date of the marriage and the place at which it was performed;
3. The names, ages and addresses of all living children, natural or adopted, common to the parties and whether the wife is pregnant;

---

* Indicates this is a "no-fault" ground.

4. The details of any agreements between the parties as to support, custody and visitation of the children and maintenance of spouse;
5. The relief sought."

Court: Superior Court
Property distribution rule upon divorce: By community property rule
Statute: Arizona Revised Statutes 25-312.
Residence: 1 year

ARKANSAS
Grounds:
*1) Living separate and apart for 18 consecutive months regardless of fault; marital misconduct relevant only when the wife seeks alimony or property division; 2) Impotence at the time of the marriage and up until commencement of the action; 3) Desertion for one year; 4) Prior existing marriage; 5) Conviction of a felony or other infamous crime; 6) Habitual drunkenness for one year prior to commencement of action; indignities to or cruel and inhuman treatment of the other spouse; 7) Adultery; 8) Living separate for three years because of the adjudicated insanity of the spouse, or because of his (her) confinement to an institution for 3 years prior to the action; 9) Willful non-support by spouse.

Court: Chancery Courts
Statute: Arkansas Statutes Annotated 34-1202.
Residence: 3 months

CALIFORNIA
Grounds:
*1) Irreconcilable differences, which have caused the irremediable breakdown of the marriage; 2) Incurable insanity.

The term "irreconcilable differences," has been interpreted as the existence of a level of marital problems which have impaired the marriage relationship to the point where the legitimate objects of matrimony have been destroyed and for which there is no reasonable possibility of elimination, correction or resolution. In re: Walton's Marriage, 104 Cal. Rptr. 472, 28 C.A. 3d 108.

Court: Superior Court
Property distribution rule upon divorce: By community property rule
Statute: California Civil Code 4506.
Residence: 6 months

COLORADO
Grounds:
*1) Irretrievable breakdown of the marriage.

According to the relevant section of the statute, this is how the term 'irretrievable breakdown', should be applied by the state courts: "If both of the parties by petition or otherwise have stated under oath or affirmation that the marriage is irretrievable broken, or one of the parties has so stated and the other has not denied it, there is a presumption of such fact, and, unless controverted by evidence, the court shall, after hearing, make a finding that the marriage is irretrievably broken."

Court: District Court
Statute: Colorado Revised Statutes 14-10-101.
Residence: 1 year

---

* Indicates this is a "no-fault" ground.

CONNECTICUT
Grounds:
*1) The marriage has broken down irretrievably and there is no reasonable prospect of reconciliation; *2) The parties have lived apart for a continuous period of at least eighteen months prior to the service of the complaint by reason of incompatibility; 3) Adultery; 4) Fraudulent contract of marriage; 5) Desertion for one year with total neglect of duty; 6) Disappearance for 7 years without being heard from; 7) Habitual intemperance; 8) Repeated cruelty; 9) Conviction of a felony or sentence to life imprisonment; 10) Institutional confinement for judicial insanity for a period of five years.

Court: Superior Court
Residence: 1 year
Statute: Connecticut States Annotated 46-32.

Connecticut's divorce law, Sec. 46-47 of the General Statute, gives the following rule for determining when a marriage has broken down: "When the parties (i.e., the husband and the wife) submit a written stipulation that their marriage has broken down irretrievably, or when both parties are physically present in court and have submitted an agreement concerning the custody, care, education, visitation, maintenance and support of their children, the testimony of either party in support of that conclusion shall be sufficient and the court shall make a finding that such marriage breakdown has occurred . . ."

DELAWARE
Grounds:
*1) The court shall enter a decree of divorce when it finds that the marriage is irretrievably broken.
   A marriage is irretrievably broken where there has been a voluntary separation, or a separation caused by respondent's misconduct, or separation caused by respondent's mental illness, or separation caused by incompatibility, where reconciliation is improbable.

Court: Family Court
Statute: Delaware Code Annotated 13-1505.
Residence: 6 months

DISTRICT OF COLUMBIA
Grounds:
*1) Voluntary separation for one year without cohabitation; 2) Adultery; 3) Actual or constructive desertion for one year; 4) Conviction of felony and sentence of not less than two years for which spouse served in whole or in part; 5) Decree of divorce from bed and board which resulted in continued separation of the parties for one year may be converted into a decree of absolute divorce on the application of the innocent spouse.

Court: Superior Court
Statute: D.C. Code Annotated 16-904.
Residence: 1 year

FLORIDA
Grounds:
*1) Irretrievable breakdown of marriage; 2) Adjudication of one of the parties as mentally incompetent at least three years prior to the proceedings for dissolution of marriage.

Court: Circuit Court
Statute: Florida Statutes 61.052.
Residence: 6 months

---

* Indicates that this is a "no-fault" ground.

GEORGIA

Grounds:

*1) Irretrievable breakdown of the marriage; 2) Incestuous intermarriage; 3) Lack of comprehension or mental capacity at the time of the marriage; 4) Force, menace, duress or fraud in obtaining the marriage; 5) Impotence at the time of the marriage; 6) Pregnancy caused by another man at the time of marriage; 7) Adultery; 8) Desertion for one year; 9) Conviction for a crime involving moral turpitude for which the spouse is sentenced to imprisonment for two years immediately prior to the commencement of the divorce action; 10) Habitual drunkenness; 11) Physical or mental cruelty; 12) Adjudicated insanity or incurable mental illness and confinement to an institution for two years prior to the commencement of the action; 13) Habitual drug addiction.

Irretrievable breakdown is interpreted as where either or both parties are unable or refuse to cohabit and there are no prospects for reconciliation. (223 S.E. 2d 802.)

Court: Superior Court
Statute: Georgia Code Annotated 30-102.
Residence: 6 months

HAWAII

Grounds:

*1) The marriage is irretrievably broken; 2) The parties have lived apart for a continuous period of two years or more, and there is no reasonable likelihood that cohabitation will be resumed; 3) The parties have lived separate and apart under a decree of separation from bed and board entered by any court of competent jurisdiction, and the term of separation has expired, and no reconciliation has been effected; 4) The parties have lived separate and apart for a period of two years or more under a decree of separate maintenance entered by any court of competent jurisdiction, and no reconciliation has been effected.

Court: Circuit Court
Property distribution rule upon divorce: By community property rule
Statute: Hawaii Revised Statutes 580-41.
Residence: 6 months

IDAHO

Grounds:

1) Adultery; 2) Extreme cruelty; 3) Desertion; 4)Willful neglect for 1 year; 5) Habitual intemperance for 1 year; 6) Conviction of a felony; 7) Idiocy or insanity for which the spouse is confined in an insane asylum for three years or more prior to the commencement of the divorce action. *8) Irreconcilable differences. (Irreconcilable differences are those grounds which are determined by the court to be substantial reason for not continuing the marriage and which make it appear that the marriage should be dissolved.) *9) Living separate and apart continuously without cohabitation for five years prior to the commencement of the divorce action.

Court: District Court
Property distribution rule upon divorce: By community property rule
Statute: Idaho Code 32-603.
Residence: 6 weeks

---

* Indicates this is a "no-fault" ground.

ILLINOIS

Grounds:

*1) Irreconcilable differences have caused the irretrievable breakdown of the marriage or reconciliation has failed or further attempts at reconciliation are impractical and the spouses have been living separate and apart without cohabitation for 2 years. (If both spouses consent, the time period becomes 6 months) 2) Impotence of either party at the time of marriage and prior to commencement of the divorce action; 3) Prior existing marriage; 4) Adultery; 5) Desertion for one year; 6) Alcoholism or drug addiction for two years; 7) Attempt on the life of the other spouse by poison or other means showing malice; 8) Repeated physical or mental cruelty; 9) Conviction of a felony; 10) Infected the other with a communicable venereal disease.

Court: Circuit Court
Statute: Illinois Hurd Annotated Statutes 40-401.
Residence: 90 days

INDIANA

Grounds:

*1) Irretrievable breakdown; 2) The conviction of a felonious or infamous crime during marriage; 3) Impotence at the time of the marriage; 4) Idiocy or insanity of either party for a period of a least two years.

Court: Superior Court/Circuit Court
Statute: Indiana Statutes Annotated 31-1-11.5-1.
Residence: 6 months

IOWA

Grounds:

*1) Breakdown of the marriage relationship to the extent that the legitimate objects of matrimony have been destroyed and there remains no reasonable likelihood that the marriage can be preserved.

Court: District Court
Statute: Iowa Code Annotated 598.17.
Residence: 1 year

KANSAS

Grounds:

*1) Incompatibility; 2) Abandonment for one year; 3) Adultery; 4) Mental or physical cruelty; 5) Habitual drunkenness; 6) Willful neglect; 7) Conviction and imprisonment of felony during marriage; 8) Confinement in an institution for mental illness for a period of three years, which need not be continuous; or a judicial determination of mental illness or incapacity for more than three years with a finding by at least two of three physicians appointed by the court before whom the action is pending, that the defendant has a poor prognosis for recovery.

Court: District Court
Statute: Kansas Statutes Annotated 60-1601..
Residence: 60 days

KENTUCKY

Grounds:

*1) Irretrievable breakdown.
A finding of irretrievable breakdown is a determination that there is no reasonable prospect of reconciliation.

Court: Circuit Court
Statute: Kentucky Revised Statutes Annotated 403.110.
Residence: 180 days

---

* Indicates this is a "no-fault" ground.

LOUISIANA

Grounds:
*1) Continuous separation for one year; *2) That a spouse (or both) desires a divorce; 3) Adultery; 4) Conviction and sentence for felony to a death sentence or imprisonment at hard labor; 5) If there is no reconciliation one year from judgment of bed and board divorce, plaintiff in that action is entitled to obtain absolute divorce; if plaintiff does not act, the other spouse may obtain divorce one year and sixty days from the bed and board divorce.

Court: District Court
Property Distribution upon divorce: Based on community property rule.
Statute: Louisiana Civil Code Annotated 9-301.
Residence: 6 months

MAINE

Grounds:
*1) Irreconcilable marital differences; 2) Adultery; 3) Impotence; 4) Mental or physical cruelty; 5) Desertion for three consecutive years prior to the commencement of the action; 6) Habitual drunkenness or drug addiction; 7) Nonsupport or neglect to provide suitable maintenance for needy spouse; 8) Confinement in a mental institution for at least seven consecutive years prior to the commencement of the divorce action.

For the 'irreconcilable marital differences' ground, both parties are required to have received counseling by a professional counselor, approved by the court as qualified, and a copy of the counselor's report made available to the court.
Court: District Court
Statute: Maine Revised Statutes Annotated 19-691.
Residence: 6 months

MARYLAND

Grounds:
*1) Voluntary living apart for twelve consecutive months without reasonable expectation of reconciliation; *2) Living separate and apart without cohabitation or interruption for three years; 3) Impotence at the time of marriage; 4) Any cause rendering marriage void, e.g. a prior existing marriage or bigamy; 5) Adultery; 6) Continuous abandonment for twelve months which is without reasonable expectation of reconciliation; 7) Conviction of a felony or misdemeanor, with sentence of at least three years or an indeterminate sentence with 12 months already served; 8) Idiocy or insanity for which the other spouse is confined in an institution for not less than three years.

Court: Equity Courts
Statute: Maryland Annotated Code 16-24.
Residence: 1 year

MASSACHUSETTS:

Grounds:
1) Adultery; 2) Impotence; 3) Desertion for one year; 4) Alcoholism or drug addiction; 5) Mental or physical cruelty; 6) Willful neglect or nonsupport of wife by husband when he is able to do so; 7) Sentence to the federal penal institutions or reformatory institution for life or for five years or more; *8) An irretrievable breakdown of marriage.

Court: Superior Court/Probate Court
Statute: Massachusetts Laws Annotated Chapter 208.
Residence: 1 year

---

* Indicates this is a "no-fault" ground.

MICHIGAN
Grounds:
*1) Breakdown of the marriage relationship to the extent that the objects of matrimony have been destroyed and there remains no reasonable likelihood that the marriage can be preserved.

The Michigan statute makes it deliberately easy to prepare the divorce papers by providing that in the preparation of a complaint for divorce, all that a petitioner is required to do is to repeat the above statement used in the statute. The complaint or petition, it states, "shall make no other explanation on the grounds for divorce than by the use of the statutory language."

Court: Circuit Court
Statute: Michigan Statutes Annotated 25-86
Residence: 6 months

MINNESOTA
Grounds:
*1) Irretrievable breakdown of the marriage relationship. The court is required to make a finding of "irretrievable breakdown" upon presentation of evidence of *any* of the following:
a. A course of conduct harmful to the relationship of the party seeking dissolution; or
b. Sentence to imprisonment during the course of marriage; or
c. Habitual drunkenness or drug addiction for a period of one year prior to the commencement of divorce action; or
d. Commitment to mental institution; or
e. Uninterrupted separation, under an order or decree of separate maintenance, for one year prior to the commencement of the divorce action; or
*f. Serious discord between the marital parties.

Court: District Court
Statute: Minnesota Statutes Annotated 518-06.
Residence: 6 months

MISSISSIPPI
Grounds:
1) Impotence at the time of marriage; 2) Adultery; 3) Imprisonment; 4) Desertion for a continuous period of one year; 5) Habitual drunkenness 6) Drug addiction; 7) Repeated cruel and inhuman treatment; 8) Insanity or idiocy at the time of the marriage; 9) Prior existing marriage; 10) Pregnancy caused by another man at the time of marriage; 11) Incestuous marriage; 12) Confinement in an institution for at least three years for insanity; *13) Irreconcilable differences.

Court: Chancery Court
Statute: Mississippi Code Annotated 93-5-1.
Residence: 6 months

MISSOURI
Grounds:
*1) Irretrievable breakdown of the marriage with no likelihood that the marriage can be preserved.

Court: Circuit Court
Statute: Statutes Annotated Missouri Statutes 452.305.
Residence: 90 days

---

* Indicates this is a "no-fault" ground

MONTANA
Grounds:
*1) Irretrievable breakdown of the marriage and serious marital discord which adversely affects the attitude of both spouses toward the marriage and no reasonable prospect of reconciliation, and living separate and apart for 180 days prior to filing for divorce.

Court: District Court
Statute: Montana Revised Code Annotated 48-316.
Residence: 90 days

NEBRASKA
Grounds:
*1) Irretrievable breakdown of the marriage.
A marriage 'irretrievably breaks down' when a personal relationship between the married parties has deteriorated to the point that the parties can no longer live together.

Court: District Court
Property distribution upon divorce: based on community property rule.
Statute: Revised Statutes of Nebraska 42-361.
Residence: 1 year

NEVADA
Grounds:
1) Insanity existing for two years before the commencement of the action. *2) Living separate an apart for one year without cohabitation; *3) Incompatibility.

Court: District Court
Distribution of Property Upon divorce: based on community property rule
Statute: Nevada Revised Statutes 125.010.
Residence: 6 months

NEW HAMPSHIRE
Grounds:
1) Impotence; 2) Adultery; 3) Repeated mental or physical cruelty; 4) Conviction and actual confinement in prison for a felony; 5) Disappearance without being heard from for two consecutive years; 6) Habitual drunkenness for two years; 7) Joining religious sect disbelieving in marriage and refusal by such spouse to cohabit with the other for six months; 8) Abandonment without cause by either party and refusal to cohabit for two years; 9) Nonsupport by husband; 10) Voluntary absence of wife from her husband without his consent for two years; 11) Wife going to live outside of the state and remaining away from husband for ten years, without his consent and without returning to claim her marriage rights; 12) Husband being an alien or citizen of another state, and wife living separate in the state of New Hampshire for two years while the husband left the United States to become a citizen of some foreign country and did not return to the state or make suitable provision for the wife's support.
*13) Irreconcilable differences which have caused the irremediable breakdown of the marriage. If one spouse resolutely refuses to continue and it is clear from the passage of time or other circumstances that there is no reasonable possibility of a change of heart, there is an irremediable breakdown of the marriage. Desrochers v. Desrochers, 347 A.2d 150.

Court: Superior Court
Statute: New Hampshire Revised Statutes 458.7.
Residence: 1 year

---

* Indicates this is a "no-fault" ground

NEW JERSEY

Grounds:

*1) Separation for eighteen consecutive months, with no apparent reasonable prospect of reconciliation existing; 2) Adultery; 3) Willful and continued desertion for twelve months or more and no cohabitation; 4) Extreme physical cruelty or mental cruelty which endangers the safety or health of the plaintiff and makes cohabitation by the complaining party improper or unreasonable; 5) Drug addition or habitual drunkenness for twelve consecutive months after marriage; 6) Institutionalization for mental illness for twenty-four consecutive months after the marriage; 7) Imprisonment of the defendant for eighteen consecutive months after the marriage; if action is not commenced until after the defendant's release, proof that the parties have not resumed cohabitation is required; 8) Deviant or unnatural sexual conduct by the defendant without consent of the plaintiff.

Court: Superior Court

Statute: New Jersey Statutes Annotated 2A:34-2.

Residence: 1 year

NEW MEXICO

Grounds:

**1) Incompatibility. 2) Cruel and inhuman treatment; 3) Adultery; 4) Abandonment.
Incompatibility exists when the level of marital discord or conflict of personalities is so high that it prevents any reasonable expectation of reconciliation.

Court: District Court

Property Distribution upon Divorce: based on community property rule

Statute: New Mexico Statutes Annotated 22-7-1.

Residence: 6 months

NEW YORK

Grounds:

1) Mental or physical cruelty; 2) Abandonment for a continuous period of one year; 3) Adultery; 4) Confinement of defendant in prison for three or more years after the marriage; 5) Living apart for a period of at least one year pursuant to a decree or judgment of separation. 6) Living apart for a period of at least one year pursuant to a written separation agreement.

Court: Supreme Court

Property Distribution upon Divorce: based on equitable distribution rule.

Statute: New York Domestic Relations Laws, Section 170.

Residence: 1 year

NORTH CAROLINA

Grounds:

*1) Continuous separation and living apart for one year; 2) Adultery; 3) Impotence; 4) Pregnancy caused by another man at the time of the marriage; 5) Engaging in deviant sexual intercourse or unnatural behavior, such as intercourse with a person of the same sex or a beast; 6) Living apart for 3 consecutive years without cohabitation by reason of incurable insanity of one spouse and his confinement in an institution for 3 consecutive years; certified incurable insanity, whether confined or otherwise.

Court: Superior Court

Statute: North Carolina General Statutes 50-5.

Residence: 6 months

---

* Indicates this is a "no-fault" ground

NORTH DAKOTA

Grounds:

*1) Irreconcilable differences. Irreconcilable differences are those grounds which are determined by the court to be substantial reason for not continuing the marriage; 2) Adultery; 3) Repeated cruelty; 4) Willful desertion for a period of one year; 5) Willful neglect or nonsupport by spouse for a period of one year; 6) Alcoholism for a period of one year; 7) Conviction of a felony; 8) Confinement for insanity for a period of 3 years in an institution; 9) Decree of separation in existence for more than four years and reconciliation improbable.

Court: District Court
Statute: North Dakota Code 14-05.03.
Residence: 6 months

OHIO

Grounds:

*1) Incompatibility, unless denied by the other spouse; or *2) Uninterrupted living apart for one year without cohabitation; 3) Prior existing marriage; 4) Willful absence for one year; 5) Adultery; 6) Impotence; 7) Extreme cruelty; 8) Fraudulent marriage contract; 9) Willful neglect of duty; 10) Habitual drunkenness; 11) Conviction and actual imprisonment of a spouse as of the time of the filing of the petition for divorce; 12) Procurement of a divorce outside the state. (This releases the party who procures it from the obligations of marriage, while such obligations remain binding upon the other party.)

Court: Courts of Common Pleas
Statute: Ohio Revised Code Annotated 3105.01.
Residence: 6 months

OKLAHOMA

Grounds:

*1) Incompatibility; 2) Abandonment for a period of one year; 3) Adultery; 4) Impotence; 5) Pregnancy caused by another man at time of marriage; 6) Repeated acts of cruelty; 7) Fraudulent marriage contract; 8) Habitual drunkenness; 9) Willful neglect or nonsupport by spouse; 10) Imprisonment for felony; 11) Procurement of divorce decree outside the state which does not in this State release the other party from the obligations of the marriage; 12) Idiocy or insanity for five years.

Court: District Court
Property Distribution upon Divorce: based on community property rule
Statute: Oklahoma Statutes Annotated 12-1271.
Residence: 6 month

OREGON

Grounds:

*1) Irreconcilable differences between the parties have (in the judgment of one or both parties) caused the irremediable breakdown of the marriage.

Court: Circuit Court
Property Distribution upon Divorce: based on community property rule
Residence: 6 months

PENNSYLVANIA

Grounds:

*1) Irretrievable breakdown of the marriage with the spouses living separate and apart without cohabitation for 2 years; or *2) irretrievable breakdown of the marriage and the spouses have both filed affidavits that they consent to the divorce. 3) Prior existing marriage; 4) Adultery; 5) Desertion for one year; 6) Repeated

---

* Indicates this is a "no fault ground.

acts of cruelty; 7) Indignities to the person so as to render the condition of the injured spouse intolerable and life burdensome; 8) Conviction and actual imprisonment for two years; 9) Insanity or serious mental disorder with confinement in a mental institution for at least 18 months immediately before the filing of the complaint.

Court: Courts of Common Pleas
Property Distribution upon Divorce: based on community property rule
Statute: Pennsylvania Statutes Annotated 23-10.
Residence: 6 months

RHODE ISLAND
Grounds:
*1) The parties have lived separate and apart for three years without cohabitation; *2) Irreconcilable differences which have caused the irremediable breakdown of the marriage; 3) Impotence; 4) Adultery; 5) Repeated acts of cruelty; 6) Willful desertion for five years or for a shorter period "in the discretion of the court."; 7) Habitual or prolonged drunkenness; 8) Drug addiction; 9) Nonsupport by husband for one year; 10) Prior existing marriage or incestuous contract.

Court: Family Court
Statute: Rhode Island General Laws Annotated 15-5-1.
Residence: 1 year

SOUTH CAROLINA
Grounds:
*1) Living apart without cohabitation for one year; 2) Adultery; 3) Desertion for one year; 4) Physical cruelty; 5) Habitual drunkenness or narcotic addiction.

Court: Circuit Court
Statute: South Carolina Code Annotated 20-101.
Residence: 1 year

SOUTH DAKOTA
Grounds:
*1) Irreconcilable differences which have caused the irretrievable breakdown of the marriage; 2) Adultery; 3) Repeated acts of cruelty; 4) Desertion for one year; 5) Nonsupport or willful neglect for one year; 6) Habitual intemperance; 7) Conviction of a felony.

Court: Circuit Court
Statute: South Dakota Compiled Laws Annotated 25-4-2.
Residence: must be resident of State at time of filing.

TENNESSEE
Grounds:
*1) Irreconcilable differences; or *2) living separate and apart without cohabitation for 2 years when there are no minor children; 3) Impotence at the time of the marriage; 4) Prior existing marriage; 5) Adultery; 6) Willful desertion — for one year; 7) Conviction of a felony; 8) Attempt on the life of the spouse by poison or other means; 9) Pregnancy caused by another man at the time of the marriage; 10) Habitual drunkenness or use of narcotic drugs during the course of marriage; 11) Cruel and inhuman treatment;

Court: Circuit Courts/Chancery Court
Statute: Tennessee Code Annotated 36-801, 802.
Residence: 6 months

---

* Indicates this is a "no-fault" ground.

TEXAS

Grounds:

*1) **Insupportability.** On the petition of either party to a marriage, a divorce may be decreed without regard to fault if the marriage has become insupportable because of discord or conflict of personalities that destroys the legitimate ends of the marriage relationship and prevents any reasonable expectation of reconciliation. 2) Living apart without cohabitation for at least three years; 3) Cruelty; 4) Adultery; 5) Conviction of a felony since marriage and imprisonment for at least one year without pardon; 6) Abandonment for at least one year; 7) Confinement of spouse in a mental hospital for mental disorder for at least three years without prospect of recovery by spouse.

Court: District Court
Property Distribution upon Divorce: based on community property rule
Statute: Texas Family Code 3.01.
Residence: 1 year

UTAH

Grounds:

*1) Irreconcilable differences in the marriage; or *2) living separated and apart without cohabitation for 3 years under a judicial decree of separation. 3) Impotence at the time of the marriage; 4) Adultery; 5) Willful desertion for more than one year; 6) Willful neglect or nonsupport by spouse who is capable of providing support; 7) Habitual drunkenness of defendant; 8) Conviction of defendant for felony; 9) Mental or physical cruelty to plaintiff by defendant; 10) Incurable insanity which is adjudicated to be so by legal authorities of this or some other state.

Court: District Court
Statute: Utah Code Annotated 30-3-1.
Residence: 3 months

VERMONT

Grounds:

1) Adultery; 2) Sentence and actual confinement in prison for three years or more at the time of the action; 3) Intolerable severity or extreme cruelty; 4) Willful desertion; 5) Nonsupport, refusal or neglect to provide suitable maintenance for the other; 6) Incurable insanity and confinement in a mental institution; *7) Living apart for six consecutive months and court finding that resumption of marital relations is not reasonably probably.

Court: Superior Court
Property Distribution upon Divorce: based on equitable distribution
Statute: Vermont Revised Statutes Annotated 15-551.
Residence: 6 months

VIRGINIA

Grounds:

1) Adultery, sodomy or buggery; 2) Conviction and actual confinement in prison for felony where cohabitation was not resumed after such confinement; 3) Willful desertion for one year; *4) Continuously living separate and apart from the spouse without any cohabitation for one year.

Court: Circuit Court
Statute: Code of Virginia 20-91.
Residence: 1 year

---

* Indicates this is a "no-fault" ground.

WASHINGTON

Grounds:

*1) The marriage is irretrievably broken.

"When a party who is a resident of this state or who is a member of the Armed Forces and is stationed in this state, petitions for a dissolution of marriage, and alleges that the marriage is irretrievably broken and when ninety days have elapsed since the petition was filed and from the date when service of summons was made upon the respondent or the first publication of summons was made, the court shall . . . enter a decree of dissolution (if the other party either joins in the petition or does not deny that the marriage is irretrievably broken) . . ."

Court: Superior Court

Property Distribution upon Divorce: based on community property rule

Statute: Washington Revised Code 26.09.030.

Residence: Spouse filing for divorce must be a resident of state at time of filing.

WEST VIRGINIA

Grounds:

1) Adultery; 2) Conviction of a felony; 3) Willful abandonment or desertion for six months; 4) Cruel and inhuman treatment whether mental or physical in nature, which make continued cohabitation unsafe or intolerable; 5) Habitual drunkenness during the course of marriage; 6) Narcotic addiction during the course of marriage; 7) One year living separate and apart without cohabitation and interruption, whether by voluntary act of one party or by mutual consent; 8) Incurable insanity for which the party is confined in an institution for three years prior to the filing of complaint; 9) Abuse or neglect of a child of the parties;

*10) Irreconcilable differences.

Court: Circuit Court

Statute: West Virginia Code Annotated 48-2-4.

Residence: 1 year

WISCONSIN

Grounds:

*1) Irretrievable breakdown of the marriage.

The irretrievable breakdown of the marriage may be shown by: 1) a joint petition by both spouses requesting a divorce on this ground; or 2) living separate and apart for 12 months immediately prior to filing; or 3) if the court finds an irretrievable breakdown of the marriage with no possible chance of reconciliation.

Court: Circuit Court

Statute: Wisconsin Statutes Annotated 247.07.

Residence: 6 months

WYOMING

Grounds:

*1) Irreconcilable Differences.

2) Confinement for incurable insanity for two years.

Court: District Court

Statute: Wyoming Statutes Annotated 20-2-104.

Residence: 60 days

---

* Indicates this is a "no-fault" ground.

APPENDIX C

Some Relevant Glossary Of Legal Terms

ABANDONMENT- The act of leaving a husband or wife. Also called "desertion."

ABATEMENT- A lessening or decrease (e.g., tax abatement)

ACKNOWLEDGMENT- A declaration, in front of a person who is legally qualified to administer an oath (such as a Notary Public), that a document bearing your signature was actually signed by you.

ACTION- A lawsuit or proceeding in a court of law.

ADDENDUM- Something added afterwards.

AD VALOREM- Latin for "based upon the value." Example: property taxes.

ADVERSE POSSESSION- The occupancy or enjoyment of property, in spite of and against the will of the person who has legal title.

AFFIDAVIT- A statement in writing, sworn to before a person authorized to administer oath, such as a Notary Public.

ALLEGATIONS- The claims or charges made in a lawsuit against the other party.

ALIMONY- The allowance ordered by the court to be paid by a husband for the support and maintenance of his wife (as opposed to the children) usually after both parties have separated or divorced.

ANSWER- A formal response to the allegations made in a complaint or petition.

ANNULMENT- A legal action which has the result of treating a marriage as if it had never occurred.

ANTE-NUPTIAL CONTRACT OR AGREEMENT- Contract made before marriage, setting out the rights and obligations of each if the marriage ends in divorce. Same as pre-nuptial.

APPEAL- A resort to a higher court for the purpose of obtaining a review of a lower court decision and a reversal of the lower court judgment or the granting of a new trial.

APPEARANCE- The coming into a case by a party summoned in a court action; to come into a case upon being summoned, either by one's self or through one's attorney; to voluntarily submit one's self to the jurisdiction of the court (made either in person or by filing a formal document, such as an answer or a waiver).

ASSIGNEE- The person to whom a property or the rights to it are transferred.

ASSIGNOR- The person who assigns (transfers) a property right to another person.

BASTARDY PROCEEDINGS- Court action against the father of a child born out of wedlock to compel support for the child.

BIGAMY- The crime (under U.S. law) of having two living legal spouses at the same time.

BREACH OF CONTRACT- Failure to perform a duty or fulfill an obligation called for in a contract.

CASE LAW- The body of law created by appellate court decisions. The case law may interpret written laws, or it may create law where there are no statutes.

COHABITATION- The act of living together by two persons of opposite sex who are not married to each other.

COLLATERAL- Something that is additional or incidental to the main issue that is being discussed e.g., child custody or support payments are 'collateral issues' in dissolving marriages.

COLLUSION- A secret agreement to defraud someone, or to do certain things that are illegal or against public morality.

COMMINGLING (OF ASSETS)- A situation where a husband and wife have so mixed up the separate property of each that it is difficult to know which one separately belongs to whom.

COMMON LAW MARRIAGE- A marriage in which there has been no formal ceremony or marriage license.

COMMUNITY PROPERTY- As defined by most states which have adopted the "community property" system, community property is any property or asset acquired by the husband and/or the wife from the time of their marriage onward (usually excluding the property acquired either before the marriage or by gift or inheritance). As of this writing, community property states are the following: Arizona, California, Idaho, Louisiana, Nevada, New Mexico, Texas, Washington and Wisconsin.

COMMUNITY PROPERTY RULE- The rule that the sum total of whatever is considered the community of a married couple, would be divided *equally* between both spouses, under the theory that both spouses make equal contribution to a marriage, the husband as a breadwinner, and the wife as the homemaker so that the husband is freed to engage in his job.

COMPETENT PERSON- A person who is mentally fit, and therefore considered legally capable of entering into a contract.

COMPLAINT-The main document in a civil case court action made out by the plaintiff ("complainant") listing the complaints and allegations and other relevant facts related to the plaintiff's case. The person who first makes out the complaint against another, is called the complainant or plaintiff, and the party against whom he makes out the complaint is the defendant or respondent. (Same as PETITIONER)

CONCLUSIONS OF LAW- A judge's opinion of what the law says which applied in a given situation.

CONFORMING THE COPIES- Filling in information from the original pleading or document on the reproduced copies of the document. When conforming a copy as to a signature, it's customary to put an /s/ in front of the name to indicate it was not an original signature on the copy.

CONSIDERATION- The thing of value that is given or offered to induce a person to enter into a contract or agreement.

CONTESTED- Differences that must be settled before a court.

CONTESTED DIVORCE- A divorce where at least one issue has not been settled prior to court.

CONTINUANCE- A postponement granted by the judge of a scheduled matter to a later date on the court's calendar.

CONTRIBUTORY RETIREMENT PLAN- Where both the employee and the employer contribute funds to a retirement plan for the benefit of the employee.

CORE CONSIDERATIONS- Those basics considered by the courts in making a property division and/or awarding alimony in a divorce case: age, health, sex, education, earning capacity, future prospects, children to care for, and any other similar relevant considerations, such as fault in causing the breakdown of the marriage in some states.

COUNTER CLAIM- A complaint (or petition) filed by a defendant (or respondent) which states claims against the plaintiff (or petitioner).

CUSTODIAL PARENT-The parent who has custody of the child; the one with whom a child normally lives.

DECREE- The title of the final ruling in a case, as in FINAL DECREE OF DIVORCE.

DEFAULT ORDER/JUDGMENT- An order or judgment of a court based only on the plaintiff's (or petitioner's) case. One party (the petitioner) shall have filed suit and served the defendant (or respondent) with notice of the suit, and the defendant (or respondent) shall not have answered the allegations or made an appearance in the case.

DEFENDANT- The person who defends against a lawsuit brought against him or her by another. (Same as RESPONDENT.)

DEPOSITIONS- Questions asked by both plaintiff and defendant (or their attorneys) and answered by a prospective witness, before a court reporter, and under oath. A form of "discovery."

DISCOVERY- The right of either party to learn from all who have information, anything which is relevant to the suit. Any of the formal procedures for obtaining information important to a case, such as notice to produce documents, written interrogatories, and depositions.

DISCRETION- Using one's own good judgment, within reasonable bounds.

DISSOLUTION OF MARRIAGE- A legal judgment that terminates a marriage. (Same as divorce).

DIVORCE- Legal dissolution (termination) of a marriage.

DOCKET- The court's book containing a brief entry of the important events in each case with their dates. Also, a list or calendar of cases set for hearings.

DOMICILE- One's permanent or legal home, as opposed to one's temporary place of abode.

EARNED INCOME- Money which is received in return for labor. Interest, alimony, child support, retirement pay, Social Security payments, welfare payments and trust income are not "earned income."

ENTIRETY- The phrase "ownership (or tenancy) by the entirety" is used to describe a situation when two ore more persons (but more commonly a husband a wife) jointly own a real property, so that the property cannot be divided between themselves. Hence, if one of the parties should die, the whole property goes to the survivor(s).

EQUITABLE CLAIMS- This refers to a right or claim which is enforceable although not based upon a written contract.

EQUITABLE DIVISION- A method of property division in a divorce (or dissolution of marriage) which is generally based on a variety of factors in an attempt to allocate a fair and just amount of property to each spouse.

EQUITY- Fairness and justice.

ESTATE- The sum total of the property, both real and personal, owned by a decedent (the dead person) at the time of his death.

ESTATE BY THE- When two people own property in this manner, each of them owns the whole property. Ordinarily husbands and wives own property by the entirety with the right of survivorship so that when one dies, the other simply becomes the sole owner of the whole property.

EX-CONTRACTU- Latin term meaning "from contract." Used to describe a court action or obligation that arises out of a contract or contractual obligation.

EXECUTION- The completion of a document (such as a will, contract, or agreement) by officially signing it.

FAULT- As used in divorce proceedings, "fault" refers to the actions of the parties with respect to the cause or reason for divorce, such as adultery, alcoholism, and so on.

FAULT-BASED DIVORCE- A divorce which may only be granted on a showing that one of the spouses was guilty of some form of marital misconduct.

FINDINGS OF FACT- This is a statement by a judge as to his or her belief of the facts presented during the trial.

FOREIGN DECREE- Ordinarily, refers to a decree of another state. For example, a New York decree would be a foreign decree to the California court.

FIRST IMPRESSION- An original question in a particular state which has not been decided by an appellate court in that state.

GROSS INCOME- The total income a person receives before deductions for taxes, retirement, insurance, and so on.

GROUNDS- The legal basis or reasons for the divorce (or *dissolution of marriage*). The grounds may be no-fault or fault-based.

HEARING- Any proceeding before a court where testimony is given or arguments heard.

HOLD-HARMLESS- A phrase used to describe an agreement by which one person agrees to assume full liability for an obligation and protect another from any loss or expense based on that obligation.

INCORPORATED INTO- As used mostly in settlement agreements or divorce judgements, the term refers to the parties' agreement to a divorce which is specifically referred to in the court decree and which actually becomes a part of the decree.

INDEMNITY- An "indemnity" provision between two parties provides that if the one who agreed to assume a liability does not pay, the other must pay, instead. If this happens, the one who should have paid must reimburse the paying party. It is frequently used to cover debt obligations, tax liability or mortgage payments in a divorce agreement.

INTEGRATED BARGAIN- A term used by the courts in interpreting divorce agreements from which a later dispute has arisen. It is well settled that generally a court cannot change a property division, but generally a court can change support payments. Most divorce agreements cover both provisions. If the court feels that both types of provisions were part of a total bargain, it will not change the support provision.

INTERROGATORIES- Questions one party asks another, in writing, which must be answered, in writing, under oath. A form of "discovery," but may only be used by one named party to the suit to another named party to the suit.

IMPLIED CONTRACT- Implied contracts are of two basic types: implied "in fact" and implied "in law." A contract implied "in fact," is one whose terms are inferred (implied) from the acts, conducts, and apparent intentions of the parties in a given situation. (Example: Mr. A steps into a taxicab and hands the driver a certain address. If the driver transports Mr. A to that address, Mr. A is reasonably expected, by implication "in fact," to pay a fare, although he had not expressly promised to do so). A contract is implied "in law" when, under certain circumstances, Mr. A has conferred a benefit upon Mr. B, which therefore implicitly entitles Mr. A to receive a reasonable value from Mr. B in return, if Mr. B's retention of the benefit would constitute an unjust enrichment at Mr. A's expense. (Example: Dr. A, a physician, renders first aid to Mr. B while Mr. B is unconscious as a result of an accident. Mr. B is expected, by contract implied "in law", to pay Dr. A the fair value of the service he received from him.)

IRRETRIEVABLE BREAKDOWN- Differences that cannot be reconciled; the ground for requesting a dissolution of marriage under no-fault system.

JOINT LEGAL CUSTODY- A form of custody of minor children in which the parties share the responsibilities and major decisions relating to the child. Generally, one parent is awarded actual physical custody of the child and the other parent is awarded liberal visitation rights.

JOINT PHYSICAL CUSTODY- A form of custody of minor children in which the parents share the actual physical custody of the child, generally alternating the custody.

JOINT PROPERTY- Property which is held or titled in the name of more than one person. (See *joint tenancy, community property* and *marital property.*)

JOINT TENANCY- The phrase "joint tenancy" or "joint ownership" is used to describe a situation when two or more persons (usually non-marital parties) own or hold a property in joint names, so that if any of them should die, the entire property goes to the remaining survivors.

JURISDICTION- The power or authority of a court to decide in a particular case.

LITIGATION- A court action or contest.

LEGAL SEPARATION A lawsuit to live apart and for support while the spouses are living separate and apart. May often deal with the same issues as in a divorce, but does not dissolve the marriage.

LUMP-SUM ALIMONY- Spousal support that is made in a single payment or in a fixed amount, but paid in specific installments.

MAINTENANCE- Support for a spouse provided by the other spouse. Same as alimony or spousal support.

MAJORITY- Refers to the age at which the child becomes an adult. This is governed by state statutes and generally varies from age 18 to 21. Child support generally ends when a child reaches majority.

MARITAL PROPERTY- Generally the property acquired during the marriage by the efforts of both spouses which is subject to division by a court upon divorce or dissolution.

MARITAL SETTLEMENT AGREEMENT- A written agreement entered into by divorcing spouses that spells out their rights and agreements regarding property, support, and children, etc. (Same as *separation agreement.*).

MATURED RETIREMENT FUND- If an employee has met all of the conditions for retirement so that he could retire and receivce his retirement payments, then his retirement has "matured", i.e., is payable.

MERGE WITH- See "incorporate into."

MOTION- A written or oral request to a court for some type of action, such as a motion to continue a trial to a later date.

NO-FAULT DIVORCE- Now adopted in almost every state in the nation, this is a concept of marital dissolution which is governed by one fundamental philosophy: replacement of the traditional concept that fault must be found with one (or both) spouses as the only basis for a divorce, with a new concept which only seeks to establish merely that the marital relationship has failed or broken down. To be awarded a divorce under most no-fault laws, you are only required to show (or just to make the claim) that you and your spouse have developed some "irreconcilable differences which have caused the irremediable breakdown of the marriage"— in other words, that there is plain inability of the parties to get along or live amicably with each other.

NON-CONTRIBUTORY- A retirement plan wherein only the employer contributes money to the account of the employee for his eventual retirement.

NON-MARITAL PROPERTY- Term used to describe separate property in some states that provide for the equitable distribution of property; generally consists of property acquired prior to a marriage and by individual gift or inheritance, either before or during a marriage. (See *marital property, community property,* and *separate property.*)

NOTARY PUBLIC- A person authorized, under the laws of the state, to administer oaths and accept acknowledgement of signatures to documents. (Such persons may usually be found in banks, in and around courthouses, real estate and lawyer's offices, often in drugstores, etc.)

NULL AND VOID- An act or pronouncement that has no legal binding or effect. (Void ab initio means the act or statement had no legal binding or effect *from the beginning.*)

ORDER- A court's ruling on some matter before it, generally, in writing and signed by the judge.

PALIMONY- The payment of support by one lover to another when the persons were never married.

PARTITION- Divide.

PARTY- A person directly involved in a lawsuit; either a plaintiff/petitioner or a defendant/respondent.

PERSONAL JURISDICTION- The power or authority of a court to make orders regarding a certain person and to have those orders legally enforced.

PETITION- A written statement, often sworn to by the maker before a Notary Public, in which the maker (the "petitioner" or "plaintiff") lists all the facts on which he bases his court action, and the remedies he demands of the court. Basically the same as a "complaint."

PETITIONER- The person who initiates a lawsuit by filing a petition with the court. (Same as plaintiff).

PENDENTE LITE- Latin expression which means "while the action or litigation is pending." Therefore, orders made by the court (e.g., about custody, support, or alimony) pendente lite, are in fact temporary orders which will continue from the time beginning when a suit is filed and ending when there is a final decree.

PERMANENT ALIMONY- Same as "alimony."

PLAINTIFF- Same as "complainant" or "petitioner."

PLEADINGS- The plaintiff's complaint *and* the "answer" (reply) of the defendant constitute, together, the pleadings — that is, the complete allegations of both sides in a case.

POSTHUMOUS CHILD- A child born after the father's death.

POSTNUPTIAL- Something entered into by the parties *after* their marriage. Separation agreement is a form of postnuptial agreement.

PRAYER- That portion of a complaint or petition which contains the action or relief that the plaintiff or petitioner is requesting of the court.

PRESUMPTION- Where the court assumes something is true until one of the parties proves otherwise.

PRIMARY CARETAKER- The parent who provides the majority of the day-to-day care for a minor child.

PRO SE- Latin term meaning "for himself" or "on his own behalf." Term used generally to describe a non-lawyer who is acting for himself or representing himself in a court case.

PUBLIC POLICY- The general principles of good and evil which prevail in the society, e.g., the requirement that contracts may not undermine the institution of marriage.

QUANTUM MERUIT- Latin term meaning "according to what he / she deserves." This is a legal doctrine whereby the parties involved in an issue or dispute over the amount to be paid for a service, are considered to be entitled to receive the "reasonable" value assessed for the service rendered. Thus, for example, the court may use this doctrine to determine that a partner in a marital or non-marital relationship is entitled to receive the "reasonable" value of the household services rendered, minus the reasonable value of the compensation and support she already receives.

REHABILITATIVE ALIMONY- Alimony which is granted for a short or limited period of time, usually just long enough for the ex-spouse to get on his / her feet and get a job. It states a specific time to end, and can be extended only for good cause shown to the court.

RELIEF- Whatever you are asking the court to do for you, e.g., to grant you a divorce, award you custody or support, etc.

RESPONDENT- Same as defendant.

RESPONSE- The formal document filed by a respondent in answer to the allegations in a petition. (Same as an *answer.*)

RIGHT OF SURVIVORSHIP- The right of joint owners of a piece of property to automatically be given the other's share of the property upon the death of the other owner. For this right to apply, it must, generally, be specifically stated on any documents of title. (Example: 'joint tenancy with the right of survivorship.')

RESULTING TRUST- A trust relationship that is not expressed in any document or specifically set up, but which arises from the acts, conducts, and apparent intentions of the parties. (Example: When the title to a piece of real estate is taken in the name of Mr. A but the purchase price is paid by Mr. B who is in no way obligated to A, then a trust "results" in which A holds the property as a trustee for the benefit of B, the provider of the purchase funds.)

SEPARATE MAINTENANCE- A lawsuit for support in a situation where the spouses live separate and apart but are not presently pursuing a divorce or dissolution. (Same as *legal separation.*)

SEPARATE PROPERTY- Property belonging to only one spouse in which the other generally has no claim.

SEPARATION (LEGAL SEPARATION)- The act of living apart by a husband and wife either by a written agreement or by a court order.

SERVICE OF PROCESS- The actual act of presenting the defendant or respondent in a lawsuit with a summons (or other legal papers) to notify him or her of the lawsuit.

SETTLEMENT AGREEMENT- The written version of a settlement which resolves certain issues.

SIGNATURE- A signed name or mark on a document to identify the person who made the document.

SODOMY- Perverted sexual intercourse e.g., an intercourse with an animal.

SOLE CUSTODY- A form of child custody in which one parent is given both physical custody of the child and the right to make all of the major decisions regarding the child's upbringing, with the other parent generally awarded reasonable visitation rights. (See *joint custody* and *split custody.*)

SPLIT CUSTODY- A form of child custody in which the actual time of physical custody is split between the parents, with both retaining the rights to participate in decisions regarding the child. (See *joint custody* and *sole custody.*)

SPOUSAL SUPPORT- Financial support for a spouse provided by the other spouse. (Same as alimony or maintenance.)

STIPULATION- An item or provision in a contract; a preliminary agreement separately worked out between husband and wife with a view to incorporating the terms of that agreement into a later divorce decree.

STATUTORY LAW- Those laws written by the state legislatures which are collected in the state law Code.

SUBJECT-MATTER JURISDICTION- The power or authority of a court to decide issues relating to certain subjects. For example: a Family Court may decide issues relating to the affairs of families; divorces, annulments, separations, custody, etc.

SUBPOENA- A document which is served upon (delivered to) a person who is not directly involved in a lawsuit, requesting that he or she appear in court to give testimony.

SUMMONS- A document which is served upon (delivered to) a person who is named as a defendant or respondent in a lawsuit. The summons notifies the person that the lawsuit has been filed against him or her and tells them that they have a certain time limit in which to file an answer or response in reply.

TEMPORARY SUPPORT- This is support granted by the court (or by agreement) to the wife/husband and/or children until a final decree is granted.

TENANCY BY THE ENTIRETY- See "Entirety" above.

TENANCY IN COMMON- The holding or ownership of property by two or more persons in such terms that each of them has an *undivided* interest in the property, and on the death of a tenant, his undivided interest automatically passes to his heirs or devisees, and *not* to the other survivors in the partnership.

TENDER YEARS- A presumption that all else being equal, a child of "tender years" should go to the mother under the theory that the mother is the better custodian, especially of a small child. Most states have now discarded "tender years" and there is generally no presumption between the parents.

UNCONTESTED- Differences are settled by agreement which is presented to the court. A court decree is granted without a trial of the issues.

VENUE- Venue has to do with the county (parish, or whatever) within a state where a court action should take place as all courts of "general jurisdiction" within a state have "power" over all the residents of the state.

VERIFICATION- Written confirmation that a written statement or document is true, usually accomplished by swearing to the written confirmation.

VESTED PENSION RIGHTS- A person's pension rights are "vested" if that person has already acquired the right to retire at some future time upon certain conditions set forth in the individual plan. This gives the worker the option to let his or her contributions remain in the retirement plan and receive the benefits of retirement payments at the designated time rather than withdrawing his or her contributions and forfeiting all future rights under the retirement plan.

VISITATION- The right of a parent who does not have custody of a minor child to visit the child or have a child visit with him or her.

VOID- An act, deed, or pronouncement, which has no legal force, effect or legitimacy from the very beginning. Same as "void ab initio." When something is voidable, it means it has a legal effect or legitimacy *until* and unless someone takes an action that makes it void, or a court declares it so.

WAIVE- To relinquish or give up a right.

WAIVER- The intentional giving up of a right, usually made in writing (or implied from one's conduct).

APPENDIX D
Some Relevant BIBLIOGRAPHY

1. "A Judicial Recognition of Illicit Cohabitation," 25 Hastings Law Journal, 1226 (1974)

2. "Validity of Prenuptial Contracts which Fix Alimony," 14 Georgia State Bar Journal 18 (1977)

3. "Rights in Respect of Engagement and Courtship Presents When Marriage Does Not Ensue," 46 American Law Reports, 3rd 578.

4. "Legal Import of Informal Marital Separation: A Survey of California Law and a Call for Change," 65 California Law Review 1015 (1977)

5. Marvin v. Marvin, 18 Cal. 3rd 660, 134 Cal. Rptr. 815, 818, 557, p. 2d 106.

6. Adams v. Jensen-Thomas, 18 Wash. App. 757, 571, p. 2d 958

7. Drafting the Marital Settlement Agreement: Strategies and Techniques (Practicing Law Institute, New York: 1977)

8. Tax Aspects of Divorce and Separation, 26 Tulane Tax Institute 27 (1977)

9. "Pro Se Marriage Dissolution in Connecticut — Some Considerations," 51 Connecticut Bar Journal 15 (1977)

10. "No Fault Divorce: 10 Years Later, Some Virtues, Some Flaws," The N.Y. Times, March 30, 1979 p. A22

11. "Sociologists Plumb the Secrets of Compatibility," The N.Y. Times, Nov. 14, 1978 p. C7.

12. "*A Legal Guide for Gay/Lesbian Couples*," (Addison-Wesley Publishing Co/NoLo Press)

13. "Learning to Mix Love and Money," The N.Y. Times, Feb. 16, 1981 p. B4

14. "Lawyers Troubled by Rehabilitation Concept in Marvin Decision," The N.Y. Times, April 20, 1979 p. A18

15. "To Have and To Hold — Short of Marriage," The N.Y. Times, July 8 1980 p. B8

16. Gail J. Koff, *Love and The Law*: *A legal Guide To Relationship In The '90's* . Simon & Schuster, N.Y. (1989)

17. Tom Biracree, *How To Protect Your Spousal Rights* (Contemporary Book, Chicago: 1991)

18. N.O.W. Legal Defense and Education and Renee Cherow-O'Leary, *The State-By-State Guide To Women's Legal Rights* (McGraw-Hill, New York: 1987)

19. Lloyd T. Kelso, *North Carolina Divorce, Alimony & Child Custody With Forms* 2nd ed. (The Harrison Co. Norcross, Ga: 1989)

20. Johnette Duff and George G. Truitt, *The Spousal Equivalent Handbook*, (Sunny Beach Publications, Houston, Tx: 1991)

21. *Arkansas Domestic Relations Handbook*, Vol. I (Arkansas Bar Association), esp. Chapters 9 and 14 on Property settlement and pre-marital agreements.

22. *Amer. Jurisprudence Legal Forms* 2d, Chaps. 17, 89 & 90, "Alimony And Separation Agreements;" and "Divorce and Separation," respectively.

23. "Denver Extends Health Coverage To Partners Of Gay City Employees," N.Y. Times, Sept. 18, 1996, p. A17

24. "Gay Partners of I.B.M. Workers to Get Benefits," N.Y. Times, Sept. 20, 1996, p. A18

25. James Novak, *Wisconsin Father's Guide To Divorce And Custody* (Prairie Oak Press, Madison Wis: 1996)

26. Leonard L. Loeb, Sharon A Drew, And Gregg M. Herman, *System Book For Family Law, A Forms And Procedures Handbook* (two volumes), CLE Book: The State Bar of Wisconsin, Madison Wis.

APPENDIX

ORDERING YOUR PRE-MARITAL AGREEMENT FORMS

The following is a list of some standard forms for drafting your own PRE-MARITAL AGREEMENT obtainable from Do-It-Yourself Legal Publishers, the nation's original and leading self-help law publisher.

(Customers: For your convenience, just make a Xerox copy of this page and send it along with your order. All prices quoted here are subject to change without notice.)

TO: Do-It-Yourself Legal Publishers (legal Forms Division)
    60 Park Place, Suite 1013
    Newark, NJ 07102

Please send me the publisher's standard "forms package for drafting a premarital written agreement" as follows:
[Prices $25.00 per set]

FORM	QUANTITY (sets)	PRICE
For a Premarital Agreement without provisions for Minor Children.............	_____	$_____
For a Premarital Agreement with provisions for Anticipated Minor Children.....	_____	$_____
For a Premarital Agreement of a General, Less Formal Shorter nature............	_____	$_____
(Prices: $25.00 per set) Subtotal......................................		$_____
Postage @ $4.00 per set......................		_____
Sales Tax*......................................		_____
GRAND TOTAL..........................		$_____

ANSWER THE FOLLOWING:

There's a substantial amount of pre-marital property involved. Yes_____ No_____
There are minor children anticipated in the marriage? Yes_____ No_____
I bought your book, or read, learned about it, from this source (bookstore, library, medium):_____

_____
(Name & address, please)

_____

Enclosed is the sum of $_____ to cover the order, which includes $4.00 per set for shipping, and local sales tax,* as applicable. *Send this order to me:*
    Mr./Mrs./Ms./Dr._____
    Address:_____
    City & State:_____Zip_____Tel.# (   )_____
*New Jersey residents enclose 6% sales tax.

IMPORTANT: Please do NOT rip out the page. Consider others! Just make a photocopy and send it.

APPENDIX F

PUBLICATIONS FROM DO-IT-YOURSELF LEGAL PUBLISHERS/SELFHELPER LAW PRESS

The following is a list of publications from the Do-it-Yourself Legal Publishers/Selfhelper Law Press of America. (Customers: For your convenience, just make a photocopy of this page and send it along with your order. All prices quoted here are subject to change without notice.)

1. Peaceful Divorce or Separation: How To Draw Up Your Own Settlement Agreement
2. Tenant Smart: How To Win Your Tenants' Legal Rights Without A Lawyer (New York Edition)
3. How To Probate & Settle An Estate Yourself Without The Lawyers' Fees ($35)
4. How To Adopt A Child Without A Lawyer
5. How To Form Your Own Profit/Non-Profit Corporation Without A Lawyer
6. How To Plan Your 'Total' Estate With A Will & Living Will, Without a Lawyer
7. How To Declare Your Personal Bankruptcy Without A Lawyer ($29)
8. How To Buy Or Sell Your Own Home Without A Lawyer or Broker ($29)
9. How To File For Chapter 11 Business Bankruptcy Without A Lawyer ($29)
10. How To Legally Beat The Traffic Ticket Without A Lawyer (forthcoming)
11. How To Settle Your Own Auto Accident Claims Without A Lawyer ($29)
12. How To Obtain Your U.S. Immigration Visa Without A Lawyer ($25)
13. How To Do Your Own Divorce Without A Lawyer [10 Regional State-Specific Volumes] ($35)
14. How To Legally Change Your Name Without A Lawyer
15. How To Properly Plan Your 'Total' Estate With A Living Trust, Without The Lawyers' Fees ($35)
16. Legally Protect Yourself In A Gay/Lesbian Or Non-Marital Relationship With A Cohabitation Agreement
17. Before You Say 'I do' In Marriage Or Co-Habitation, Here's How To First Protect Yourself Legally
18. The National Home Mortgage Escrow Audit Kit (forthcoming) ($15.95)

Prices: Each book, except for those specifically priced otherwise, costs $26, plus $4.00 per book for postage and handling. New Jersey residents please add 6% sales tax. **ALL PRICES ARE SUBJECT TO CHANGE WITHOUT NOTICE**

CUSTOMERS: **Please make and send a zerox copy of this page with your orders)**

ORDER FORM

TO: **Do-it-Yourself Legal Publishers**
      60 **Park Place**., Ste.1013, Newark, NJ 07102

Please send me the following:
1._____ copies of _____
2._____ copies of _____
3._____ copies of _____
4._____ copies of _____

Enclosed is the sum of $_____ to cover the order. *Mail my order to:*
Mr./Mrs.//Ms/Dr. _____
Address (include Zip Code please): _____
_____
Phone No. and area code: ( ) _____ Job: ( ) _____
*New Jersey residents enclose 6% sales tax.

IMPORTANT: Please do NOT rip out the page. Consider others! Just make a photocopy and send it.

INDEX